"Want to celebrate? Here is just the book to show you how and why you can, every day. The clearly written recipes and helpful wine notes will satisfy your hunger for the world's greatest duo—food and wine."

CARLO MIDDIONE, chef of Vivande Risorante and author of
Carlo Middione's Traditional Pasta and *La Vera Cucina*

"Carolyn's wine notes perfectly illuminate the considerations of wine choice for each recipe...and the recipes are mouthwatering."

ZELMA LONG, Chandon Estates

"This stunning collection of sublime seasonal dishes is indeed a feast for the senses!"

FLO BRAKER, author of *The Simple Art of Perfect Baking* and
Sweet Miniatures: The Art of Bite-Size Desserts

"Her family's four generations of wine experience and dedication to the pleasures of the table make Carolyn Wente the perfect guide into the enjoyable world of wine and food."

CAROLYN A. MARTINI, President, Louis M. Martini Winery

"The quality that has guided the Wente family's winemaking permeates this handsome book. It's not only a wonderful guide to great meals, it captures the essence of living well and joyfully in the fruitful land which they nurture for the generations to come."

JERRY DI VECCHIO, Food and Wine Editor, *Sunset* magazine

"From the fourth generation of the Wente family comes a treasure-load of adventures in wine and food. Carolyn Wente and chef Kimball Jones provide in this book a gloriously colorful invitation to enrich our lives with gastronomic journeys. A good read and a good route to fine dining!"

ROBERT BALZER, author of
The Los Angeles Times *Book of California Wines*

Sharing the Vineyard Table

*A Celebration of Wine and Food from
the Wente Vineyards Restaurant*

SHARING THE VINEYARD TABLE

A Celebration of Wine and Food from the Wente Vineyards Restaurant

CAROLYN WENTE AND KIMBALL JONES

TEN SPEED PRESS
Berkeley, California

A Kirsty Melville Book

Ten Speed Press
P.O. Box 7123, Berkeley, California 94707
www.tenspeed.com

Distributed in Australia by Simon and Schuster Australia, in Canada by Ten Speed Press
Canada, in New Zealand by Southern Publishers Group, in South Africa by Real Books, in
Southeast Asia by Berkeley Books, and in the United Kingdom and Europe by Airlift Books.

Book design by Nancy Austin
Photos on pages 2, 3, 19, 37, 43, 49, 154, 155, 161, 172, 179 and 190
by Richard Eskite, San Francisco.
Photos on pages xiv, 56, 57, 66, 75, 80, 102, 103, 107, 117, 133, and 146
by Penina, San Francisco.
Location photography by Robert Holmes.
Food styling by Sandra Cook. Prop styling by Sara Slavin.
Archival photographs courtesy of the Wente family and Wente Vineyards

Library of Congress Cataloging-in-Publication Data
Wente, Carolyn.
Sharing the vineyard table: a celebration of wine and food from the Wente
Vineyards Restaurant / written by Carolyn Wente and Kimball Jones.
p.   cm.
Includes bibliographical references and index.
ISBN 1-58008-044-8
1. Cookery. 2. Wine and wine making. I. Jones, Kimball.
II. Title.
TX714.W36   1999
641.5'09794'65—dc21   99-21374
                                                          CIP

First printing, 1999. Printed in China

1 2 3 4 5 6 7 8 9 10 — 03 02 01 00 99

Acknowledgments

Thank you to our families...

Dick and Shirley Jones, for encouraging me to follow my bliss. Morgwn and Taylor Jones, the best taste testers a dad could have.

Jean Wente, not only my mom (and a great chef), but also my mentor who challenged me to explore the world of wine and food. Buck and Bucky Layton, my loving family who are most supportive of my projects and endeavors. Eric and Philip Wente, the most wonderful siblings any gal could have, as well as the best business partners.

...and everyone else who made this endeavor possible.

Carol Salvin, our guiding light and organizational goddess whose incredible efforts made this project feasible and brought it to life! Linda Hayes, the first person who believed in us. Dan Carroll, for all of those great years cooking together. Rick Reid, for providing the environment to create. Diane Dovholuk, for inspiring us with ever-changing delights from the garden. Antonio Zaccheo, for teaching us how to make the best olive oil. All of the cooks, past and present, at Wente Vineyards Restaurant for consistently striving for perfection.

Many thanks to our recipe testers—

Irene Angelo, Virginia Cook, Liz Griest, Mille and George Griffith, Shirley Jones, Josie Little, Tony Mattera, Katie Meagher, Paige Poulos, Don Richards, Moaya Scheiman, Marilyn Schlangen, John Watanabe, Jean Wente, Donna Wilcox, Anne Woolley, and Myra Zimberoff.

CONTENTS

SPRING

SUMMER

AUTUMN

WINTER

APPENDICES

Foreword

Anthony Dias Blue

Wine country. Rows of leafy vines reaching toward the sun; warm, languid afternoons in the dappled sunlight spent sipping a new wine; serene moments of introspection and air perfumed by honeysuckle; and casual, convivial meals enjoyed outdoors with family and close friends. These two words conjure a complete lifestyle—a style of living.

This style of living is extremely appealing, stemming from the intrinsic simplicity and purity it conveys. Wine, on its own, is a substance replete with positive associations—nature, farming, the land, flavors of fruit and spice—but in the broader context of the wine country lifestyle, wine is inseparable from food. This synergism between silky fruit-driven wine and farm-fresh seasonal ingredients is a cornerstone of wine country and a tenet of the contemporary American palate. You can drink wine accompanied by a Ring-Ding, but the wine will be better served and better appreciated when matched with fresh, clean-flavored food.

The book you hold in your hands is about the wine country, but it is about much more. It is an evocation of a delightful and elucidating approach to living as seen through the eyes and hearts of Carolyn Wente and Kimball Jones, two people who live it every day.

This book is also about a restaurant's cuisine, which is the manifestation of the personalities of these two people, their energy, and the continual efforts by many to provide enjoyable culinary experiences. An early morning stroll through the unopened restaurant reveals much. A sous chef wanders through the garden, gathering fresh herbs warmed by the early sunlight. Lively chatter emanates from the kitchen staff, revealing thoughts on how to compose the daily menu. The aromas wafting from the freshly sliced peaches and berries in the pastry kitchen mingle with the mounds of freshly washed greens from the main kitchen. To an outsider, the anticipation of a luscious dining experience is in the air. Fortunately for us, this book captures the recipes of these lovely meals and the wines that accompany them.

After graduating from the California Culinary Academy, Kimball Jones spent more than two years working under Bradley Ogden, one of America's best native chefs. Here he developed his respect and understanding of fresh, local ingredients and his talent for pure, intense, balanced flavors. His approach was a delicious counterpoint to the libations served in wine country. For ten years Kimball has been executive chef of the Wente Vineyards Restaurant, one of the most celebrated dining establishments in northern California.

Carolyn Wente was born into one of America's first families of wine. While other kids were riding bikes on city sidewalks, Carolyn was riding a horse through the vineyards. But she did not let this special existence just wash over her and thus take it for granted; she learned about it, examined it, contemplated it, and found joy in it.

How did the Wentes come to be so important in the history of California wine making? The story of this wine dynasty is a remarkable recipe for success—wise decisions coupled with an abiding love and respect for the land, along with all the familiar ingredients: intelligence, ambition, and a little bit of luck.

When Carl Heinrich Wente left his family farm in Germany in 1880, he could scarcely have imagined that he was blazing a trail that would transform the Livermore Valley and, indeed, shape the course of American wine making. After spending three years working with fellow German Charles Krug, young Carl moved to Livermore and bought a 48-acre vineyard planted primarily with sauvignon blanc and sémillon from the nearby Louis Mel vineyard. Within a few years, Wente had expanded his holdings to more than 300 acres.

With the business firmly on its feet, Carl passed the winery on to his sons, Herman and Ernest. Ernest studied agriculture at UC Davis, while his brother studied enology at UC Berkeley. They made an effective team: Ernest grew the grapes and Herman made the wine. They aspired to more than just selling wine; they wanted to make better wine—to refine and improve the very process itself. Perhaps because they were removed from the Napa Valley, the Wentes were able to quietly work on their wines in an atmosphere of almost scholarly exploration.

Ernest made a critical decision in 1912 when he decided to plant chardonnay vines, which were relatively rare and unknown in America at the time. Ernest selected two sources for his vines. A neighbor, Charles Wetmore, who founded the Cresta Blanca winery, had brought "pinot chardonnay" vines (as they were then known, since some vintners mistakenly thought the grape was related to pinot noir) from Burgundy and distributed them to local vintners. He also drew from the well-known Montpelier Nursery in France.

After the repeal of Prohibition, the Wente brothers produced the first California wine to carry a Chardonnay label. As late as 1960, state records showed that there were only 230 acres of chardonnay in all of California, with Wente plantings accounting for a full 70 acres of the total. The 1959 Wente Bros. Chardonnay is considered an absolute classic, a point underscored at the time by the Michelin Guide, which declared it to be the finest white wine made in America and equal to the best Europe had to offer.

Through the years, the backbone of this family winery has been their classic French varietals—Chardonnay, Sauvignon Blanc, Cabernet Sauvignon, and Merlot.

From the 1940s to the 1960s, vintners across California selected cuttings from the Wente vineyard and planted them in their own vineyards. Working with the Foundation Plant Material Service at UC Davis, Ernest selected what he felt was the most outstanding chardonnay clone for the University nursery. Heat-treated clone #4—the "Wente" clone—has become widely propagated throughout the state. It is estimated that today eighty percent of all chardonnay in California is planted from the Wente clone.

Ernest's son, Karl, anticipated the growing demand for white wines and acquired the Riva Ranch vineyard in the Arroyo Seco region of Monterey in 1961. The Wentes were among the earliest vintners to recognize Monterey's potential as a source of quality Chardonnay and Riesling. It was from the Riva Ranch vineyard that Karl produced a series of sweet wines made from riesling grapes that were affected by the botrytis cinerea fungus that produces the great dessert wines of Europe. These were California's first naturally botrytised late-harvest wines.

Each generation of Wentes has infused their business with fresh ideas, and the current generation is no exception. Karl's children, Eric, Philip, and Carolyn, have taken the oldest continuously family-operated winery in California to an exciting new level, working with the intelligence and sensibility that seems to be in the Wente blood. The old Cresta Blanca winery has been transformed into the Wente Vineyards Visitors Center, with the restaurant nestled among its buildings. During the summer, a concert series draws over 15,000 visitors each year. A short distance from the visitor center, a spectacular championship golf course designed by PGA veteran Greg Norman weaves its way over the hills and through the vineyards.

Despite these exciting developments, Wente Vineyards remains first and foremost a winery committed to producing lovely California wines and sharing the wine country lifestyle. What follows is quite magical. It isn't just a cookbook, and it isn't a step-by-step program for living the wine country lifestyle, either. But if you read it as I did, picking up suggestions here, new ideas there, it will infiltrate your life. You will start noticing a serenity seeping into your kitchen and a mellowness in your daily dealings with the outside world. Welcome to wine country.

The Tale of
Our Vineyard Table

SINCE WINE AND FOOD have long been my family's daily passion, it was only natural that we thought about opening a restaurant to share our enthusiasm. We dreamed about a relaxed atmosphere where guests could deepen their enjoyment and understanding of the world of food and wine by experiencing the wines of the region accompanied by finely prepared meals. When the previous owners of the old Cresta Blanca winery put it up for sale, my brothers, Eric and Philip, and I had a glimpse of what the possibilities might be. Nestled in the end of its little valley, Cresta Blanca was founded in 1882 by Charles Wetmore, a year before my great-grandfather started our winery. Wente Vineyards Restaurant—one of a handful of California winery restaurants—opened in 1986 on the site of the old winery. My vision of a "white tablecloth restaurant" at the end of a country road had come to be. It was finally possible for guests to be enveloped in the wine country lifestyle, a comforting atmosphere in which the experience and enjoyment of wine and food are paramount.

When you gather around a table at the Wente Vineyards Restaurant, you'll partake of the freshest, seasonal ingredients, gathered from many sources. You'll also find an intriguing variety of sweet and savory dishes, with flavors that are balanced and authentic—honest food. Sauces and preparations enhance the fare rather than disguise it. Our presentation is straightforward, not fussy or contrived, which reflects our sense of rustic spontaneity. We've selected wines from a wide range of California appellations to complement or contrast the varied choices.

Kimball joined me as executive chef, bringing with him a passion for creating dishes with the freshest produce available. Coming from San Francisco to the rural setting of the Livermore Valley, he was excited by the possible purveyors that he knew the area must offer. Some of his early challenges lay in seeking out these suppliers as well as in convincing his "city" sources that the hour-long drive to Livermore would be worth it. The Jones silver Volvo became the worse for wear as it doubled as delivery van, filled with giant coolers of fresh fish, produce, and breads.

In Kimball's words, "I believe the best food is very simple food, where the pure, clean flavors of the ingredients shine through. I am always searching for the best and freshest. Because our style at the restaurant reflects the classic cuisines of France and Italy through New World ingredients and heirloom American dishes, our success is very dependent on the quality of our suppliers. Carolyn and I think our restaurant combines the best traditions of the Old World with the innovative spirit of the New World."

Over the years, the combined efforts of Kimball, myself, and our excellent culinary team have paid off. Our 200-seat restaurant in the midst of our vineyard estate has developed an international reputation for the excellence of its cuisine and wine collection. Many of our guests at first expect only Wente wines to be available and are astounded at the breadth of our wine list's offerings. But we want people to become familiar with the styles and flavors of wine from the various regions, to understand the differences, and to learn what their personal preferences are. Comparing three or four different wines is one of the best ways to do this.

We always have a lot of fun and often learn something new by giving people the opportunity to experiment with the different flavor combinations of wine and food. We try to do it in many ways and as often as we can. At our Winemaker's Dinners, for example, Kimball serves a multiple course dinner, which he develops with a featured California vintner to showcase the particular wines of the season. Four or five times a year, Kimball travels internationally to prepare the wines and foods of Wente Vineyards in many countries. Preparing our cuisine in some strange and challenging environments has given him enough stories to write a book. Even our monthly training classes for our waitstaff always seem to spark a spirited debate over which wines people think will best complement the dishes presented and which wines actually do.

Kimball's words express both our thoughts: "Through the restaurant, our travels, cooking classes, and seminars, Carolyn and I have seen how a little information goes a long way in furthering the appreciation of food and wine. The recipes in this collection, as well as our tips, opinions, and recommendations, are collected from our day-to-day experiences. Too often people use cookbooks as if they're full of unbreakable rules, without the information or confidence to change them. We hope we can demystify the world of wine and food, giving you the knowledge and assurance to go beyond the recipes in this book...to seek out new sources and information, to become curious about food and wine, and to express your own personal tastes and style at the table. Try, enjoy, experiment, and learn."

—CAROLYN WENTE AND KIMBALL JONES

Publisher's Notes

Two voices are present in this book. In an effort to represent each of them with least impediment to the reader we have settled on the following approach. Throughout this book, the recommendations and comments about pairing wine and food (appearing in the outer page margins) were written by Carolyn Wente, while the recipe headnotes were written by Kimball Jones. However, sprinkled among Kimball's recipes are some of Carolyn's versions of family favorites and, of course, she has written the headnotes for these (indicated by her initials, CW). Whether Carolyn or Kimball has written the sidebars about the restaurant and historical information about the vineyard and the valley, is indicated by the use of their initials, CW or KJ.

EGG ADVISORY

Some of the recipes in this book contain raw eggs. The bacterium *salmonella* may be present in raw eggs, and therefore they should not be consumed by infants and small children, pregnant women, the elderly, and any people who may be immunocompromised. When using eggs, whether they will be served raw or cooked, it is advisable that you buy only certified *salmonella*-free eggs.

ABOUT PREPARATION TIMES

Throughout this book, the recipes require a variety of preparation times. Some of the recipes are quick and simple, perfect at the end of a hectic day. Others are more involved, great for those relaxed weekends when you want to prepare a delicious repast for friends or family. Still others, such as soups and braises, have brief preparation times but longer cooking times. Be sure to review the recipe you want to prepare to make sure that it works with your schedule.

A WINE AND FOOD PAIRING HINT

If you are looking for a recipe to serve with a particular wine selection, check the index. All wine recommendations are cross-referenced with the recipes.

An Introduction to Wine

Carolyn Wente

WINE IS FOOD. Having grown up in the world of vineyards and wineries, I find this very logical. For one, wine flavors and enhances our food preparations, both as an ingredient and as an accompaniment. In much the same way that an herb chart tells you which herbs blend well with certain ingredients, there are wine charts that offer similar general information. Second, the flavors are essentially the same. Using the same descriptive aromas and flavors that we experience in food, we can describe the delicious wine just sampled. Third, the molecular structure in wine that makes it smell or taste like a particular food is actually identical to the molecular structure of that food.

In order to be able to talk about wine, we need to have a set of words to describe our experiences. The practice of describing wine using food flavors is what led Ann Noble, a professor of food science at the University of California at Davis, to create one of the best tools in the wine industry. It's called the Aroma Wheel, shown on page xxiv. The Aroma Wheel organizes the aromas and flavors identified in wine. Its usage provides a starting point for a common descriptive vocabulary for our wine experiences. We can then identify similar attributes in food recipes and begin the process of pairing wine and food flavors.

WHAT INFLUENCES FLAVOR?

The flavor in any wine starts with the grape itself and the vine on which it is grown. Most grape varieties, such as chardonnay, are grown around the world. Where they are planted becomes the ultimate flavor determinant—the soils, the climate, the viticultural practices in the vineyards where they are grown, as well as how and when they are picked. I am often asked, "What did you add to the wine to make it taste like apples and pears?" Of course, the answer is nothing; that specific smell or taste comes from the variety of grape. Once the grapes are brought to the winery, additional influences from the winemaking process, the fermenting, the aging, and the art of blending all contribute to the final style and characteristics of a wine—its flavor, weight, texture, body, and intensity.

Where a vine is planted and how it grows are key to understanding flavors in wine. Wine grapes are reasonably easy to cultivate and adapt to a wide spectrum of soils and climates. The richer the soil, the easier it is for the vine to grow, producing foliage (canopy) and bunches of grapes. The warmer the climate, the more rapidly the grapes ripen. The combination of these two factors produces a high yield of grapes with ripe flavors and low acid. Conversely, a poorer soil causes the vine to struggle, producing fewer leaves and bunches. In a cooler climate, the grapes hang on the vine longer in order to ripen. These factors combine to produce a lower grape yield with herbal, vegetal, and grassy flavors and higher acid. Additionally, if a grape is left on the vine in the sun, it will fully ripen and dehydrate, becoming a raisin, which is almost entirely sugar.

As grapes ripen, the sugar and acid content is constantly monitored to determine the best time for harvest. Grape growers and winemakers are watching for a particular sugar-acid balance and a particular development of flavors suitable for the style of wine they are producing. Not only are grapes tasted in the fields, but various sample grapes throughout a particular block are analyzed in the laboratory. Picking begins when the desired flavors, sugar, acid, and pH balance are reached throughout that block of vines.

Each grape variety takes on different qualities—including aromas, flavor variations, weight, and balance—depending on the region in which it is grown. The spectrum of flavors from a chardonnay grape grown in a cool area is crisp (higher acid), with more delicate flavors, including apple, pear, and citrus (tree fruits). In warmer years and at warmer vineyard sites, the chardonnay vine will produce riper, softer flavors (lower acid) with more ripe apple, melon, pineapple, and banana characteristics (tropical fruit flavors).

Each grape variety bears fruit of different size. The smaller the grape, the greater the proportion of skin to juice and pulp, which produces more concentrated color and flavor compounds in the juice (must). Cabernet sauvignon, one of the smallest grapes, typically is full in color and flavor as compared to a pinot noir grape, which has thin skin, more juice, and a more delicate flavor.

CALIFORNIA WINE REGIONS

In California, soils vary from very rich to very poor, and climates range from hot to cold. Throughout the state, the grapes grown will be influenced by the combination of soils and the climate of any particular region. Most of California's premium table wines come from coastal valleys and hillsides that have a wide range of soil types and climates moderated by the Pacific Ocean or the larger bays along the coastline, such as San Francisco and Monterey bays.

INFLUENCES IN WINE PRODUCTION

After grapes are harvested and brought to the winery, they are gently pressed. Then fermentation is started, which is the process of converting the grape sugar to alcohol and carbon dioxide. It is controlled and influenced by the yeast, the temperature, and the container.

Some wineries use native or wild yeasts found on the skins of the grapes. These are not easy to control, nor do they yield consistent results. Sometimes fermentation is started with the wild yeast, but most producers inoculate the grape juice with a yeast strain they have nurtured and know will provide an active fermentation. When the yeast has converted all of the grape sugar to alcohol and carbon dioxide, the result is a completely dry wine. If the fermentation is stopped before the yeast finishes converting all of the sugar, the resulting wine has some sweetness. The sweeter the wine, the more residual or natural grape sugar is present. In California, it is not legal to add sugar during the winemaking process.

Fermentation of wine usually takes place in stainless steel tanks or small oak barrels, casks, or puncheons. Stainless steel is a perfect container, which means that it does not impart any flavor to the wine, resulting in the most pure varietal characteristics. When grape juice is fermented in barrels, usually made of oak, it picks up additional flavor, which helps soften the wine. Oak is a semiporous wood that allows air to come into contact with the wine, causing the wine to mellow or oxidize slightly. This usually creates a smoother wine and helps to develop its aromas. Some of the aromas and flavors from barrel fermentation are wood, toasted oak, vanilla, smoke, and cereal grain. An oak barrel can be used numerous times, but each time it imparts less flavor. A new oak barrel imparts the most complex aromas and flavors to the wine. Both red and white wines are aged in wood barrels. A white wine aged in oak will develop more texture and flavor than the same wine that has been held in stainless steel. The most common barrel-fermented white wine is Chardonnay, while some producers will also barrel-ferment Sauvignon Blanc and Sémillon for more flavor.

The effects of temperature in the fermentation process can change the flavor profiles. A cooler fermentation preserves the varietal characteristics of the must, producing a lighter, crisper wine. Warmer fermentation temperatures, which are usually used in red wines, make the fermentation go faster but cause the loss of some of the flavors. If the temperature is too warm, the yeast dies and fermentation is not completed.

As a wine undergoes fermentation, the resulting alcohol is a critical component because it determines a wine's weight and flavor. The weight is felt on your palate. A light wine has less alcohol, 8 to 10 percent by volume, while a full-bodied wine has 13 to 14 percent alcohol by volume. Compare a light Chenin Blanc, with an alcohol content of around 10 percent, to a "big" (full-bodied) Chardonnay, with an alcohol content approaching 14 percent. This same Chardonnay may taste perceptibly sweeter because alcohol influences our perception of flavor. Usually a lower-alcohol dry wine will taste drier than its higher-alcohol counterpart.

An additional influence on wine during the winemaking process is malolactic fermentation. This is a secondary fermentation that involves the natural conversion of malic acid to lactic acid. Malic acid can be likened to the sharp, tart acid found in green (pippin) apples, while lactic acid is a softer acid found in milk, cream, and butter. When a white wine goes through malolactic fermentation, it becomes softer, reducing the tartness and adding the flavor complexities of butter to butterscotch. All red wines go through malolactic fermentation spontaneously, as do some whites. Winemakers can control it to produce a particular style of wine, inducing it when it doesn't occur naturally or stopping the spontaneous occurrence to attain a particular balance between acidity and creaminess.

When red wines are made, the juice remains in contact with the skins and seeds of the grapes for a period of time to extract color from the skin. During this time, tannin is also extracted from the skin of the grapes and the seeds. Great care is taken not to break open the seeds, which would impart even more tannin and bitterness to the juice. Tannins are more prevalent in red wines than in white wines because of this process. While tannins contribute to the longevity of a wine, their astringent characteristics are perceived as a bitterness by your entire palate.

Wine aging is a reflection of style in both red and white wines. Aging can take place in wood containers as well as in the bottle. The longer the wine is aged in a wood container, the more oak characteristics it picks up and the mellower the wine becomes. The winemaker must be very careful not to overdo oak aging. The extreme example is wine that has stayed too long in the barrel, becoming overly oxidized and turning into vinegar. Wines held in stainless steel do not age appreciably and tend to be cleaner, crisper in flavor, and lighter in texture.

Sur lie aging also influences a wine's flavor and texture. This French term refers to the practice of aging a wine on the yeast sediment (the lees) after the fermentation process has been completed. The lees enhance the flavor, texture, and complexity of the wine, adding yeasty, toasty, baked bread, and nutty characteristics. Again, the wines that are most often aged *sur lie* are Chardonnay and Sauvignon Blanc as well as Champagne when made in the traditional manner.

In addition to the techniques mentioned here, winemakers may blend different varietals to produce their particular style or vision of a wine. There is no formula to this creative process—they may combine several different varietals, a malolactic and nonmalolactic-fermented lot, or a sweet with a dry. What the winemaker is seeking is a particular balance of the various flavor components. And as is always the case, good wines start in the vineyard.

VARIETAL CHARACTERISTICS

Each particular wine varietal can usually be identified by its particular spectrum of aromas and flavors. These may vary within a given range as a result of the influences of the yearly climates, soils, and farming techniques used on the vines. However, a vocabulary can be developed to describe each grape variety, the wine it produces, and the expected flavor characteristics. Following are descriptors of the major wine grape varieties grown in California and the wines produced from them, which generally reflect the effects of the growing conditions.

WHITE WINE VARIETALS

Chardonnay is one of the world's most esteemed white wine varietals. It is noted for its range of styles, depth of flavors, and complexity. The major categories of Chardonnay's aromas and flavors as illustrated in the Aroma Wheel lean toward fruit, spice, and wood. Within the fruit category, the warmer growing regions produce wines with "riper" flavors such as pineapple, pear, banana, mango, and peach, while the cooler-region grapes demonstrate flavors from the other end of the fruit spectrum, such as green apple, lemon, and grapefruit. If the wines are barrel fermented or aged in oak, they begin to take on spice and wood attributes. These aromas and flavors include cinnamon and cloves as well as toasted oak, smoke, and vanilla. A Chardonnay that has been stainless steel fermented will maintain clean, fresh fruit flavors. Lastly, if the Chardonnay has gone through malolactic fermentation, it will alter the acidity of the wine, giving the wine a softer and rounder feeling in your mouth while adding flavor complexities of butter, butterscotch, and caramel. If the wine has been aged *sur lie*, some yeasty, nutty, and baked bread characteristics will come through. Chardonnay ranges from medium- to full-bodied in style.

Sauvignon Blanc is a varietal that has very distinct characteristics that carry through the winemaking process. The flavor spectrum most associated with Sauvignon Blanc is from greener flavors (herbs, grass, green bean) to riper ones (citrus, melon, fig). Generally, the cooler the region the greater the tendency toward herbal, grassy, and citrus notes. The warmer the region, the more the variety develops toward melon, kiwi, and fig flavors. Oftentimes, Sémillon is blended in with Sauvignon Blanc, yielding a wine with more body and even more fig and honey characteristics. This blending will also somewhat reduce the acidity. Like Chardonnay, Sauvignon Blanc can have complexity added through barrel fermentation, oak aging, and malolactic fermentation. The results are somewhat similar in that aromas and flavors of toasted oak, smoke, vanilla, butter, and butterscotch are developed in the wine. Sauvignon Blanc ranges from light-medium to full in body, depending on the winemaking style.

Johannisberg Riesling (also known as White Riesling) is generally stainless steel–fermented, which results in a wine that focuses on the fruit aromas and flavors. This grape has floral and fruit as

its main categories, with specific aromas and flavors of orange blossom, rose petals, peaches, apricots, and apples. Traditionally, this grape has been planted in cooler climates, which allows the grape variety to develop ripe fruit flavors while maintaining a good acid balance. This wine is made both dry and off-dry, which influences the perception of its body from light to medium.

Chenin Blanc is sometimes referred to as the "poor man's Chardonnay" when produced as a dry wine with some amount of barrel aging. However, the majority of Chenin Blanc wines in California are made with some amount of residual grape sugar. The varying degrees of sweetness create a wine ranging from light to medium in body. The grape variety's origins are in the Loire Valley of France, which produces the well-known Vouvrays. The aroma and fruit characteristics are predominantly in the fruit category, much like Chardonnay. Fruit notes for

Aroma Wheel

copyright © 1990 A.C. Noble

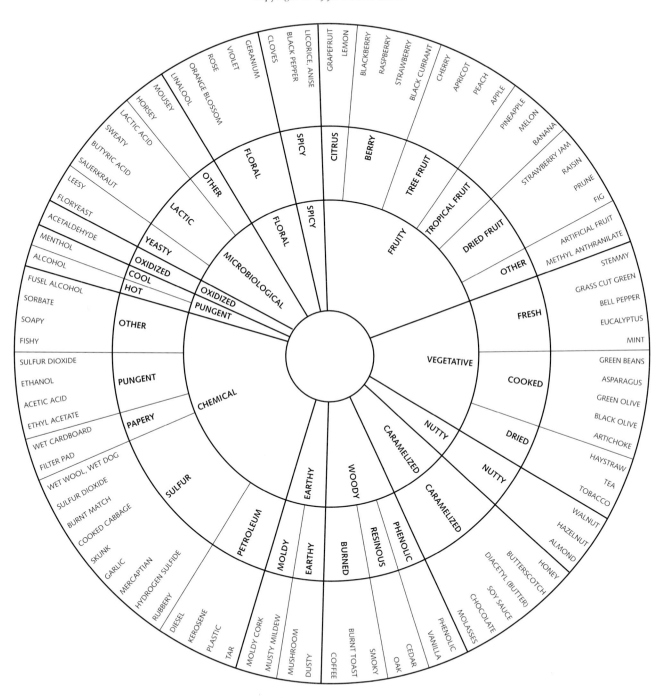

To purchase a colored plastic laminated aroma wheel, please see
Mail Order Resources, page 213, for details.

this varietal would be lemon, apple, pear, and pineapple. Chenin Blanc has a wonderful sweet-sour balance, reflecting the degree of fruit and residual sugar in the wine as well as its ample acid.

Gewürztraminer, whose origins are most closely associated with the Alsace region of France and Germany, takes its name from the traminer grape variety combined with the German word *gewürz*, meaning spicy. The vine does well in cooler climates. There is a tendency for the acid level to drop rapidly and for the pH to rise as the grape ripens. The grape grower must monitor it closely to assure that the sugar and flavor development is nicely balanced by the acid. The assertive fruit flavors tend toward grapefruit and apple, while there are spicy cinnamon and clove undertones as well. Generally, the grapes are pressed and cool-fermented in stainless steel, enhancing the fruit and spice qualities. The wine sees little or no aging. It is produced both dry and off-dry, putting it in the range of light to medium body.

RED WINE VARIETALS

Cabernet Sauvignon is considered by many to be the top red wine varietal because of its full flavor, robust character, and ability to age. This varietal has a wide complexity of aromas and flavors, influenced by the growing region, viticultural methods, age, and yield of the vine. Aromas and flavors identified with Cabernet Sauvignon are fruit (blackberry, currant, cherry, plum), herbs (black and green tea, tobacco, mint) earth (mushroom), vegetal (green and black olives, green bean, bell pepper), wood (oak, toasted oak, smoky, eucalyptus, cedar, resin), spice (vanilla, pepper, juniper berry, cloves), and floral (violet, rose). The cooler regions or vineyard sites produce grapes with more vegetal or herbal characteristics, whereas the warmer regions produce grapes with fruitier character and more spice. The wood flavors generally relate to the amount of contact with oak, such as barrel aging, that the wine has. Oak barrel aging helps to soften the wines. Because of the distinctive nature of this grape, it is often blended with Merlot, Cabernet Franc, Malbec, or Petit Verdot, each contributing to the complexity of the finished wine. Cabernet can be soft with an elegant structure, or it can be tannic, muscular, and full. It can be found in a broad range of flavors from light-medium to very full in body.

Merlot, once used mainly for blending with Cabernet Sauvignon, is now one of the more popular red varietals. The wine is distinguished in flavor and is generally produced as medium to full in body. The aromas and flavors are as wide ranging as those found in Cabernet Sauvignon; however, its appeal is its accessibility and softness. In the fruit spectrum, plum, cherry, raspberry, blackberry, currant, and blueberry can be found. The herbal tones tend to lean toward tea and tobacco as well as mint. In cooler regions, more vegetal flavors can appear in this varietal, hinting of green olive, green bean, and green pepper. Spice and wood characteristics include vanilla, black pepper, and licorice, as well as toasted oak, eucalyptus, and cedar. As with Cabernet Sauvignon, growing regions, vineyard sites, viticultural practices, and winemaking influences all contribute to the finished wine. It can range from fruity and mellow to rich and complex, making it a favorite for food pairing.

Pinot Noir is the classic red varietal from the Burgundy region in France. This varietal generally favors cooler regions and careful winemaking to ensure adequate flavor and structure. This varietal is versatile, ranging in style from light-medium to fuller in body, with corresponding flavors and texture. When grown in cooler climes along the California coast or in Oregon, it yields berry fruit flavors characteristic of raspberry, strawberry, cranberry, and currant. It can also have concentrated cherry and plum flavors. Pinot Noir will often have hints of spice, including cloves, ginger, cinnamon, nutmeg, vanilla, and black pepper. Often aged in oak, it will have nuances of toasted oak, smoke, and cedar. Pinot Noir can have a wonderful earthy quality reminiscent of mushrooms and truffles. With the broad flavor spectrums and its tendency toward medium body and elegant texture, it is one of my favorites for pairing with food.

Zinfandel is an extremely flavorful grape and is produced as a light-medium to full and rich red wine. It is also used to produce the "pink" or rosé style wine known as White Zinfandel. The Zinfandel varietal yields flavors in the berry fruit category of blackberry and raspberry but can also take on the concentrated flavors of grape and jam. The predominant spice found in this wine is black pepper, but cloves, cinnamon, and anise can also be present. The wood aromas or flavors include toasted oak, eucalyptus, pine, and smoke. The vegetal characteristics sometimes found in this wine are olive, pepper, pumpkin, and green bean. Floral notes can hint at rose, violet, and lavender.

Syrah is the major red varietal in the Rhône Valley of France and is widely planted in Australia and South Africa. Syrah as a grape variety is known for its ability to age and its depth of color and flavor. The petite sirah grape has been in California for more than a hundred years, and its origins are traced to syrah. Yet genetic testing has produced some uncertainty surrounding its origins. According to research done at the University of California at Davis, petite sirah is linked to at least three genetically distinct varieties: durif, peloursin, and one still to be distinctly recognized but probably traceable to syrah. In essence, there are vineyards throughout California that are planted with different varieties but that still make an excellent red wine known as Petite Sirah. This grape creates a wine that is concentrated in fruit such as blackberry, brambleberry, raspberry, and plum and with lots of spice, including black pepper, nutmeg, and cloves. In the wood category, it picks up oak and toasted oak, but as the wine ages a pleasant cedar bouquet will develop. Both Syrah and Petite Sirah can be full-bodied and strong in tannin while young but develop into soft, rich wines as they age. When grown in cooler regions, the intensity of color and tannins increases along with the more herbal and green flavors.

PAIRING WINE WITH FOOD

From the vineyard through the winemaking process to the bottle, the individual flavors of each grape variety will come through in the wine. These varietal characteristics are the major flavor components in a wine. Winemaking influences come into play because they also contribute to the weight, texture, and final balance of a wine—in essence, determining its style. When considering which wines to pair with a particular dish, these are the flavors I look to match or contrast.

Most of us interested in wine and food have learned some traditional guidelines, such as

"White wine with fish and white meats, red wine with red meats and heavier, more robust foods, and rosé (pink) wine with everything else," and "White before red, and dry before sweet." We have heard these for good reason—they work. Wines should be consistent with the various courses in the meal, generally building from lighter to heavier (appetizers to main course). Generally, starting wines should not be too big and rich or too filling. When you begin with a sparkling wine, its effervescence will refresh the palate, as will any wine that is light in alcohol, clean, crisp (good acidity), and flavorful. As the meal progresses, the wines can become bigger and richer, matching the food.

Today's chefs are pushing the boundaries of flavor by discovering new ingredients, preparing nontraditional dishes, and combining ethnic cuisines. In doing so, the traditional guidelines of wine and food pairing have been pushed to the limit. With all of this experimentation taking place, it is exciting to see that there is no longer one right match for a given food. Much of this trial and error is based on personal preference, having the confidence to explore, and not being shy about the outcome.

In pairing wine with food, there are certain clues I look for in the style of wine, the ingredients list, and the preparation techniques. All relate to body, weight, and texture. Starting with the traditional guidelines mentioned earlier, I also must decide if I want to complement or contrast the wine and food. What will each achieve? Which will be the better result? There are some intricacies caused by certain ingredients or by a combination of flavors or even by a particular cooking method that may create a challenge with the pairing; knowing to watch for these is helpful, too. See "Adjusting Recipes to Complement Wine" (page 91).

The wine recommendations found in this book's wine notes focus on wines made from grape varieties grown in California. The climate and soils in California are similar to many found in the premier wine grape–growing regions around the world, giving us a wonderful spectrum of wines from which to choose. At the Wente Vineyards Restaurant, we serve well over 400 wines from various appellations in the state, which reflects our food philosophy to develop memorable wine and food pairings for our guests.

The Clues

Flavor and intensity are two important elements to consider when choosing a wine to complement food. A simple approach is to identify a flavor in the food and match it in the wine, mimicking similar components. For example, a Pinot Noir can have currant flavors, so it would pair well with a currant sauce served over roasted duck. The intensity of flavor refers to the notion that both wine and food have a range of flavors, from very delicate and subtle to extremely full and powerful. A wine should be paired with a food that has equal intensity, delicate with delicate and full-bodied with big and rich. Match delicate sand dabs with a delicate, stainless steel–fermented Sauvignon Blanc, not with a winery's full-bodied, tannic reserve Cabernet Sauvignon.

Another element is the cooking techniques. If you poach a salmon, it will taste lighter and more delicate than if you grill it or roast it. If you shave fennel and dress it in a salad, it will have a different flavor than if you braise it in the oven and serve it with a stew. How a food is prepared will change the texture and flavors.

The weight and texture of both food and wine are also clues. As I mentioned earlier, a wine's alcohol content determines its weight, body, and flavor. The higher the alcohol content in a wine, the fuller the body and the higher the viscosity. Such wines have a thicker feeling on your tongue, almost coating it. The less alcohol in a wine, the lighter it feels in the mouth. A wine with 13 to 14 percent alcohol is medium to full-bodied and would pair well with a heavier dish.

Another clue to be considered is heat—not temperature, but spice. A wine higher in alcohol will increase the heat in spicy food, exaggerating the hotness. A lighter wine will diminish this effect, as will some amount of sweetness in a wine. An off-dry wine, with its slight sweetness, will moderate spicy characteristics. Food ingredients like chile peppers, black pepper, horseradish, and even raw garlic can numb the palate. When this numbing occurs, delicate or subtle flavors in a wine are lost.

Choosing contrasting flavors is decidedly more difficult than choosing complementary ones, but the same considerations apply—flavor, intensity, texture, and heat. The most prevalent example of opposites in flavor is sweet and sour. An example of this is a sweet Dungeness crab morsel served with an acidic (tart) Sauvignon Blanc. Add to this same morsel of crab a dab of aioli, which is rich and creamy with a hint of garlic, and the contrast with the Sauvignon Blanc is even more pronounced, but it still works well because the good acidity in the wine acts like a squeeze of fresh lemon, cleansing the palate of the rich crab and aioli.

Another example of contrast is salt and acid. Very salty foods pair best with high-acid wines—particularly sparkling wines. Some amount of experimentation is necessary to find the perfect contrast, but when you are successful, it can take your enjoyment of wine and food to another level. Try freshly shucked oysters in their salty brine with champagne or a crisp, dry Chenin Blanc.

Texture in both food and wine is the actual feeling on your tongue when you take a bite or a sip. As I discuss in the sidebar "How We Taste Wine and Food" (page 39), salt, sour, bitter, and sweet all have distinct locations on the tongue. Because you actually feel a sensation on your tongue, it is often easier to understand or describe texture, giving it a stronger influence than flavor.

As with flavor, texture must be in balance when pairing food and wine. In order to do this, consider each of the four tastes. Salt contrasts with bitterness and lowers the perception of bitterness in wine. As I mentioned before, salt with a highly acidic wine counterbalances the acid. Acid levels need to be less in food than in the wine it is paired with, or the wine will appear dull. A common example of this is dressing a salad with too much vinegar, causing the wine to taste flat. A young wine with a lot of astringency and some bitterness can be balanced by having a bitter component in the food, bringing out the fruit flavor of the wine. Lastly, the level of sweetness in a wine should always be equal to or greater than the sweetness of the food, or the wine will taste bitter and thin. Each of these four flavors influences the perception of texture in wine, and the same applies to food. A good match between food and wine occurs when there is a balance of all of these flavors.

Beware of food high in fat, which coats the palate and reduces the ability to perceive textures. With these foods, serve wines having the same intensity of richness, such as a malolactic-fermented, full-bodied, high-alcohol Chardonnay with a rich, creamy Alfredo sauce. Without this richness, the wine would appear light and thin. Fat can also reduce the perception of tannin or bitterness, which can be helpful when pairing "big" red wines. This is why many such wines are wonderful with cheese or with a well-marbled, rare steak. The high acid contrasts with the fattiness, and the sweet, red-blood juiciness contrasts with the bitterness of the tannins, providing balanced flavors.

The serving temperature of a wine is always important and can drastically influence the flavor of the wine. If a wine—red or white—is served too cold, some of its flavors will be masked, distorting the combinations. Certainly a chilled wine can be served as a nice contrast to spicy, hot foods. Red wines, when served too warm (warmer than 68°), can emphasize the tannins, causing a bitterness that may not complement the food. Sometimes slightly chilling a red wine will bring out its fruity nature and lessen the perception of the tannins. The ideal temperature for white wines is 45° to 55°; for reds it is 55° to 65°.

Lastly, personal preference should be the deciding factor in making a wine selection. Each person's body chemistry is unique, which results in different individual tastes and perceptions. Then there is the place and time. My response to a frequent question I am asked, "What is your favorite wine?" is very simple. It depends on my mood, the weather, the time of day, and the occasion—am I pairing it with food or sipping it as an apéritif? All of these guide my choice of wine for any given occasion.

S P R I N G

MEAT AND POULTRY

*Roast Leg of Lamb, Petite Sirah–Balsamic Sauce, and Mint Oil
with Artichoke–New Potato Gratin* 30

*Smoked Pork Chops with Ginger-Peach Chutney
and Creamy Polenta* 32

*Crispy Breast of Muscovy Duck with Maple Glaze, Cherry Sauce,
and Hazelnut Wild Rice* 34

*Quail Stuffed with Fresh Ricotta, Bacon, and Greens with
Green Garlic–Sweet Pea Purée* 36

FISH AND SHELLFISH

Pecan-Crusted Rainbow Trout with Citrus Salsa 38

Soft-Shell Crabs with Spring Vegetable Slaw and Basil Aioli 40

Halibut Poached in Fennel Broth with Dried Tomato Relish 42

*Grilled Jumbo Prawns Marinated in Ginger, White Wine,
and Lemon with Mango-Mint Salsa* 44

DESSERTS

*Mascarpone Cheesecake with Biscotti Crust
and Balsamic Strawberries* 46

Blackberry and Pistachio Shortcakes with Lime Cream 48

Warm Fruit Compote with Lavender-Vanilla Ice Cream 51

Mile High Chocolate Cake 52

Smoked Trout on Potato Chips with Lemon, Fennel, and Dill

MAKES ABOUT 20 CHIPS AND 1 CUP OF SMOKED TROUT TOPPING

❧ WINE NOTES

A crisp, slightly off-dry Gewürztraminer or Riesling would be very refreshing with these chips. These two wines usually have good acid, which will refresh the palate, and the slight residual sugar will add some body and contrast. If you prefer to complement the flavors in this recipe, the crisp herbal characteristics of a Sauvignon Blanc or a Pinot Grigio pair well with the fennel, lemon, and trout.

I used to make these potato chips with a piece of the green part of a scallion woven through the potato slices before they were fried—my staff nearly mutinied! It looked great but was very labor intensive. The smoked trout topping makes a great meal by itself, served over a bed of salad greens. You could also serve it on cucumber or tomato slices, or on toasts. Purchase the smoked trout if you can't smoke them yourself.

POTATO CHIPS

2 to 3 russet potatoes, peeled and reserved in water

Peanut oil for deep-frying

SMOKED TROUT TOPPING

2 (8-ounce) fresh trout, center bones removed, with skin

Kosher salt and freshly ground pepper

1 small bulb fennel, finely diced (reserve some tops for garnish)

1/4 cup diced red onion

2 teaspoons finely chopped lemon zest

1 teaspoon chopped fresh dill

2 tablespoons extra-virgin olive oil

3 tablespoons lemon juice, or to taste

To smoke the trout: Season the trout with salt and pepper. Smoke as described on page 62. Cool, remove the skin, and flake.

To prepare the chips: Slice the potatoes on a slicer or mandoline, about 1/8 inch thick. Rinse in a few changes of fresh water until the water is clear, removing most of the starch from the potatoes. In a high-sided pot, heat 4 inches of peanut oil to 350°. Pat the potato slices dry, and cook them in small batches in the oil, stirring often, until golden brown. Remove from oil, drain, and season with a light sprinkling of salt.

To prepare the topping: In a bowl, combine the flaked trout, fennel, red onion, finely chopped lemon zest, dill, and olive oil. Add lemon juice, salt, and pepper to taste.

To serve, spoon about 2 teaspoons of the topping onto each chip. Garnish with fennel leaves.

Spring Leek Cakes with Smoked Sturgeon, Créme Fraîche, and Chives

These cakes can be made in smaller rounds and used as hors d'oeuvres. You can also substitute other fish such as salmon, trout, caviar, scallops, or prawns. When cooking in oil, as you do in this recipe, always tip the pan away from you when turning the cakes so that any oil splatters away from you. The starch from the potatoes is what binds these cakes together. Make sure you use russet potatoes, which are high in starch and low in moisture and prepare them just before you use them. You can add a little cornstarch if the mixture is not holding together. When I made this recipe in Istanbul, I found that the potatoes there were not as starchy as ours, so I added a bit of cornstarch.

> 1 leek, white part only, washed and cut into julienne (about 1 cup)
>
> 2 russet potatoes, peeled and cut into julienne (about 2 cups)
>
> Kosher salt and freshly ground pepper
>
> 2 tablespoons olive oil
>
> 1 tablespoon cornstarch (optional)
>
> 8 slices smoked sturgeon (about 8 ounces)
>
> $1/4$ cup crème fraîche (page 199)
>
> 1 tablespoon chopped chives
>
> Lemon juice for sprinkling over cakes

In a bowl, toss together the leek and potato. Season with a salt and pepper.

Preheat the oven to 350°.

In a large nonstick frying pan over medium-high heat, heat the oil. You may need to use a bit more olive oil so that the cakes cook evenly. Form the potato mixture into 4 cakes, about $3^{1}/_{2}$ inches in diameter and about 1 inch thick. The starch from the potatoes should hold the cakes together. If they seem a little loose, add a tablespoon of cornstarch to the mixture. Carefully place the cakes in the hot oil. Reduce the heat to medium, as they'll get bitter if they cook too fast. Fry one side until golden brown, 5 to 7 minutes. Turn the cakes over and repeat. Drain on paper towels. Place on a baking sheet and bake in the oven for 10 minutes to finish cooking the insides.

To serve, divide the cakes among 4 plates. Top each cake with 2 slices of smoked sturgeon, a tablespoon of crème fraîche, a few pieces of chive, and a squeeze of lemon juice.

SERVES 4

❧ WINE NOTES

A basic concept in food and wine pairing is that wines high in acid cleanse the palate, increasing your desire for what you are eating. Echoing this concept, the effervescence of a sparkling wine or Champagne will tease your palate, while the acidity will be refreshing with this rich and oily fish. A dry sparkling wine, labeled "natural" or "brut," would be an excellent match.

5

Artichoke–Ricotta Fritters with Meyer Lemon Sauce

MAKES 10 TO 12 FRITTERS

⋙ WINE NOTES

Artichokes are notoriously difficult to pair with wine. A component in artichokes, cynarin, blocks all but the sweet taste receptors in the mouth. Pairing these fritters with a wine with good acid, such as Pinot Grigio, helps to balance out this effect.

In Northern California, we are blessed with cool, foggy nights and warm days perfect for growing artichokes. Most of the artichokes sold throughout America come from the Watsonville area, about an hour and a half south of our restaurant. In your market, look for artichokes with tight heads, a bright green color, and good weight for their size. They are the meatiest and most flavorful.

Meyer lemons, a hybrid of lemon and orange, were developed for the cooler climate of Northern California. I have seen them in greenhouse rooms as far north as Vancouver, B.C. They have a unique sweet lemon flavor with only a little of the acidity of regular Eureka lemons. These trees produce several crops throughout their long growing season, usually November through June, showing blossoms and ripe lemons on the same tree at the same time. This long, uneven growing season, combined with a thin skin, makes Meyer lemons a difficult commercial crop. If Meyer lemons are not available in your area, use equal amounts of lemon and orange juice.

Use a peeler, rather than a zester, when removing the skin. Cut away the white pith, which is bitter, and then finely chop the peel.

MEYER LEMON SAUCE

1 tablespoon diced shallot

1/2 cup dry white wine

1/4 cup champagne vinegar

1/4 cup heavy whipping cream

1/2 cup unsalted butter, at room temperature

1 teaspoon Meyer lemon juice

1/2 teaspoon finely chopped Meyer lemon zest

Dash of kosher salt

ARTICHOKE-RICOTTA FRITTERS

4 or 5 large artichokes (to yield about 2 cups coarsely chopped artichoke hearts)

1/2 lemon

2 cups ricotta (to make your own, see page 200)

1 tablespoon grated Parmesan cheese

1 tablespoon baking powder

2 large eggs, lightly beaten

1/4 teaspoon ground cayenne pepper

1 1/2 tablespoons Eureka lemon juice

Kosher salt and freshly ground pepper

About $1/2$ cup flour

Peanut oil for deep-frying

Flat-leaf parsley sprigs, for garnish

To prepare the sauce: In a non-reactive saucepan over medium heat, combine the diced shallot, white wine, and vinegar and bring to a simmer. Continue to cook at a low simmer until most of the liquid is gone, approximately 15 minutes. Add the cream, bring the mixture back to a simmer, and reduce for 5 minutes, or until it coats the back of a spoon. Remove from the heat and slowly whisk in the butter, a little at a time. Make sure that each addition of butter is completely blended into the mixture before adding more. If the sauce gets too cool while adding the butter, place the pan back over low heat for a few seconds before continuing. Thin with the lemon juice. Add the finely chopped lemon zest. Season with salt to taste. Set aside in a warm area.

To prepare the fritters: By hand, tear off the outer leaves of the artichokes, until you reach the lighter-colored inner leaves. With a sharp paring knife, trim away these inner leaves and the outer stem until just the hearts of the artichokes remain. (To prevent discoloration, wait until after cooking to remove the fuzzy choke.) Rub the artichoke hearts with the cut side of a lemon half.

In a saucepan, cover the hearts with water and bring to a boil. Lower the heat to a simmer and cook until tender and a knife easily pierces the center, approximately 15 minutes. Remove from the water, drain, and cool. Remove the fuzzy choke from the center of each heart with a spoon, then coarsely chop the hearts.

In a bowl, mix together the artichoke hearts, ricotta, Parmesan, baking powder, eggs, cayenne, and lemon juice. Season with salt and pepper. Add enough flour to lightly bind the mixture together.

In a high-sided 4-quart pot, add peanut oil to a depth of 2 inches. Heat the oil to 375°.

To test for seasoning, spoon a small portion of the mixture into the hot oil. Cook until golden brown, turning if necessary. Drain on paper towels. Let cool and then taste. Add salt, pepper, cayenne, or lemon juice to the mixture, as needed.

Dip a large spoon or a $1/4$-cup measuring cup into the oil and then into the fritter mixture. (This prevents the batter from sticking to the spoon or cup.) Using another spoon dipped in oil, push the batter into the hot oil. You want about $1/4$ cup of batter per fritter. Cook both sides until golden brown, turning once. Serve immediately, placing 2 fritters and 2 tablespoons of the sauce on each plate. Garnish with a few sprigs of parsley.

Asparagus and Roasted Shallot Custard with Smoked Salmon and Greens

SERVES 8

WINE NOTES

Because of the creaminess of the custard, the saltiness of the salmon, and the little bit of acid from the vinaigrette, I would serve a brut sparkling wine, a Sauvignon Blanc, or a crisp Chardonnay with this dish.

Many people don't think of preparing a savory custard; they just think of the sweetened dessert version. You can substitute almost anything for the asparagus—I've used corn, a mixture of colored peppers, and chiles. Try serving the custards with fish and meats such as walnut-crusted trout or prosciutto. I've even served a roasted garlic version with slices of rabbit and frisée greens.

The ingredients for this recipe and the asparagus salad are very similar, yet they are distinctively different dishes. This is a great example of using different cooking techniques to prepare the same ingredients and ending up with totally different dishes.

1 tablespoon olive oil

2 or 3 shallots, peeled

Kosher salt and freshly ground pepper

$^1/_4$ cup vegetable or chicken stock (page 205 or 206)

1 cup heavy whipping cream

2 extra-large eggs, lightly whipped

1 teaspoon Dijon mustard

$1^1/_4$ teaspoons grated lemon zest

8 spears fresh asparagus, green part only, sliced thinly on a slight angle

1 tablespoon grated Parmesan cheese

GREENS

1 teaspoon champagne vinegar

1 tablespoon extra-virgin olive oil

$^1/_4$ teaspoon Dijon mustard

$^1/_4$ pound mixed baby greens

8 (1-ounce) slices smoked salmon

Chopped chives and chervil, for garnish

To prepare the custards: Preheat the oven to 350°. In an ovenproof sauté pan over medium heat, heat the olive oil. Add the shallots to the pan and season lightly with salt and pepper. Place in the oven and roast for 15 to 20 minutes, or until the shallots start to caramelize. Add the stock and continue to cook until the shallots are soft, about 10 minutes. Remove from the oven, let cool, and slice thinly. Set aside.

Reduce the oven temperature to 325°.

In a small bowl, mix together the cream, eggs, mustard, and lemon zest, and season with salt and pepper.

Divide the asparagus, shallots, and Parmesan cheese evenly among eight 2-ounce ramekins. Divide the cream and egg mixture evenly among the ramekins. Place in a deep-sided baking pan in the oven. Add hot water until it is halfway up the sides of the ramekins. (It's easier to do this when it is already in the oven.) Bake for about 30 minutes, or until the custard is set. Remove from the oven and cool.

To prepare the greens: In a large bowl, mix together the vinegar, olive oil, and mustard. Season with salt and pepper. Add the greens and toss.

To serve, place a piece of smoked salmon in the middle of each of 8 plates. Run a sharp knife around the edge of each custard. Remove the custard from the mold by turning it over onto your hand and giving it a gentle shake. Flip the custard back over and place it on top of the smoked salmon. Scatter the salad greens around the plate, and garnish with chopped chives and chervil.

THE SPRING GARDEN

When the ground finally dries out and a walk in the garden doesn't end with wet feet, Diane Dovholuk, the energy and focus behind the restaurant's organic gardens, and I are well into planning the spring additions. The ever-changing symbiosis between the kitchen and the garden necessitates working together to plan the garden's harvests. Diane is often searching for some new or unusual variety of herb or vegetable—and the space to plant it—to fulfill a kitchen request.

Spring also means planting herbs and greens. For the home gardener, as well as for us, many of the hard-to-find or expensive "spring things" are easy and simple to grow in the garden (or in a pot). For example, in some areas, green garlic just isn't available, but it is very easy to grow. Diane simply separates the cloves of a garlic bulb—organic is better because it hasn't been treated with anything to prevent sprouting—and pushes each clove into the dirt until the tip is at soil level, with the broad root side down. Shortly after, green shoots sprout. The clove will begin to disappear as it feeds the new plant. Watch it closely! It is best used just as the plant begins to form a new bulb. At this point it looks a lot like a scallion. Green garlic has the garlic flavor without the strong, acidic taste.

We have to make sure we will have plenty of the perennial herbs: thyme, chives, oregano, tarragon, sage, rosemary, lavender, and savory. Then we plant lots of the annuals as well, such as basil, parsley, and cilantro. Of course, each season has a couple of new requests from the kitchen. Chervil, which has a wonderful peppery flavor and can be quite expensive, was a great addition. We use it mixed with salad

greens to add extra punch. It's also added to the chopped, mixed herbs in pasta dishes. Chervil and chives are very tasty with the house smoked salmon. A couple other additions were curly cress plus another variety, upland cress. Upland cress is not curly and has a more hearty, spicy flavor. Both of them are spicier versions of watercress and are a great foil for sweeter things, such as fresh figs, melon, and prosciutto.

Most of the baby greens in a mesclun mix, such as red romaine, Oak Leaf lettuce, and spinach, are quick starts. Mizuna is very fast and easy. Diane waits seven days for the seeds to sprout and then another twenty days of growing before she brings it to us for our salads.

Diane also plans for many edible flowers, which add lots of splash and color to the greenery. The flowers of many herbs and greens have distinctive flavors and are great additions to salads and desserts. The flowers of rocket, or arugula, taste like peanuts and can be used in salads. Calendulas have a nice, peppery bloom, as do nasturtiums. The kitchen uses the spicy flowers of the mustard plant to finish a wonderful yellow, creamy soup. Mustard flowers are also good in salad or as garnishes. The blooms from stock, which taste like radishes, add a lovely fragrance and lots of color to a salad. Try the lavender-colored chive blooms in salads, too. Many flowers, such as nasturtiums, violets, and lavender, can be candied before they are used. Paint them with egg white, sprinkle with a bit of sugar, and let them dry. Don't forget to let some of the blooms go to seed. Plants with flavorful seeds include mustard, chives, and cilantro, also known as coriander. —KJ

Mozzarella Toasts
with White Mushrooms

This recipe was inspired by a friend, Paula Lambert, who owns and operates the Mozzarella Company in Dallas, Texas. Every cheese she makes is hand-crafted and is very special in flavor. I particularly love her mozzarella cheese and often try to find a place to showcase it in a meal. To me, spring means fresh herbs from the garden, so I use a potpourri of them in this recipe. Serve this dish as an appetizer or as an accompaniment to a mixed baby green salad with minced spring onions simply dressed with lemon and extra-virgin olive oil. If you want, use different breads such as sundried tomato and rosemary bread, olive bread, or focaccia. —CW

5 tablespoons butter

1 pound button mushrooms, sliced

$1/2$ teaspoon chopped fresh oregano leaves

$1/2$ teaspoon chopped fresh lemon thyme leaves

1 teaspoon fresh chopped parsley

12 slices whole-grain bread, crusts trimmed

12 $1/4$-inch-thick slices mozzarella cheese

2 tablespoons olive oil, more as needed

Sprigs of herbs, for garnish

In a skillet over moderate heat, melt the butter and sauté the mushrooms until tender, about 6 minutes. Do not overcook, as the liquid will be extracted from the mushrooms, making them dry. Stir in the oregano, lemon thyme, and parsley and immediately remove from the heat. Set aside.

On a cutting board, place 6 of the trimmed bread slices. Place a slice of mozzarella on each of the pieces of bread. With a slotted spoon, divide the mushrooms evenly among the 6 pieces of bread and cheese. Place another slice of cheese on top of the mushrooms and then top with the remaining slices of bread, pressing down gently. Brush the top pieces of bread lightly with half of the olive oil.

Place the sandwiches in a skillet, oiled side down, and pan-fry over medium-high heat until lightly toasted and cheese begins to melt. Brush the top pieces of bread with the remaining olive oil, turn, and toast the other side. Remove and slice into finger food–sized pieces, approximately 1 inch by 3 to 4 inches. Place on a serving platter and garnish with sprigs of herbs.

MAKES ABOUT 18 TOASTS

WINE NOTES

An off-dry Chenin Blanc, with its light body, slight fruitiness, and pleasing acid balance, will enhance the cheese, herb, and mushroom combination. If you prefer a dry wine to start, a Sauvignon Blanc has many of the complementary flavor notes of this recipe, particularly if you serve the toasts with a salad.

Carrot–Ginger Soup
with Spring Onion Cream

SERVES 8

🎋 WINE NOTES

The texture and weight of the carrot soup needs the balance of a medium to fuller-bodied white wine. Tropical or citrus flavors would also complement the ginger and the sweetness of the carrots. A full-bodied, crisp Chardonnay from a cooler region or an oak-aged Sauvignon Blanc from warmer coastal appellations would have these characteristics.

The true spring onion looks similar to a scallion. The difference is that the bulb at the base of the onion has begun to grow but is still young and tender. As with green garlic, the essential flavor is there, but without the assertive tanginess of a mature onion. If you can't find spring onions, substitute scallions.

In this recipe, the vegetables are "sweated" (see glossary) before any liquid is added. This technique deepens their flavors and releases them into the broth.

SPRING ONION CREAM

1 spring onion (green part only)

1/2 cup crème fraîche or sour cream (page 199)

Kosher salt to taste

Meyer lemon juice to taste

ROASTED SPRING ONION AND FRIED CARROT GARNISH (OPTIONAL)

8 spring onions

Olive oil

Kosher salt and freshly ground pepper

2 cups peanut oil for frying

1 carrot, peeled and cut into very thin julienne
    or matchsticks

CARROT-GINGER SOUP

2 tablespoons unsalted butter

1 onion, sliced

2 pounds carrots, sliced
    (reserve 1 whole carrot for optional garnish)

4 sprigs lemon thyme

1 bay leaf

2 cloves garlic, peeled

1 tablespoon sliced fresh ginger plus 1 tablespoon
    grated fresh ginger

2 white potatoes, peeled and diced

6 cups chicken stock (page 206)

1 teaspoon finely chopped Meyer lemon zest

1/2 cup heavy whipping cream

Kosher salt and freshly ground white pepper

3 tablespoons Meyer lemon juice

To prepare the cream: Carefully wash the green end of the onion and chop finely. (You may use the white end in the garnish.) In a small bowl, combine the chopped onion and crème fraîche. Season with salt and lemon juice to taste. Whisk in a little water so that the cream is easily drizzled. Set aside.

To prepare the spring onion garnish: Preheat the oven to 350°. Separate the green and white ends of the spring onions, leaving about 2 inches of the stem. Discard the greens. Carefully wash the white ends, dry, and rub with olive oil, salt, and pepper. Roast in the oven until tender, about 15 minutes. Remove the outer skin, if tough, and slice in half lengthwise. Set aside.

To prepare the carrot garnish: In a medium sauté pan, heat the peanut oil to 375°. Add the julienned carrots and fry until light golden brown. Remove from oil and drain on a paper towel. Do not overcook—they become bitter.

To prepare the soup: In a nonreactive pot over low heat, melt the butter. Add the onion and carrots. Cover and cook until the vegetables start to release some liquid, about 10 minutes, stirring occasionally. Tie the thyme sprigs and bay leaf together and add to the pot, along with the garlic, sliced ginger, and potatoes. Continue cooking for another 5 minutes. Do not let the vegetables take on any color.

Add the chicken stock and bring to a simmer. Cook at a low simmer for 15 to 20 minutes, or until the carrots and potatoes are tender.

Remove the thyme sprigs and bay leaf. Strain. Purée the solids in a food mill or food processor and add back to the cooking liquid. Add the grated ginger, finely chopped lemon zest, and cream and return to medium heat. Bring to a simmer and season with salt, white pepper, and lemon juice.

Serve the soup in heated bowls with a drizzle of the spring onion cream, two halves of roasted spring onion, and a small mound of fried carrots in the center of each bowl.

Arugula Salad with Morel, Prosciutto, and Homemade Ricotta

SERVES 4

The dominant flavors in this recipe are the morels, the prosciutto, and the arugula—one has strong, earthy tones, one a salty, rich, fatty flavor, and the third a peppery, spicy flavor. I suggest a wine with light to medium body, fruity and spicy and probably red. Red wines have a bit more tannin and weight, matching the weight and texture in this dish. A Pinot Noir or Beaujolais would fit this description, or try a lighter-style Zinfandel.

Spring brings the first morels of the year from my home state of Oregon. Look for morels that are hollow, with the stem adjoining the base of the cap. Morels with the stem attached on the inside, much like a regular mushroom, are not true morels and, in fact, are toxic to some people. Try to purchase morels that are dry and meaty, as the flavor is more intense. To clean morels, see page 209. This salad is equally wonderful with other spring vegetables in place of the arugula, such as asparagus, English peas, or fava beans. You could also use dried morels or other wild mushrooms if you can't find them fresh. The homemade ricotta needs to drain overnight, so prepare it a day ahead. Homemade ricotta is easy to make and well worth the effort, containing none of the additives found in commercial ricotta.

VINAIGRETTE

2 tablespoons olive oil

1 tablespoon extra-virgin olive oil

1 tablespoon balsamic vinegar

$^1/_2$ teaspoon Dijon mustard

1 teaspoon minced garlic

Kosher salt and freshly ground pepper

1 tablespoon olive oil

$^1/_2$ pound fresh morels, cleaned

1 shallot, minced

4 slices whole-wheat sourdough bread

1 tablespoon extra-virgin olive oil

1 pound arugula, preferably small leaves, washed and dried

8 very thin slices prosciutto

$1^1/_2$ cups homemade ricotta (page 200)

To prepare the vinaigrette: In a small bowl, combine oils, balsamic vinegar, mustard, and garlic. Season with salt and pepper. Set aside.

To prepare the salad: In a sauté pan over medium-high heat, heat the olive oil. Add the morels and sauté for a few minutes, until softened. Add the shallot and cook until lightly golden. Season to taste with salt and pepper.

Brush one side of each slice of the bread with extra-virgin olive oil and toast in the oven or on a grill. Cut in half diagonally.

To serve, toss the arugula in a bowl with the vinaigrette, and divide among 4 plates. Divide the morels and prosciutto among the plates, arranging them over the greens. Crumble the ricotta over the top. Place 2 pieces of toast on each plate. Serve immediately.

THE EARLY CALIFORNIA WINE INDUSTRY

Since the first grape plantings done by the Spanish missionaries, California's wine industry has followed cycles of boom and bust. In the late 1800s, many of the founders of California's oldest wineries were drawn into the fervor surrounding the industry. These founding fathers planted *vitis vinifera* vineyards, which were the noble or most premium grape varieties brought over from Europe. Among these pioneers were Agoston Haraszthy of Buena Vista in Sonoma; Etienne Thee of Almaden, Paul Masson and Pierre Pellier of Mirassou in San Jose; Gustav Niebaum, Jacob Schram and Charles Krug in Napa; and Charles Wetmore, Carl Wente, and Joseph Concannon in the Livermore Valley. These gentlemen made the Bay Area a major grape-growing region. Their objective was to produce the finest wines in the world. In their view, it was California versus the European countries, which were leading the charge at that point. —CW

Carl Wente, founder of the Wente Vineyards (1913)

New Potato, Leek, and Fennel Soup with Apple Oil

❧ WINE NOTES

Rieslings can be made dry or off-dry and are packed with intense fruit character. Many of the coastal white Rieslings have apple and peach aromas and flavors, which echo the flavors in this recipe. Their good acid content also goes exceptionally well with this creamy potato soup.

The apple oil adds a beautiful visual touch to this dish, as well as contributing intense flavor. Because it takes a bit of time to dry the apple skins, you can prepare the apple oil and the soup a day ahead or in the morning for serving that evening. Letting the flavors in the soup marry for a bit before you serve it will make it more flavorful. It is also possible to dry the skins in a dehydrator. Try to use organic or local apples—commercial apples often have a waxy film to help preserve them. The last time I made this soup I added mussels that had been cooked in water with a bit of Riesling added to it. I substituted this cooking liquid for some of the chicken stock, resulting in a delicious variation.

APPLE OIL

Skins of 2 Granny Smith apples (use apples in soup)

$1/2$ teaspoon lemon juice

$1/4$ cup extra-virgin olive oil

Kosher salt and freshly ground white pepper

NEW POTATO, LEEK, AND FENNEL SOUP

2 tablespoons olive oil

2 Granny Smith apples, peeled, cored, and diced

2 fennel bulbs, finely diced (reserve some tops for garnish)

2 cups sliced leeks (white part only)

2 tablespoons Pernod

2 pounds new red potatoes, peeled and diced
  (reserve in water until used)

4 cups chicken stock, more if needed (page 206)

Bouquet garni containing 1 teaspoon fennel seed,
  2 teaspoons white peppercorns, 2 bay leaves, and
  2 sprigs fresh thyme (page 211)

$1/2$ cup heavy whipping cream

Kosher salt and freshly ground white pepper

To prepare the Apple Oil: Preheat the oven to 200°. Place the apple skins on a baking sheet. (Placing the peeled apples in water with a little lemon juice keeps them from discoloring until you need them for the soup.) Dry in the oven for 4 to 5 hours. They will be very crumbly. In a blender or spice grinder, pulverize them. In a small bowl, combine with the lemon juice and extra-virgin olive oil. Season with salt and white pepper.

To prepare the soup: In a nonreactive pot over medium-low heat, heat 1 tablespoon of the olive oil. Sauté 2 tablespoons each of the diced apple and fennel. Reserve for garnish.

Heat the remaining 1 tablespoon of olive oil in the same pot. Add the leeks and the rest of the apple and fennel. Cover and cook until tender, about 10 minutes, stirring occasionally. Do not brown this mixture. Add the Pernod and flame it (page 209) to burn off the alcohol.

Add the potatoes, chicken stock, and bouquet garni. Cook for 30 to 40 minutes. The texture of the soup should be medium thick. Add more stock if necessary. Remove the bouquet garni and purée the soup with a hand blender or food processor.

Add the cream and bring to a simmer. Season the soup with salt and white pepper to taste.

To serve, ladle into bowls and garnish each bowl with some of the sautéed fennel-apple mixture, fennel tops, and a spoonful of Apple Oil.

Grilled Asparagus with Prosciutto, Roasted Shallot Vinaigrette, and Eight-Minute Egg

SERVES 4

🎋 WINE NOTES

The balsamic vinegar in the vinaigrette has a natural sweetness that can be paired with a slightly sweet, fruity wine. Make sure that the wine has sufficient acid to refresh the palate. A Johannisberg Riesling will meld the flavors nicely. If you prefer a dry wine, try a light, fruity red such as a Gamay or Grenache.

This salad is one of the first delicious signs of spring. If the weather does not allow you to crank up your grill this early, you can roast the asparagus instead. Just toss the spears in the vinaigrette, season with salt and pepper, and spread on a baking sheet. Roast in a preheated 350° oven, turning every few minutes until light golden brown, approximately 10 minutes.

Asparagus tastes best when eaten soon after it is picked. Look for tightly closed heads, as those that have begun to flower will have a stronger grassy flavor. You can peel the asparagus stems to remove some of these flavors, which helps when trying to marry asparagus with wine.

ROASTED SHALLOT VINAIGRETTE

1 tablespoon olive oil

3 shallots, peeled

1 tablespoon Dijon mustard

2 tablespoons balsamic vinegar

1/4 cup extra-virgin olive oil

Kosher salt and freshly ground pepper

2 large eggs

2 bunches thin asparagus, approximately 40 spears

8 very thin slices prosciutto

1 tablespoon coarsely chopped fresh flat-leaf parsley leaves, for garnish

To prepare the vinaigrette: Preheat the oven to 350°. In an ovenproof sauté pan over medium heat, heat the olive oil. Add the shallots. Place in the oven and roast for approximately 30 minutes, turning occasionally so that they brown evenly. Remove from the oven and cool. Remove any papery outer layers and slice. Place in a mixing bowl with the mustard and vinegar. Slowly whisk in the olive oil. Season with salt and pepper. Set aside.

To prepare the eggs and asparagus: Build a medium-hot fire in your barbecue.

Put the eggs in a saucepan and cover with cold water. Bring to a boil. Turn off the heat and let stand for 8 minutes. The center of the yolk should be just cooked through. Immediately after cooking, place the eggs in a bowl of ice water until cool. This releases the shell from the egg. Peel and coarsely chop. Set aside.

Snap off the white woody ends of the asparagus, leaving only the tender, edible parts.

Toss the asparagus in the vinaigrette and season with salt and pepper. Grill until lightly golden brown.

To serve, divide the asparagus among 4 plates, crisscrossing it. Drizzle with some of the vinaigrette so that the asparagus is nicely moistened. Lay 2 pieces of prosciutto over each pile of asparagus. Garnish with parsley and chopped egg.

Green Garlic and White Bean Soup
with Oregano Pesto

SERVES 4 GENEROUSLY

🍷 WINE NOTES

Because of the flavors of oregano and fennel and the underlying bitter component of Swiss chard, this wonderful spring soup is a challenging match. Experiment with Meritage white wines, which are blends of classic Bordeaux grape varieties such as sauvignon blanc and sémillon. The blending creates a richer, creamier wine that complements the weight of this soup.

I am forever inspired by what our head gardener, Diane Dovholuk, grows in early spring. All of these vegetables are planted in our winter garden and harvested at the first rays of spring sunshine. This basic recipe can be used with lots of different vegetables, such as parsnips, leeks, celery, spinach, and kale. If you can't find green garlic, substitute a half-and-half blend of regular garlic and the white parts of scallions.

GREEN GARLIC AND WHITE BEAN SOUP

2 tablespoons olive oil

1 cup minced green garlic, white part only (about 4 stalks)

$1/2$ cup peeled, diced carrot

$1/2$ cup diced onion

$1/2$ cup diced fennel bulb

2 teaspoons minced garlic

1 cup Great Northern beans, soaked overnight

5 cups chicken stock, more if needed (page 206)

Bouquet garni with 2 flat-leaf parsley stems (leaves removed),
    2 oregano stems (leaves removed), $1/2$ teaspoon black peppercorns,
    and 1 bay leaf (reserve the parsley and oregano leaves
    for the pesto) (page 211)

1 cup chopped Swiss chard

OREGANO PESTO

2 tablespoons fresh oregano leaves

2 tablespoons fresh flat-leaf parsley leaves

1 tablespoon pine nuts, toasted (page 210)

$1/4$ cup extra-virgin olive oil

1 tablespoon finely grated Parmesan cheese

1 tablespoon minced green garlic, white part only

1 teaspoon minced garlic

Kosher salt and freshly ground pepper

To prepare the soup: In a pot over medium heat, heat the olive oil. Add the green garlic, carrot, onion, and fennel. Cook for 10 minutes, stirring often. Do not brown. Add minced garlic and cook, stirring, for 1 minute. Add the drained beans, chicken stock, and bouquet garni to the sautéed mixture.

Bring the mixture to a simmer and cook at a low simmer until the beans are tender, about 90 minutes. The texture of the soup should be medium thick. Add more chicken stock if needed.

To prepare the Oregano Pesto: While the soup is simmering, place the oregano, parsley, pine nuts, and extra-virgin olive oil in a blender or mini-chopper and purée until smooth. By hand, blend in the grated Parmesan, green garlic, and garlic. Season with salt and pepper to taste.

Just before serving, add the Swiss chard to the soup and cook at a simmer until the chard is wilted, about 1 to 2 minutes. Ladle the soup into bowls and drizzle with the Oregano Pesto.

REBUILDING AFTER PROHIBITION

Prohibition wiped out much of the efforts of California's early vintners. When winemaking resumed, those who had managed to stay in business had an edge. Not only were their wineries up and running and able to bring the wines to market but they also had older vineyards, which produced higher-quality, fuller-flavored grapes. Those who had to replant had to wait at least three years before a first crop or, as commonly believed, ten years before the full flavor intensity of a mature vine would be reached.

Beginning after Prohibition in the 1930s and continuing on through the 1940s, the focus of California's vintners was to heighten the awareness of their world-class wines. It was necessary to clean up the morass of poor wine that had flooded the market after Prohibition. Much of this wine had been in stock and was marketed under generic names. In an effort to distinguish the quality inherent in the new releases, varietal labeling was introduced. This made it possible for consumers to know what they were buying as well as promote the higher-quality wines. For the first time, a consumer would be assured that a wine labeled Chardonnay was indeed made from the noble chardonnay grape from Burgundy, and was not merely the generic Chablis, which in California could contain any white wine. —CW

Karl, Ernest, and Herman Wente. Herman's wife Edith is seated.

Pizzettas with Pancetta, Leeks, Wild Mushrooms, and Herb Pesto

MAKES 8 PIZZETTAS

🐌 WINE NOTES

This recipe has several wine possibilities. The rich, earthy essence of the mushrooms and the complex flavors suggest a medium-bodied red Pinot Noir or Merlot. A Sauvignon Blanc with herbal hints and good fruit would also pair nicely with the herbs, leeks, and salty pancetta.

This is not your typical American pizza held together with cheese and tomato sauce—I look at pizza dough as a foundation on which to build flavors. These pizzettas are small, each meant to be eaten by one person. To eat, dust them with Parmesan and fold them up New York style.

HERB PESTO

1 tablespoon fresh, coarsely chopped parsley

1 teaspoon fresh, coarsely chopped oregano

1/2 teaspoon fresh, coarsely chopped thyme

2 tablespoons minced garlic

1 tablespoon pine nuts, toasted (page 210)

1/4 cup grated Parmesan cheese

1/2 cup extra-virgin olive oil

1/2 teaspoon crushed red pepper flakes

1 cup chicken stock (page 206)

2 leeks, white part only

1/2 pound pancetta, thinly sliced

1/2 pound wild mushrooms such as chanterelle, black trumpet, or hedgehog, cut into bite-sized pieces

Pizza dough (page 203)

To prepare the pesto: In a mini-chopper or blender, combine the parsley, oregano, thyme, garlic, pine nuts, and Parmesan. Add the olive oil and blend until smooth. Add the chile flakes. Set aside.

To make the pizzettas: Preheat the oven to 350°. In an ovenproof sauté pan, bring the chicken stock to a simmer. Add the leeks and season with salt and pepper. Place in the oven and cook until tender, about 25 minutes.

While the leeks are cooking, place the sliced pancetta on a baking sheet and cook in the oven with the leeks until nicely browned, about 10 minutes. Drain the fat from the pancetta, reserving 1 tablespoon, and crumble the pancetta.

Remove the leeks from the stock and chop coarsely. Set aside. Save the stock for another use.

In a sauté pan over high heat, heat the reserved pancetta fat. If your pancetta didn't render enough fat, add olive oil to measure a total of 1 tablespoon. Add the mushrooms, season with salt and pepper, and sauté until golden brown, shaking the pan often.

As described on page 204, prepare and preheat the oven to 550°, divide the dough into 8 pieces, and shape. Spread Herb Pesto over the bottoms of the shaped dough. Arrange the pancetta, leeks, and mushrooms on top, dividing evenly among the pizzettas. Immediately slide the pizzettas off the paddle onto the pizza stone in the bottom of the oven. Bake until golden brown, 8 to 10 minutes. Remove from the oven and serve immediately.

Orzo with Caramelized Onions and Asiago

With spur-of-the moment dinner guests, I always seek out or develop dishes that are flavorful yet easy to prepare. I like to spend time with my company enjoying the conversation, not always in the kitchen preparing dinner. This orzo dish definitely hits the target, as there is very little preparation and cooking time for this tasty side dish. For small family dinners, I often prepare this recipe as a main course instead of a risotto. Orzo, like risotto, can have many ingredients, such as vegetables, meats, and poultry, added to change the flavor and increase the substance of the dish. —CW

SERVES 4

WINE NOTES

For a classic match of weight, texture, and flavors, try a medium-bodied, ripe-flavored Chardonnay with a hint of oak and buttery richness.

6 to 7 cups chicken stock (page 206)

1 tablespoon extra-virgin olive oil

1 tablespoon unsalted butter

1 large yellow onion, coarsely chopped

Kosher salt and freshly ground pepper

3 cups orzo pasta

1 1/2 cups grated, aged Asiago cheese

1 cup fresh cilantro leaves (reserve several leaves for garnish)

In a large saucepan, bring the chicken stock to a slow boil.

In a large skillet or a saucepan over medium heat, melt and combine the olive oil and butter. Add the onion and sauté until translucent, about 5 minutes. Season the onion lightly with salt and pepper. Add the orzo and continue to sauté until it begins to brown lightly.

Carefully add the hot chicken stock to the skillet. Bring to a boil and cover. Turn off the heat and let stand for 20 minutes. The orzo will absorb the liquid. If any liquid remains, continue to cook over low heat until it has been absorbed. Stir in the cheese and cilantro. Garnish with the reserved cilantro.

Green Garlic and Spring Onion Pizzas with Fennel Sausage

MAKES FOUR 12- TO
14-INCH PIZZAS

❧ WINE NOTES

Pizzas carry a lot of flavorful ingredients. The more ingredients, the more complex and robust the wine needs to be. I think a hearty Zinfandel or Cabernet Sauvignon with hints of herb, spice, oak, berry, and currant flavors meet the test of the young garlic, spring onions, and sausage in these pizzas.

Oven-drying the tomatoes first greatly intensifies their flavor and helps to keep the crust of the pizza crisp, not soggy. I have made wonderful sausage for this pizza using different meats such as duck, venison, turkey, and chicken. Just remember to keep the fat content the same and the results will be fantastic. The origins of this sausage recipe date back to my Italian Cuisine instructor at the California Culinary Academy, Carlo Middione, who contributed much to my culinary education. If grinding your own meat, have everything, including the grinder, ice cold. The meat is then cut cleanly rather than mashed. If you want to make this pizza in another season, substitute a mixture of scallions and regular garlic for the green garlic and scallions, and use regular onion in place of the spring onion. You could also use a little leek.

1 (32-ounce) can whole, peeled plum tomatoes, drained

FENNEL SAUSAGE

1 pound ground pork (about 15% fat)

1 tablespoon minced garlic

1 teaspoon crushed red pepper flakes

2 tablespoons white wine

2 teaspoons fennel seeds, toasted (page 210)

Kosher salt and freshly ground pepper

1 cup chicken stock (page 206)

4 whole spring onions, trimmed

4 stalks green garlic

Pizza dough (page 203)

Olive oil

1 tablespoon fresh whole tarragon leaves

1 cup grated mozzarella

To dry the tomatoes: Preheat the oven to 275°. Cut the tomatoes in half and remove the seeds. Place cut side down on a parchment-lined baking sheet. Roast in the oven for about 1 hour, or until the tomatoes are dried out but not browned.

To prepare the sausage: In a bowl, combine the ground pork, garlic, chile flakes, wine, and fennel seeds. Season with salt and pepper. Cut off a small piece, fry it, and taste for seasoning. Adjust if necessary.

To prepare the onions and garlic: In a small pot, combine the chicken stock and spring onions, and bring to a simmer. Cook until tender, approximately 20 minutes. Remove the onions from the stock and chop coarsely. Save the stock for another use.

Remove the root and green ends of the green garlic and discard. Mince the white part and reserve.

To make the pizzas: As described on page 204, prepare and preheat the oven to 550°, divide the dough into 4 pieces and shape. Brush the 4 pizza shells with olive oil. Divide the tomatoes, onions, and spring garlic evenly among the shells. Sprinkle with tarragon. Pull the sausage mixture apart into little pieces and divide among the doughs. Top with the mozzarella. Slide off the paddle onto the pizza stone in the bottom of the oven. Cook until golden brown, 6 to 8 minutes. Remove from the oven, cut into wedges, and serve immediately.

THE VERSATILITY OF PIZZA DOUGH

Meals made from pizza dough are often seen as casual affairs. However, this highly adaptable dough has many guises and can be used for almost any occasion. For example, you can make it into breadsticks for a dinner party by cutting it into strips and rolling them in poppy or caraway seeds. As flatbread, another prebaked dough, it can accompany the hors d'oeuvres or be served with the main course. Roll out the dough as you would for a pizza, brush with olive oil, bake, and cut into wedges as it comes out of the oven. Flatbread is also perfect at a brunch, served with smoked salmon.

Another of pizza dough's wonderful guises is focaccia. Flavor the dough by kneading chopped herbs, such as rosemary or sage, into it. Focaccia makes wonderful sandwiches, plain or herbed. Cut up a large, flat sheet of baked focaccia or, when shaping the dough, make it into smaller, sandwich-sized "loaves." At the restaurant, we usually make a savory focaccia, but for Sunday brunch we sweeten it with things like grapes, raisins, or chunks of figs and top it with a sprinkling of coarse sugar.

Then there is the ever-versatile pizza, my lifesaver when cooking with my kids. Each kid-sized pizza can be customized to individual tastes. Use whatever is on hand. Pizza is adaptable to many sauces and toppings. Consider any ingredient. Carolyn's Grilled Pizza with Figs, Goat Cheese, and Pancetta (page 77) is hard to beat. Or add a goat cheese filling, fold the dough over, and it's a calzone. I think pizza is all about imagination!

Pizza dough can also go to a barbecue. Arrange the coals in the grill so that there is a hot side and a cool side. Have all of the toppings prepared and the dough shaped into 8-inch rounds. Put everything close to the grill—it goes very fast. Place a round of dough over the hot side of the grill until it has browned. Flip it over to the cool side and add the toppings. Move it back toward the heat to melt the cheese and warm the toppings. Watch it very carefully to avoid burning. Kids young and old love pizza prepared this way.

When making pizza in an oven, it's essential to get the oven as hot as possible. I turn my oven up as far as it will go. A pizza stone or bricks placed on the bottom of the oven to cook directly on are also helpful. If you don't have a stone, make the pizza on a pizza pan or baking sheet and put it right on the bottom of the oven, not on the rack; the result will be a nicely browned crust.

For basic instructions for making pizza dough and for shaping and baking pizzas, see page 203. —KJ

Ravioli with Braised Lamb, Eggplant, and Citrus Gremolata

﹋ WINE NOTES

The wonderful rich fruit flavors, medium to heavy body,
and sufficient tannins of a
Petite Sirah enhance the flavors of this lamb ravioli. Lamb
and Petite Sirah are nearly syn-
onymous for my family. One of
our memorable pairings is my
mother's braised lamb shanks,
which were always accompanied by Concannon Vineyard's
Petite Sirah. Concannon was
the first producer of Petite
Sirah in the early 1960s and, as
they are a neighboring winery,
we have always enjoyed their
wines.

Traditionally, spring was the time new lambs were born. The meat from
these young lambs is the most tender since they have not fully developed
their muscles. With the use of artificial insemination, lamb is available to us
year-round, but I still believe that the flavor and texture of true spring lamb
is superior.

If the raw garlic in the gremolata recipe is too strong for you, there are
ways to tame it. You can cut the cloves in half and remove the inner sprout
from each clove. Or you can lightly sauté the minced garlic in a little olive
oil for about a minute and let it cool before adding it to the gremolata.

CITRUS GREMOLATA

1 tablespoon chopped fresh parsley

1 tablespoon minced orange zest

1 teaspoon finely chopped lemon zest

1 tablespoon minced garlic

LAMB AND EGGPLANT STUFFING

1/2 large globe eggplant, about 1/2 pound
     (a little over 1/2 cup
     when cooked)

1/2 pound lamb shoulder, trimmed of fat
     and cut into 1-inch cubes

Kosher salt and freshly ground pepper

1 tablespoon olive oil

1/4 cup peeled, diced carrot

1/4 cup diced onion

1 tablespoon minced garlic

1 cup red wine

1 cup chicken stock (page 206)

2 tablespoons fresh orange juice

1 tablespoon fresh lemon juice

Bouquet garni with 2 teaspoons black peppercorns,
     2 sprigs thyme, 2 parsley stems (leaves removed),
     and 2 bay leaves (page 211)

2 tablespoons finely grated Parmesan cheese

Double recipe pasta dough (page 202)

2 tablespoons finely grated Parmesan cheese, for garnish

To prepare the gremolata: In a small bowl, combine the parsley, orange and finely chopped lemon zest, and minced garlic. Set aside.

To prepare the stuffing: Salt the cut side of the eggplant half and let it sit for 1 hour.

Preheat the oven to 325°. Season the lamb with salt and pepper. In a $2^{1}/_{2}$-quart ovenproof pan over medium-high heat, heat the olive oil. Add the lamb, carrot, and onion and sauté until golden brown. Add the minced garlic and cook, stirring constantly, for 1 minute.

Add the red wine, chicken stock, and orange and lemon juice. Stir over medium heat to scrape up the browned bits of lamb and vegetables from the bottom of the pan. Add the bouquet garni, bring to a simmer, and braise, uncovered, in the oven for about 1 hour, or until tender. While the lamb and vegetables are braising, blot the liquid off the eggplant with a clean towel. Rub the cut side with olive oil and place on a baking sheet, cut side down. Roast in the oven (along with the lamb and vegetables) for about 30 minutes, or until tender.

When cooked, remove the eggplant, lamb, and vegetables from the oven. Strain the lamb and vegetables from the liquid, discarding the bouquet garni. Bring the braising liquid to a simmer, skim off the fat, and pass through a fine-meshed sieve. Set aside.

When the lamb and vegetables are cool, cut into a small dice.

When the eggplant is cool, scoop out the inside. Combine with the diced lamb, vegetables, and the Parmesan. Check for seasoning and set aside.

To assemble the pasta: Bring a large pot of salted water to a boil to cook the pasta. Separate the pasta dough into 4 pieces, keeping them covered. Roll out a piece in a pasta machine set to the thinnest setting, as described on page 202. Cut in half to form 2 rectangular pieces the width of the pasta machine. Lay a piece down on a flat surface and place $^{1}/_{4}$ cup of filling in the center of the dough, about $2^{1}/_{2}$ inches from a short edge. Continue placing $^{1}/_{4}$ cup of filling every 5 inches along the length of the dough. Moisten the edges of the pasta dough, including the spaces between the filling, lightly with water. Place the other rectangular piece over the piece with the filling, slowly and gingerly stretching it so that it covers the filling and dough. Press down on the edges to seal, and cut between the stuffing, forming 5-inch square ravioli. Trim any loose edges. Repeat with the remaining 3 pieces of dough.

Cook the stuffed pasta in the boiling water for about 5 minutes, or until the pasta is tender. Drain.

In a sauté pan over medium heat, combine the stuffed pasta with the reserved braising liquid. Cook for another 2 minutes.

Serve the pasta in bowls in the braising liquid, topped with the gremolata and the remaining 2 tablespoons Parmesan.

Fettuccine with Green Garlic Cream, Home-Smoked Salmon, Peas, Fava Beans, and Asparagus

SERVES 4

✿ WINE NOTES

The weight of the heavier pasta, rich cream, and smoky salmon, plus the texture of the peas, favas, and asparagus, suggests a wine that is weighty and full-bodied, with toasty oak flavors. A full-bodied Chardonnay meets these criteria. Many Pinot Blancs are also produced in this "Chardonnay-like" style. This means that they are barrel fermented, imparting the toasty oak character, and that they have gone through malolactic fermentation, which creates a creamy, buttery wine.

Wild king salmon is the stuff of legend in my family. I grew up with my mother's stories of summers in her native Oregon, catching and barbecuing fresh Pacific salmon on the beach. In this recipe I have substituted the smoker for the grill, but the salmon truly is the star.

In Northern California, our salmon season begins around May 1. The flavor and texture of the wild salmon is far superior to those of farm-raised salmon. King salmon, also sometimes called Chinook, is the richest of all of the Pacific salmons. (Others include Coho or silver, sockeye, chum, and pink salmon.) It has a high oil content and flakes into moist, meaty chunks. More fragile than Atlantic salmon, the flesh of the king salmon requires delicate handling. In some areas of the country you can buy hot-smoked salmon, which you can use in this recipe, if it isn't possible to smoke your own.

When entertaining, this dish is easy to prepare ahead of time. Make the Green Garlic Cream, blanch the vegetables, and smoke the salmon. After guests have arrived, just cook the pasta, heat the cream, warm the vegetables and salmon in the cream, toss together with the pasta, and serve.

$1/2$ **pound fresh salmon, skin on**

GREEN GARLIC CREAM

2 tablespoons olive oil

$1/2$ cup sliced green garlic, about $1/2$ bunch, or
    $1/4$ cup sliced scallions and $1/4$ cup sliced garlic

4 cloves garlic, sliced

2 cups heavy whipping cream

$1/4$ cup fresh, shucked English peas

$1/4$ cup fresh, shucked fava beans

1 bunch asparagus, peeled and cut diagonally into
    1-inch pieces (15 to 20 spears)

2 tablespoons extra-virgin olive oil

Kosher salt and freshly ground pepper

1 pound dried fettuccine

$1/2$ cup finely diced green garlic, about $1/2$ bunch

3 tablespoons lemon juice

2 teaspoons finely chopped lemon zest

Season and smoke the salmon as described on page 62. Once the grill is ready, it will take you about 30 minutes to smoke the fish, depending on the type and size of your grill. When cooked, remove and discard the skin and flake the flesh. Set aside.

To prepare the Green Garlic Cream: In a saucepan over low heat, heat the olive oil. Add the sliced green garlic and the sliced garlic cloves. Cover and cook for about 5 minutes. Add the cream, bring to a low simmer, and cook for about 20 minutes. The cream should thicken slightly. Purée and set aside.

To prepare the pasta: Bring 2 pots of salted water to a boil, one to cook the fettuccine and the second to blanch the vegetables. The water used for blanching should be highly salted, approximately 2 tablespoons salt per quart of water.

Blanch the peas, fava beans, and asparagus separately in the highly salted water. The peas will take 3 to 4 minutes, the favas 2 to 3 minutes, and the asparagus about $1^1/2$ minutes. While still warm, toss all of the vegetables together in the extra-virgin olive oil. Season with salt and pepper to taste. Set aside.

Cook the fettuccine in salted, boiling water until al dente. Drain.

In a large saucepan over medium-high heat, heat the garlic cream and add the diced green garlic. Add the fettuccine to the cream and cook for 2 to 3 minutes. Add the salmon, vegetables, lemon juice, and finely chopped lemon zest, and season to taste with salt and pepper. Divide among 4 plates and serve immediately.

Roast Leg of Lamb,
Petite Sirah–Balsamic Sauce, and Mint Oil
with Artichoke–New Potato Gratin

SERVES 8 TO 10 GENEROUSLY

☙ WINE NOTES

Many recipes call for wine to be used as an ingredient in marinades, sauces, and stock. The common assumption that a lower-quality wine can be used in cooking doesn't really work. If you wouldn't drink a wine, it may not be the best enhancement for your recipe. In this case, you can certainly use the same wine in cooking as you serve for dinner.

This recipe is perfect for a dinner party, as it calls for a leg of lamb, but you can easily buy just half a leg and cut the recipe in half. The Mint Oil and Petite Sirah–Balsamic Sauce can be prepared a day ahead. Rich veal stock can be purchased at a deli if you don't want to make your own. The better flavored the stock, the tastier the sauce. I prefer to use American lamb; it is a little larger, usually fresher, and better flavored than Australian or New Zealand lamb. Ask your butcher to clean and score the lamb and to remove the shank and sirloin bones. Save the bones for use in the sauce. When the sauce is done, don't throw away the nicely braised shank. It is great for lamb hash the following day. Concannon Petite Sirah from the Livermore Valley is superb in this dish. As I always say, "If it's good enough for drinking, it's good enough for cooking!"

MINT OIL

1/4 cup extra-virgin olive oil

3 or 4 sprigs mint

LEG OF LAMB

12 cloves garlic, thinly sliced

1/4 cup balsamic vinegar

1/4 cup Petite Sirah

1/4 cup extra-virgin olive oil

1 bunch fresh thyme

1 leg of lamb (4 pounds), bones removed and reserved

PETITE SIRAH–BALSAMIC SAUCE

2 carrots, peeled and coarsely chopped

1 stalk celery, coarsely chopped

1 onion, coarsely chopped (about 1 cup)

2 or 3 sprigs thyme

1/2 cup balsamic vinegar

2 tablespoons olive oil

1 cup Petite Sirah

2 cups veal demiglace (page 206)

Kosher salt and freshly ground pepper

1/4 cup unsalted butter

ARTICHOKE–NEW POTATO GRATIN

2 cups heavy whipping cream

1 tablespoon chopped garlic

1 tablespoon chopped fresh thyme

2 teaspoons chopped fresh flat-leaf parsley

4 pounds large red potatoes, thinly sliced

1 tablespoon kosher salt

Freshly ground pepper

3 cups fresh artichoke hearts (page 209)

1 cup finely grated Parmesan cheese

To prepare the Mint Oil: In a small saucepan, warm the extra-virgin olive oil. Add the mint and cook slowly for 10 minutes. Let steep for 4 to 5 hours. Strain.

To marinate the lamb : In a small bowl, mix together the garlic, vinegar, wine, extra-virgin olive oil, and thyme. Put the lamb in a nonreactive pan and pour the marinade over the lamb. The marinade will penetrate more if the lamb leg is opened fully when boned. Marinate in the refrigerator for at least 4 hours, turning the lamb every 30 minutes.

To prepare the sauce: Preheat oven to 350°. In an ovenproof pan, combine the lamb bones, carrots, celery, onion, thyme, vinegar, and olive oil. Roast in the oven, stirring every 10 minutes or so to assure that everything browns evenly. Roast until all of the ingredients are nicely browned, about 30 minutes.

Pour the fat from the roasting pan. Add the wine, and stir over medium heat to scrape up the browned bits from the bottom of the pan.

Place the roasted vegetables and bones and the wine in a large saucepan and add enough water to cover the lamb bones, about 4 cups. Bring to a simmer, and simmer for 2 to 3 hours. Skim off the fat that rises to the top as it cooks. Strain.

Return the liquid to the saucepan, add the veal demiglace, and simmer until reduced by half, approximately 1 hour. Taste for seasoning. Set aside. (Butter will be added just before serving.)

To prepare the gratin: In a bowl, combine the cream, garlic, thyme, and parsley. Add the potatoes and toss. Season with salt and pepper.

Put half of the potato mixture in the bottom of a 2^{1}/2-quart baking dish. Layer the artichoke hearts on top of the potatoes. Sprinkle with half of the Parmesan. Layer the rest of the potatoes on top. Pour the cream remaining in the bowl over the last layer. Top with the rest of the Parmesan. Set aside to bake with the lamb.

To bake the lamb and gratin: Remove the lamb from the refrigerator 30 minutes before roasting. Preheat the oven to 425°. Remove the lamb from the marinade, season with salt and pepper on both sides, roll up, and tie with butcher's twine. Place in a roasting pan and roast for about 15 minutes, turning once.

Lower the oven temperature to 350°. Continue roasting the lamb, and place the potato-artichoke gratin in the oven with the lamb.

Bake both the lamb and the gratin for 45 minutes. When done, the gratin should be bubbling and the potatoes browned and tender when pierced with a sharp knife. The internal temperature of the lamb should reach 120° when checked with an instant-read thermometer. Let the lamb rest for 5 minutes after removing from the oven.

To serve, heat the sauce until it simmers. Add the 1/4 cup of butter to round out the flavors. Ladle 1/4 cup of the sauce onto each plate. Cut the gratin into 8 portions and divide among the plates. Slice the leg of lamb thinly and place on top of the gratin. Drizzle with the Mint Oil. Serve immediately.

Smoked Pork Chops with Ginger-Peach Chutney and Creamy Polenta

SERVES 4

❧ WINE NOTES

We teach food and wine pairing to our waitstaff in the restaurant, which allows them to taste different wines with foods they serve. Many thought this dish would pair well with a red wine, and they were surprised to find that the residual sugars of Gewürztraminer or Riesling were a better complement to the sweet pork and chutney.

I am often asked how new dishes are created. The smoked pork chop, one of our signature items on the menu, is a great example. I wish I could take all the credit for its invention, but in fact there are two other people who were insturmental in its inception—Dan Carroll and Stu Edgecombe (sous-chefs in the restaurant). We were standing in the back of the kitchen one day talking food (what else!), when I brought up the idea of slowly cooking a 2-inch-thick pork chop in the smoker. (I love to smoke meats.) Dan thought creamy polenta would go great with it and Stu had been working on a chutney that would fit perfectly. We tried it all together the next day, put it on the menu, and have been unable to remove it ever since!

If you want to prepare this dish for a dinner party, make the chutney and smoke the pork chops the day before. Because the chops are steamed while smoked, they can be slowly reheated in a 250° oven and still remain moist and flavorful. The polenta can be prepared just before guests arrive and kept warm over a hot water bath.

4 (12-ounce) double-cut pork loin chops (2 inches thick)

Kosher salt and freshly ground pepper

1 scallion, green part only, cut into julienne, for garnish

GINGER-PEACH CHUTNEY

2 teaspoons olive oil

1/2 cup chopped onion

1 clove garlic, minced

2 tablespoons minced fresh ginger

1/2 red bell pepper, diced

1/2 yellow bell pepper, diced

1 jalapeño pepper, seeded and diced (page 210)

1 cup apple cider vinegar

1 cup brown sugar

1 tablespoon mustard seeds

1/2 teaspoon ground allspice

1/4 teaspoon ground cayenne pepper

3 cups fresh peeled, sliced peaches, prepared right before
    needed to prevent discoloration

Creamy polenta (page 204)

To smoke the pork chops: Salt and pepper the outside of the pork chops. Let them rest in the refrigerator for 1 hour. Smoke the pork chops on a grill or smoker, as described on page 62, until the pork reaches an internal temperature of 145°, about an hour. Depending on the type and size of your smoker, the cooking time may vary. Once the chops have the good smoky flavor, you may finish them in a 250° oven until done.

To prepare the chutney: You can make the chutney while the chops are smoking, or up to a day in advance. In a nonreactive saucepan over medium heat, heat the olive oil and add the onion, garlic, ginger, red and yellow bell pepper, and jalapeño pepper. Cover and cook until tender, about 10 minutes. Do not let the mixture brown. Add the vinegar, brown sugar, mustard seeds, allspice, and cayenne. Cook, uncovered, over medium heat until the mixture starts to thicken and has formed a good sweet-sour flavor, approximately 45 minutes. Remove from the heat and set aside.

Prepare creamy polenta as directed on page 204, and keep it warm over a hot water bath.

To serve, just before the pork chops are ready, add the peaches to the chutney mixture. Taste for seasoning. Chutney can be served warm, at room temperature, or cold. Serve the pork chops on top of the polenta with the chutney spooned over the top. Garnish with a fine julienne of scallion.

Crispy Breast of Muscovy Duck with Maple Glaze, Cherry Sauce, and Hazelnut Wild Rice

SERVES 4

🐾 WINE NOTES

The complexity of ingredients and rich layers of flavors in this dish demand a wine with intense fruit and full body. My mouth waters for a Syrah or a Cabernet Sauvignon from warmer regions. The wines from these areas develop much fruitier flavors (cherry, currant), with fuller body and softer acidity.

This dish combines three of my favorite native North American foods—Muscovy duck, maple syrup, and wild rice.

Muscovy duck, native to Mexico, was crossbred in southern France with both the Rouen and Nantes ducks. I prefer its meatier, almost wild, flavors. The Muscovy duck we serve in our restaurant is raised in Stockton, about an hour from Livermore, by a French company, Grimaud Farms.

Maple syrup is one of the few foods produced only in the New World. In precolonial America, it was the preferred sweetener. Its popularity gave way to honey and then molasses as colonists tried to replicate the familiar flavors left behind. In this well-balanced marinade, maple syrup adds a wonderful sweet note against the acidity of the balsamic vinegar.

Wild rice really isn't rice at all but a grass native to the northern Great Lakes area of the United States and Canada. The best rice still comes from there and is grown and harvested by Native Americans. It has a wonderful nutty flavor with a crunchy but smooth texture.

4 Muscovy duck breasts, with skin on (can use other ducks)
2 tablespoons maple syrup

MARINADE AND CHERRY SAUCE
1 cup red wine
1/2 cup pitted Bing cherries, or 1/4 cup dried cherries
2 tablespoons balsamic vinegar
2 tablespoons maple syrup

2 cups duck or chicken stock, reduced to 1 cup (page 206)
2 tablespoons unsalted butter, cut into small pieces

HAZELNUT WILD RICE
2 tablespoons olive oil
1/2 carrot, peeled and finely diced
1/4 onion, finely diced
1 stalk celery, finely diced
1/2 apple, finely diced
1 cup wild rice
3 cups chicken stock
Bouquet garni with 2 sprigs fresh thyme, 2 bay leaves, 2 parsley stems (leaves removed) and 2 teaspoons black peppercorns (page 211)

Kosher salt and freshly ground pepper

**¹/₄ cup hazelnuts, toasted, skinned,
    and coarsely chopped (page 210)**

To marinate the duck breasts: Trim the duck of any excess fat. Score the skin in a ¹/₄-inch crosshatch pattern, being careful not to cut all the way through the skin. In a nonreactive pan over medium heat, bring the red wine and half of the cherries to a simmer. Cook until the cherries are soft, 10 to 15 minutes. Remove from the heat.

When cool, add the vinegar and maple syrup. Pour the mixture into a glass baking dish and add the duck breasts, skin side up. (Duck skin marinated in maple syrup tends to darken or burn when cooked.) Marinate for at least 4 hours in the refrigerator.

To prepare the wild rice: In a pot over medium heat, heat the olive oil. Add the carrot, onion, celery, and apple. Sauté for a few minutes, stirring constantly. Add the rice, chicken stock, and bouquet garni and bring to a boil. Reduce the heat to a gentle simmer and cook until the wild rice starts to open up, about 45 minutes. Add enough hot water to just cover the rice, and season with salt and pepper. Cover and remove from the heat. Let stand 15 minutes. This will allow the rice to absorb a little more liquid and salt without overcooking. Remove the bouquet garni. Drain the remaining water, if any. Set aside in a warm place.

To prepare the cherry sauce: Remove the duck from the marinade, season the duck with salt and pepper, and set aside.

In a nonreactive saucepan, combine the reduced duck stock and the marinade and bring to a boil. Lower to a simmer and let it reduce for approximately 15 minutes. Stir occasionally. (Butter and remaining cherries will be added just before serving.)

To roast the duck breasts: Preheat the oven to 450°. Heat an ovenproof sauté pan over medium heat and add the duck, skin side down. Cook for 5 to 6 minutes. Remove the duck fat as it renders in the bottom of the pan. With the duck still skin side down, place the sauté pan in the oven. Roast until there is just a little pink left on the exposed side of the duck breast, approximately 10 minutes. Remove from the oven. Turn the duck breasts over and brush the skin with 2 tablespoons maple syrup. Let rest in the warm pan.

To serve, return the wild rice to low heat for 10 minutes, stirring occasionally. Stir in the hazelnuts.

Strain the reduced cherry sauce, and discard the solids. Add the remaining cherries and bring to a simmer. Remove from the heat and swirl in the butter, several pieces at a time, by slowly moving the pan in a circular motion. Check for seasoning.

With a carving knife, slice the duck breasts lengthwise into thin pieces. Divide the wild rice among the plates. Fan the duck slices on top of the rice and spoon the sauce over the duck.

Quail Stuffed with Fresh Ricotta, Bacon, and Greens with Green Garlic–Sweet Pea Purée

SERVES 4

🍂 WINE NOTES

Quail is not as gamy or "wild" as some fowl, and the flavors are often influenced by ingredients or cooking method. A Pinot Blanc, which has the body of a red wine with the acidity of a white, complements the fuller flavors of the quail and bacon as well as the herbs and greens in the stuffing.

My kids are the inspiration for this dish. My son Taylor decided at the tender age of ten that quail were his favorite birds, but he would always lament, "Why can't they make them a little bigger?" I like to serve at least two per person because they are so small. Be careful not to overcook the birds, as they tend to lose their juiciness. Ask your butcher for semi-boned quail, which have had all of the bones removed except the very small ones in the thigh, leg, and wing. If you can't find frisée, use a mixture of spinach and chard. I made the pea purée for my older son, Morgwn, when he was a baby. It was probably his first solid food.

GREEN GARLIC–SWEET PEA PURÉE

1 tablespoon olive oil

2 stalks green garlic, white part only, finely diced

4 cups sugar snap peas, strings removed

Kosher salt and freshly ground pepper

STUFFING

1 head frisée

2 tablespoons olive oil

1 teaspoon minced garlic

2 strips bacon, diced

1/2 cup fresh ricotta cheese (to make your own, see page 200)

1 tablespoon grated Parmesan cheese

1/4 teaspoon minced fresh chervil

1/4 teaspoon minced fresh flat-leaf parsley

Kosher salt and freshly ground pepper

8 quail, semi-boneless

2 tablespoons olive oil

Pea sprouts, for garnish

To prepare the pea purée: Bring a pot of heavily salted water (2 tablespoons salt per quart) to a boil.

In a sauté pan over medium heat, heat the olive oil. Add the garlic and sauté, stirring occasionally, for 5 minutes. Remove from the heat and set aside.

Blanch the peas for 3 or 4 minutes in the boiling water. Drain and purée in a food processor or pass through a food mill. Combine with the sautéed garlic. Taste for seasoning. Set aside.

To prepare the stuffing: Wash the frisée, remove the stem, and discard the tough outer leaves. In a sauté pan over medium heat, heat the olive oil.

Sauté the frisée until it begins to wilt, about 2 minutes. Add the garlic and continue to sauté until the greens are just wilted, 1 to 2 minutes. When cool enough to handle, chop coarsely.

In a sauté pan over medium-low heat, cook the bacon until golden brown. Drain on a paper towel. Discard the fat. Combine the bacon with the ricotta, Parmesan, herbs, and greens-garlic mixture. Season to taste with salt and pepper.

To prepare the quail: Preheat the oven to 400°. Season the inside of the quail with salt and pepper. Make a slit in the left leg of each quail and slip the right drumstick end through the incision in the left.

Fill a piping bag with the stuffing, and pipe the stuffing into the quail opposite the drumsticks, between the wing bones. (Using a piping bag makes it easier. If you don't have one, use a small plastic bag and cut off a corner. You could also spoon the stuffing into the birds.) Do not overfill. Tie the wings together.

In a sauté pan over medium-high heat, heat 2 tablespoons olive oil and brown the quail on both sides. Place them on a rack in a roasting pan. Roast in the oven for 12 to 15 minutes, or until the juices run clear when the thigh is poked with a sharp knife.

To serve, in a sauté pan over low heat, reheat the pea purée for a few minutes. Divide among 4 plates. Remove the string from the wings of the quail, and place 2 quail on each plate, on top of the purée. Garnish with pea sprouts.

Pecan–Crusted Rainbow Trout
with Citrus Salsa

SERVES 4

I learned this basic technique for preparing trout—marinating in buttermilk and coating with nuts—while working with Bradley Ogden at Campton Place Hotel in San Francisco. The meat of the fish stays wonderfully moist, while the pecans and cornmeal add a nice crunchy texture. Do not leave the trout in the buttermilk longer than a day. The acid in the buttermilk will break down the tissues of the trout, making it mushy.

4 boneless trout, head, tail, and pin bones removed, split

1 cup buttermilk

CITRUS SALSA

1 grapefruit

1 lime

1 orange

1 tangerine

3 tablespoons lemon juice, more if necessary

1 teaspoon Dijon mustard

1/4 jalapeño pepper, seeded and diced (about 1 teaspoon) (page 210)

1 teaspoon minced shallot

1 tablespoon extra-virgin olive oil

Kosher salt and freshly ground pepper

2 cups ground pecans

1 cup cornmeal

1 cup flour

1 teaspoon ground cayenne pepper

Peanut oil for frying

Marinate the trout in the buttermilk for about 1 hour.

While the trout is marinating, prepare the Citrus Salsa: Peel and section the grapefruit, lime, orange, and tangerine, as described on page 209. Squeeze any juice that remains from the membrane and add it to the peeled segments. Combine the lemon juice, mustard, pepper, shallot, and olive oil with the citrus segments. Taste for seasoning and acidity, adding salt and pepper to taste and a little more lemon juice, if necessary. Set aside.

To prepare the trout: Combine the pecans, cornmeal, flour, and cayenne. Remove the trout from the buttermilk and season with salt and pepper. Dredge the trout in the pecan mixture, making sure that all parts are well coated.

In a large sauté pan over medium-high heat, heat $^1/_8$ inch of oil until almost smoking. Add the trout. (You may need to cook it in batches, adding oil as needed.) Lower the heat to medium. Cook on each side until golden brown, 3 to 4 minutes per side. Remove from the oil and drain on paper towels. Serve promptly, topped with the Citrus Salsa.

HOW WE TASTE WINE AND FOOD

Early on in life, I became aware that much of what we taste is derived from what we smell. I learned this from tasting wines with my grandfather and father. They would stick their nose into a glass of Sauvignon Blanc, searching for aromas, and describe it as smelling of fresh-cut oat hay, citrus, and ripe melon. Since I lived on a ranch, I certainly knew the smells of fresh-cut oat hay. Harvesting the oranges and lemons in the orchard also made me aware of the citrus smells, and I also cut open my share of fragrant ripe melons during the hot summer months. Without consciously realizing it, my familiarity with these smells gave me a description of what my grandfather and father were tasting.

Our brain is a memory bank that stores and remembers aromas and tastes. Every one of us has stored smells and tastes since early childhood. In order for us to talk about food and wine, we must draw upon our memory and articulate aromas and flavors that are reminiscent of actual life experience. Of the five senses, smell is the most evocative of memories and can influence more than 85 percent of what we taste.

My definition of flavor is a combination of the sensations of taste, smell, and touch in the mouth and nasal passages. Taking this one step further, how do we taste? The basic components of food are sweet, sour, salt, and bitter. These components are physically felt on your tongue—sugar at the front tip, sour on the sides, salt down the center, and bitter across the back. Imagine biting into a sugar cube; you will immediately feel the sweetness at the tip of your tongue. Biting into a lemon wedge will cause you to pucker your mouth; it's the acid/sour sensation on the sides of your tongue. Salty french fries are felt mostly in the center of the tongue, while the bitterness of unsweetened chocolate causes almost a gagging feeling at the back of your mouth.

The basic components of wine are sugar (fruit), acid (sour), alcohol (body), and tannin (bitterness or astringency). When tasting wine, I contemplate a particular wine's sensations on my tongue just as I would with food. For example, when tasting an off-dry wine—a wine that still has a bit of residual grape sugar—I feel its sweetness on the front tip of my tongue. A wine with an acid content will be felt at the sides of my tongue, while a wine with some amount of tannin will be felt not only at the sides of my tongue, due to the acid and astringency, but also at the back as I perceive some bitterness in the tannin.

The influence of aromas on taste, as well as the sensations stimulated in the mouth by certain components, begin to identify the characteristics that make up particular foods and wines. This in turn enables us to match the flavors of wine with food, and vice versa.

As a cook and a winemaker, my goal is to balance the basic components of sweet, sour, salt, and bitter in the wines we produce, in the meals I prepare, and in the wines and food I pair together. I believe that by drawing on your own personal senses—your own personal memory bank—you develop your own individual taste. Developing the confidence to follow your own taste is the single most important thing when cooking and when enjoying fine wines. —CW

Soft-Shell Crabs with Spring Vegetable Slaw and Basil Aioli

SERVES 4

WINE NOTES

I would pair for similarity, not contrast, in this recipe. A Sauvignon Blanc with citrus and grassy, herbal flavors similar to those in the slaw would be wonderful. The crispness and light body would also work well with the crabs. When soft-shell crabs are served on their own, a wine that has undergone a stainless steel fermentation, such as a Chenin Blanc or Chardonnay, creates a light, clean, crisp wine with ample acid to match the subtle flavor of the crab.

We start getting soft-shell crabs, or softies as we call them, around the beginning of May from the Chesapeake Bay. The shells are soft because the crabs are going through their molting season. You can eat the whole thing if prepared properly. You might want to ask your fishmonger to clean them. The vegetable slaw and aioli in this recipe can be prepared in advance. Many people plunge vegetables into cold water after blanching them, but I think this can make them taste watery. I prefer to toss them lightly in olive oil, which also stops the oxidation process, keeping them green. I do this especially with spring vegetables such as carrots, peas, and favas. I also salt them when they are warm so they absorb the seasoning.

SPRING VEGETABLE SLAW

20 spears asparagus, peeled and trimmed to 4-inch lengths

1 teaspoon extra-virgin olive oil

2 small carrots, peeled and cut into julienne, about 1 cup

2 stalks celery, strings removed and cut into julienne, about 3/4 cup

1/2 red onion, thinly sliced, about 1/4 cup

1/2 English cucumber, peeled, seeded, and cut into julienne, about 1 cup

3 tablespoons sour cream

1 teaspoon granulated sugar

1 tablespoon plus 1 teaspoon apple cider vinegar

1 tablespoon chopped fresh chives

Kosher salt and freshly ground pepper

Basic Aioli (page 207)

10 basil leaves

4 soft-shell crabs

1 cup buttermilk

Semolina flour for dredging

Ground cayenne pepper

Kosher salt and freshly ground pepper

Olive oil for frying

To prepare the Spring Vegetable Slaw: Bring a pot of salted water (1 tablespoon salt per quart water) to a boil.

Cook the asparagus in the water for $1^1/_2$ minutes. Remove from the water and drain well. While still warm, place in a bowl, drizzle with extra-virgin olive oil, and sprinkle with a little salt. Toss thoroughly. Slice each of the asparagus spears in half lengthwise. Add the carrots, celery, onion, and cucumber to the asparagus and toss lightly. Add the sour cream, sugar, vinegar, and chives and toss again. Add salt and pepper to taste. Refrigerate if not using right away.

To prepare the Basil Aioli: Before making the aioli, place the basil and olive oil in a blender or mini-chopper and purée until smooth. Continue as described on page 207, using the olive oil–basil mixture in place of the plain olive oil.

To prepare the crabs: Clean the crabs by cutting off the front of the top shell with a pair of scissors. Lift the top shell up on each side and remove the gills. Lift the tail piece up and remove. Place the crabs in the buttermilk.

Make a mixture of semolina flour flavored with cayenne, salt and pepper to taste. Remove the crabs from the buttermilk and dredge in the seasoned semolina flour.

In a sauté pan over medium-high heat, heat $^1/_8$ inch of olive oil. When the oil is hot but not smoking, add the crabs. Cook until golden brown on both sides. Drain on paper towels.

To serve, divide the slaw among 4 plates. Place a crab atop each bed of slaw, and spoon a dab of aioli on the side.

Halibut Poached in Fennel Broth
with Dried Tomato Relish

SERVES 4

◈ WINE NOTES

Depending on which flavors you want to enhance, there are several different wine choices for this recipe. The broth is a light-bodied liquid, pairing well with a dry white wine with light body and a fair amount of acid, such as a Sauvignon Blanc or Pinot Grigio. These wines will feel clean and crisp in your mouth. Other possible matches would be a Gamay, a Sangiovese, or even a rosé. These red wines will intensify the anise flavor of the fennel and the sweetness and acidity of the tomatoes.

This is a very easy dish to cook once you have all of the ingredients prepared. I always get in trouble for using every pot in the kitchen (what else are they there for?), but miraculously, you need only one pot for this dish! The French refer to this type of dish as *à la nage*, or in the swim, because the fish is served in the liquid in which it is cooked.

FENNEL BROTH

2 tablespoons olive oil

1 leek, white part only, cleaned and thinly sliced

1 yellow onion, thinly sliced

1 stalk celery, diced

2 cups sliced fennel bulbs, approximately 2 to 3 bulbs (save the tops for garnish)

1 bulb garlic, separated into cloves and peeled

2 cups water

1 cup canned peeled tomatoes, seeded and chopped with juice

1 1/2 cups white wine

Bouquet garni with 1 lemon, cut in half; 1 teaspoon white peppercorns; 1 tablespoon fennel seeds; and 2 bay leaves (page 211)

DRIED TOMATO RELISH

1 (16-ounce) can whole tomatoes, drained

1 teaspoon balsamic vinegar

1 teaspoon sherry vinegar

1 tablespoon extra-virgin olive oil

1 tablespoon olive oil

1 teaspoon chopped capers

1/4 teaspoon chopped anchovy

1/2 teaspoon minced garlic

4 (6-ounce) halibut fillets

Kosher salt and freshly ground pepper

4 slices whole-wheat sourdough bread

To prepare the broth: In a nonreactive stockpot over medium heat, heat the olive oil. Add the leek, onion, celery, fennel, and garlic and sauté for 10 minutes, stirring often. Add the water, tomatoes and their juice, white wine, and bouquet garni. Bring to a simmer. Simmer lightly for 30 minutes. Remove the bouquet garni and strain, discarding the vegetables. Set the broth aside.

To dry the tomatoes: Preheat the oven to 275°. Cut the tomatoes in half and remove the seeds. Place cut side down on a parchment-lined baking sheet. Roast in the oven for about 1 hour, or until the tomatoes are dried out but not browned. Remove from the oven, cool, and dice.

To prepare the relish: Mix the dried tomatoes, balsamic vinegar, sherry vinegar, extra-virgin olive oil, olive oil, capers, anchovy, and garlic together and taste for seasoning. Set aside.

To cook the halibut: Season the halibut with salt and pepper and let sit in the refrigerator for 20 minutes. Bring the fennel broth to a simmer, and poach the halibut in it at a very low simmer until cooked through, 5 to 7 minutes. Depending on the thickness of the halibut, you may have to flip it to cook evenly.

While the halibut is poaching, toast the bread. To serve, put a slice in the bottom of each of 4 bowls. Place the poached halibut fillets on top of the bread, ladle the broth over the fish, and garnish with the tomato relish and fennel tops.

Grilled Jumbo Prawns
Marinated in Ginger, White Wine, and Lemon with Mango–Mint Salsa

SERVES 4

❧ WINE NOTES

There are lots of flavors here—the subtle spiciness and smoky taste of the grilled marinated prawns and the fruitiness of the salsa. A Chardonnay from a cooler coastal region can have lots of fruit and spice and has a hint of smokiness when aged in oak, making it a perfect match. A good acid backbone in the wine will assure that the palate is refreshed and will also balance the lemon flavor. You can also serve the same wine as you used in the marinade.

My husband is originally from New Orleans, and its proximity to the Caribbean allowed him to spend a great deal of time there. My inspiration for this dish was his love for prawns and fruit salsas we have tasted throughout the Caribbean, and the fresh ingredients from our own garden. Preparation can be done in advance, leaving only the brief grilling to take place after guests have arrived. All in all, this falls into the category of delicious flavors and easy preparation—a good combination for entertaining. I like to serve this with rice. —CW

MANGO-MINT SALSA

2 cups peeled, pitted, cubed ripe mango

1 cup peeled, cored, cubed fresh pineapple

3 tablespoons chopped fresh mint

1 teaspoon minced fresh ginger

2 tablespoons diced red onion

2 tablespoons diced red pepper

2 tablespoons chopped cilantro

3 tablespoons freshly squeezed lemon juice

24 jumbo prawns, approximately 1¼ pounds

MARINADE

3 tablespoons extra-virgin olive oil

¼ cup freshly squeezed lemon juice

½ cup dry white wine

1½ tablespoons grated fresh ginger

2 teaspoons minced garlic

Kosher salt and freshly ground pepper

To prepare the salsa: Combine the mango, pineapple, mint, ginger, onion, red pepper, cilantro, and lemon juice in a bowl. It is best to do this in advance and refrigerate, to give the flavors time to marry.

To butterfly the prawns: Place the prawns in a colander, rinse, and drain. With a small pair of sharp, pointed scissors (I use my kitchen shears), cut the shell from the head along the back to the tail. Using a sharp knife, place the prawn on a cutting board and cut through the flesh to the underside of the shell. Be careful not to cut all the way through. Remove the vein from under the shell. The prawn will open flat, like a butterfly, when placed on the grill.

To marinate and grill the prawns: In a large bowl, combine the olive oil, lemon juice, wine, ginger, garlic, and salt and pepper to taste. Add the butterflied prawns and toss lightly to coat. Cover and refrigerate for at least 2 hours, tossing several times while marinating.

Remove the prawns from the marinade and place them, flesh side down, on the grill. After 2 to 3 minutes, turn and baste with the marinade. Continuing basting until done. Total grilling time is 5 to 8 minutes. Serve with Mango-Mint Salsa on the side.

THE CALIFORNIA WINE INDUSTRY SINCE WORLD WAR II

After World War II, supplies and equipment needed by wineries and vineyards were hard to find. Repairs were difficult. But as the '50s unfolded, technical innovations emerged. In the winery, Millipore filters and microfilters were introduced, which made it possible to produce a higher quality wine. Wine production could maintain higher quality standards with the introduction of sterile techniques and operations. Centrifuges were introduced to remove solids from the wine, reducing bitterness and making wine that was more varietally true than filtered wine. The introduction of stainless steel and jacketed stainless steel fermentors allowed for temperature-controlled, cooled fermentation, creating better white wines in particular.

In the fields, chemical fertilizers and pesticides were heralded.

Prior to the 1950s, vineyards were almost all tended by dry farming. There was very little irrigation. With the introduction of aluminum pipes and sprinklers, large-scale irrigation was possible. In low-lying areas where frost was a potential danger, sprinkler systems even provided a degree of frost protection.

In the 1970s, my dad worked with Chisholm Ryder and UpRight Harvester to develop the first experimental mechanical harvesting machines. He re-trellised a section of the vineyards so that the grapes would line up with the insides of the various machines. He was involved with the first lots of wine picked by machine. This innovation made it possible to pick only the ripest grapes, based on their liquid weight, leaving the green berries and dried raisins behind in the

vineyard. The result was higher-quality grapes arriving at the winery.

During the 1960s, a major expansion began into underdeveloped or new grape-growing regions, such as Monterey County and the Santa Barbara–Paso Robles region. By the 1980s, Monterey County had more acreage planted in grapes than Napa. But as the boom-bust cycle of California's wine industry turned once more, the bottom dropped out of the market and many of the newly planted vines were pulled up. Many of the wineries that had expanded into the Monterey area changed ownership as well. But the downsizing was short lived. Prior to 1970, there were fewer than 100 wineries in the California wine industry. Now, in the current growth cycle, there are over 850. —CW

Mascarpone Cheesecake with Biscotti Crust and Balsamic Strawberries

MAKES ONE 9-INCH CAKE

❧ WINE NOTES

Kimball suggests something similar to a red Vin Santo, a sweet Italian dessert wine with a sugar content equal to the cheesecake. Or try a late-harvest Zinfandel. The wine itself is rich and, because of its "red" nature, it does have berry undertones, which enhance the strawberries in the dish.

This is a very creamy cheesecake with a distinctive, not too sweet flavor. The basic mixture was developed by Michelle Lyons, our former restaurant pastry chef and now owner of her own bakery, Home Slice. I've tweaked the cheesecake by adding the biscotti crust and balsamic strawberries. You could also use amaretti cookie crumbs in the crust. Instead of a springform pan, I use a regular 2-quart round baking pan so I can cook the cheesecake in a water bath. This moistness in the oven helps prevent the top from cracking.

1 1/2 cups ground biscotti crumbs
    (crushed with a rolling pin or food processor)

6 tablespoons unsalted butter, melted

2 pounds cream cheese (approximately 4 cups),
    at room temperature

1/2 pound mascarpone (approximately 1 cup),
    at room temperature

1 1/4 cups granulated sugar

2 eggs

BALSAMIC STRAWBERRIES

2 cups hulled and quartered strawberries

¹/₄ cup balsamic vinegar

Confectioners' sugar for sweetening berries

To make the cheesecake: Butter the bottom of a 2-quart round baking pan and line with a circle of parchment paper.

In a bowl, mix together the biscotti crumbs and butter and fill the bottom of the pan with the mixture, packing it down with your fingertips. Chill in the refrigerator for 30 minutes.

Preheat the oven to 325°.

In the bowl of a mixer, using the paddle attachment, cream together the cream cheese, mascarpone, and sugar. Mix until light; the mixture will become lighter in both color and texture and a bit fluffy. Add the eggs, one at a time, making sure that the first egg is fully blended in before adding the second. Scrape the sides of the bowl a few times while adding the eggs.

Pour the mixture over the biscotti crust. Smooth the top. Place inside a larger pan and fill the larger pan one-third of the way up the sides with warm water. Place in the oven and bake for 1 hour. When the cake is done, the top of the cake will appear to move as one piece, but the cake will not be totally firm, when you shake the pan. (If you do not have a water bath in which to cook the cheesecake, or if you want to use a springform pan, bake at 275° for 60 to 70 minutes.)

Turn the oven off and prop the door open with a spoon. Let the cake cool in the oven for 20 to 30 minutes to prevent the top from cracking. Then cool for 2 to 3 hours in the refrigerator.

To prepare the strawberries: Mix the strawberries and balsamic vinegar together and add confectioners' sugar to taste. The amount of sugar will depend on how sweet the berries are and how good the balsamic vinegar is, as you are trying to balance the sweetness and acidity of the topping.

To serve, when the cake has cooled completely, remove it from the pan. This will be easier if you place the pan in a warm water bath for a minute and then run a hot knife around the inside edge of the cake pan. Carefully invert the cake onto a plate, remove the parchment paper, and then invert again onto another plate.

To slice the cake, heat your knife under hot tap water, wipe clean, and cut a slice. Repeat for each cut. Serve each slice topped with strawberries.

Blackberry and Pistachio Shortcakes with Lime Cream

SERVES 4

🐟 **WINE NOTES**

Not every dessert pairs well with wine. The sweetness of the dessert often causes the wine to taste sour or bitter. With desserts that have a fruit component, I look for a wine with similar fruit attributes—very fruit-intense and immediately recognizable as the same fruit. Generally, wines made from red grapes, such as Merlot, Zinfandel, Pinot Noir, and Cabernet Sauvignon, have berry flavors such as blackberry, raspberry, and strawberry. Select a wine that is light in style with moderate acid and low tannin, such as a Grenache or Gamay. This accentuates the fruitiness, making it seem sweeter. For a wonderful experience, serve it slightly chilled.

Vinexpo, the largest wine trade show in the world, is held in Bordeaux, France, every two years. Working with our French importer, we create a special dinner at Château Pape-Clément in the beautiful Graves region for all of our worldwide wine agents. I had planned to serve shortcake with strawberries, peaches, and raspberries for dessert. We went to the market and bought the most incredible fruit, both in looks and flavor. But the first shortcakes were a disaster! In France, the flour is milled much finer than ours. My shortcakes were flabby rather than flaky. In our broken French, we pleaded with a local restaurateur for help. The flour that he supplied us had more body. Our dessert was finally a rousing success.

We use the same shortcake dough in the restaurant to make scones. A real treat is to make the scones with dried cranberries instead of the pistachios. Sprinkle with rock sugar and bake for the same time at the same temperature.

LIME CREAM

1/2 recipe pastry cream (page 199) flavored with
    11/2 teaspoons lime zest

SHORTCAKES

2 cups all-purpose flour

1/2 teaspoon kosher salt

1 tablespoon baking powder

1/4 cup granulated sugar

1/2 cup cold unsalted butter, cut into pieces

1/2 cup shelled pistachios

3/4 cup plus 2 tablespoons heavy whipping cream

1 egg, lightly whipped and thinned with
    an equal amount of water

1 cup crème fraîche or 1 cup heavy whipping cream (page 199)

Granulated sugar to taste

4 cups blackberries

Confectioners' sugar, for dusting (optional)

Finely chopped lime zest for garnish (optional)

Prepare the pastry cream, flavoring it with the lime zest.

To prepare the shortcakes: In a bowl, mix together the flour, salt, baking powder, and sugar. With your hands, work the chilled butter into the dry

ingredients until most of the butter chunks are pea-sized. Some larger chunks of butter are fine; they will add to the flakiness. Mix in the pistachios. Add the cream and mix quickly. Do not overmix. Wrap and refrigerate for 1 hour.

On a lightly floured surface, roll the dough out approximately 1 inch thick. Cut into 4 shortcakes with a $3^1/2$-inch round cutter. Place the shortcakes on a baking sheet and let rest in the refrigerator for 1 hour.

Preheat oven to 425°. Remove the shortcakes from the refrigerator and brush the tops with the egg-water mixture (also known as an egg wash). Place the baking sheet on a second sheet. This helps prevent the bottoms from becoming too brown. Bake for approximately 20 minutes, or until golden brown. Cool on racks.

To serve, whip the crème fraîche to soft peaks, adding sugar to taste. Split the shortcakes and place a spoonful of lime pastry cream and berries on each bottom half. Place another spoonful on the inside of the top half of each shortcake and place on top of the berries. Dust the top with confectioners' sugar and a dollop of the sweetened crème fraîche. Sprinkle with lime zest.

Warm Fruit Compote
with Lavender–Vanilla Ice Cream

This is a simple dessert that I used to prepare before I became a chef. Of course, I bought the ice cream back then! You can omit the lavender and still have a delicious homemade ice cream. It is fun to experiment with different fruits and liqueurs. I like using fresh peaches in season, figs, nectarines, and even apples and pears. I try to match the alcohol to the fruit so that the flavors complement each other. Any liqueur that is on the sweet side will work, but I use the rum every time.

LAVENDER-VANILLA ICE CREAM

1 whole vanilla bean

¹/₂ cup fresh lavender leaves and flowers

**Ice cream (page 199); steep cream first as described below
   before preparing**

2 cups strawberries, hulled

2 tablespoons granulated sugar

2 cups blackberries

2 small mangoes or 1 large mango, peeled and sliced

¹/₄ cup rum

2 tablespoons orange liqueur, such as Grand Marnier

2 tablespoons butter

To prepare the ice cream: Combine the vanilla bean, fresh lavender, and cream and bring to a boil. Remove from the heat and let steep for 30 minutes. Continue making the ice cream as described on page 199.

To prepare the compote: If the strawberries are very large, halve them. In a large sauté pan over high heat, heat the sugar until it starts to caramelize. Add ¹/₂ cup of each of the fruits. Remove the pan from the heat, add the rum and liqueur, and return to the heat. Flame off the alcohol, as described on page 209. Mash the fruit in the pan until it is saucelike. Lower the heat and cook until the fruit is soft, 6 or 7 minutes. Remove from the heat and swirl in the butter. Add the remaining fruit and toss. Serve immediately over scoops of Lavender-Vanilla Ice Cream.

SERVES 4 GENEROUSLY

WINE NOTES

My father was the first in California to produce a late-harvest Riesling with botrytis, a "good" mold found in our vineyard in the Arroyo Seco district of Monterey. The first late-harvest wine he produced back in 1969 was likened to many of the fine Spätleses and Ausleses originating in Germany. These wines can be paired with many desserts, as they are characterized by a broad range of flavors such as honey, peaches, apricots, orange blossoms, and hints of spice.

Mile High Chocolate Cake

SERVES 16

🍂 WINE NOTES

Many of my friends in the wine industry believe that one of the best matches with a chocolate dessert is a rich, full-bodied red wine with undertones of chocolate in the aftertaste, such as a Cabernet Sauvignon. However, I think either a non-vintage port or a vintage port can best enhance your chocolate dessert experience.

This recipe is based on a cake made by my friend Michelle Lyons. I like to use the best cocoa I can—Dutch-processed and high in cocoa fat. (Ghirardelli chocolate from San Francisco is one of the highest at 22 percent cocoa fat.) It makes a better tasting, richer, and moister cake. The frosting recipe is quite generous. There is definitely enough for the kids to lick the bowl!

$1^1/_2$ cups cocoa powder

$1^1/_4$ cups boiling water

$1^1/_2$ cups cake flour

$1^1/_2$ cups all-purpose flour

$1^1/_4$ teaspoons baking soda

$1^1/_4$ teaspoons baking powder

Pinch of kosher salt

$^3/_4$ cup unsalted butter, at room temperature

$2^3/_4$ cups brown sugar

4 large eggs

$1^1/_4$ cups buttermilk

$1^1/_4$ teaspoons vanilla extract

FROSTING

4 ounces bittersweet chocolate, chopped

8 ounces unsweetened chocolate, chopped

1 cup unsalted butter, at room temperature, cut into small cubes

$3^1/_2$ cups confectioners' sugar

Pinch of kosher salt

2 teaspoons vanilla extract

$^7/_8$ cup ($^3/_4$ cup plus 2 tablespoons) warm milk

Preheat the oven to 350°. Butter the inside of two 9 by 2-inch round cake pans, and line the bottoms with parchment paper. Dust the sides of the pans with flour.

In a small bowl, combine the cocoa powder and boiling water with a few quick strokes.

In another bowl, sift together the cake flour, all-purpose flour, baking soda, baking powder, and salt. Set aside.

In the bowl of a mixer, using the paddle attachment, cream the butter and brown sugar at medium speed until smooth and well blended. Add the cocoa liquid to the butter-sugar mixture and mix until well blended.

In a bowl, lightly whisk the eggs and combine with the buttermilk and vanilla.

With the mixer on low, add the wet and dry ingredients alternately, a third at a time, to the butter-sugar-cocoa mixture. That is, add a third of the wet ingredients, then a third of the dry ingredients, and so on. Make sure each addition is mixed in before adding the next. Fold in the last third of the dry ingredients by hand.

Divide the batter between the 2 pans. Smooth the tops with a rubber spatula. Bake in the oven for about 35 minutes, or until a toothpick comes out clean. Let cool on baking racks for 10 minutes. Turn the layers out onto plates. Invert another plate on top of each layer and turn over again. The layers are now right side up. Set the plates back on the racks to cool.

To prepare the frosting: In a bowl over a warm water bath, melt the two types of chocolate and the butter together. Do not get the water too hot, as the steam will take the shine out of the chocolate. Also, if you heat chocolate too quickly, it can separate. Remove from the water bath and cool to lukewarm. Whisk together the confectioners' sugar, salt, vanilla, and milk. Place over a warm water bath and stir until smooth. Combine the two mixtures. Cover and cool to room temperature, about 1 hour. Stir every 20 minutes while cooling. The frosting will thicken as it cools.

To finish the cake: Trim the tops of the layers so they are both the same height. With a serrated knife, split each layer in half horizontally. You should now have four rounds of equal height. Spread a 1/4-inch layer of frosting on top of each layer. Place the first layer on a plate, and stack the remaining layers on top of each other until you have a 4-layer cake. Frost the sides of the cake with the remaining frosting. Cut into slices and serve.

SUMMER

STARTERS

🐚 WINE NOTES

A bubbly, dry Champagne would pair nicely with this dish if served as an appetizer. If you want to serve the cakes as a main course, make sure that the wine has enough structure to hold up to the flavors in the salsa. A Sauvignon Blanc that has been aged in oak would complement these grassy, herbal, rich flavors.

Pan-Seared Fish Cakes
with Avocado Salsa Verde

This is an easy and fun dish to prepare for a large dinner party. The recipe can be doubled readily to accommodate more guests. I cut the avocado in half lengthwise, remove the pit, and cut the avocado into cubes while still in its skin. Then it's a breeze to scoop the avocado meat out with a spoon and add it to the salsa verde.

AVOCADO SALSA VERDE

1 tablespoon fresh tarragon leaves

2 tablespoons fresh parsley leaves

1/4 cup extra-virgin olive oil

1 clove garlic, minced

1 jalapeño, roasted, peeled, seeded, and diced (page 210)

1/2 teaspoon chopped capers

1/2 anchovy, minced

1 green olive, minced

1 large avocado, cut into 1/2-inch dice

FISH CAKES

2 1/2 pounds fish scraps such as salmon, cod, or halibut, cut into small pieces

1/4 cup diced red pepper

1 teaspoon diced scallion

1 tablespoon minced fresh ginger

1 jalapeño, seeds and ribs removed, diced

1 tablespoon lemon juice

1 teaspoon finely chopped lemon zest

1 tablespoon lime juice

1 teaspoon finely chopped lime zest

2 extra-large eggs, lightly whipped

1/2 cup toasted fine bread crumbs, or more as needed

Kosher salt and freshly ground pepper

2 tablespoons olive oil

1 tablespoon champagne vinegar

3 tablespoons extra-virgin olive oil

1/2 pound mixed baby greens

To prepare the salsa verde: Chop the tarragon and parsley together and mix with the olive oil, garlic, jalapeño, capers, anchovy, and olive. Add the avocado and toss lightly.

To prepare the fish cakes: In a bowl, mix together the fish, red pepper, scallion, ginger, jalapeño, lemon juice and zest, lime juice and zest, eggs, bread crumbs, salt, and pepper, and taste for seasoning.

Preheat the oven to 350°. Form the mixture into 10 flat patties. Heat the olive oil in a nonstick pan over medium-high heat. In batches, cook the cakes on both sides until golden brown. Place them on a baking sheet and bake in the oven until cooked through, about 5 minutes.

To serve, in a large bowl, combine the vinegar and oil. Toss the greens in the mixture. Divide among the plates. Lean a fish cake on each mound of greens and top with the salsa verde.

Hot-Smoked Pacific Salmon Rillettes with Chives and Crème Fraîche

For many summers over the past fifteen years, my family and I have headed for Brittany, on the north coast of France. The markets are alive with the best fruit, vegetables, meats, and fish of the season. We have also enjoyed the traveling butcher vans that make outstanding sausages and incredible pork and duck rillettes. The rillettes are addictive and, unfortunately, very fattening, so we looked for a way to make something similar with salmon that was lighter. The crème fraîche replaces the duck or pork fat used in the original. You can use hot-smoked or poached salmon and add cold-smoked or cured salmon to the mix. This is a fabulous way to use up leftovers from the night before!

1 pound Pacific salmon fillet, skin on

1 tablespoon lemon juice

1 tablespoon finely chopped lemon zest

1/4 cup crème fraîche or sour cream (page 199)

1 tablespoon chopped chives

Kosher salt and freshly ground pepper

Smoke the salmon as described on page 62.

When the salmon is cool, remove the skin and brown meat on the underside and discard. Flake the salmon and combine it with the lemon juice, finely chopped lemon zest, crème fraîche, chives, and salt and pepper, and taste for seasoning.

Serve with a salad, on toasts, or in omelets.

MAKES APPROXIMATELY
2 CUPS

🔺 WINE NOTES

A chilled, crisp rosé with fruitiness reminiscent of berries would be very appealing to the palate—and the eye—against the soft pink color of the rillettes. The smoky richness of the oily salmon and crème fraîche would also contrast well with the bubbles, acidity, and toasty character of a sparkling wine.

Grilled Figs with Mascarpone, Mint, Port, and Prosciutto

MAKES 16 APPETIZERS

🐟 WINE NOTES

Look for a Cabernet Sauvignon with intense jamlike, figgy, and minty flavor components. It's different and fun to start a meal with a Cabernet (or any wine) and pair different dishes with it all the way through the meal. Kimball likes to pair these figs with a lightly chilled rosé, or a non-vintage port. It's not as heavy, rich, and tannic as a vintage port.

At a friend's house in Paris, I was served an incredible Charentais melon bathed in port, which was the inspiration for this dish. The addition of the creamy mascarpone and the salty prosciutto makes this version a little richer.

Donna Wilcox, the general manager of Concannon Vineyard, has five incredible fig trees in her backyard in Livermore. She lets me pick as much fruit as I can haul away! It's usually a race between me and the birds to see who gets there first.

8 fresh figs

1/4 cup non-vintage port

3 tablespoons mascarpone

4 very thin slices prosciutto

4 large mint leaves, for garnish

Cut off the ends of the figs and split in half lengthwise. Macerate in the port for an hour. Prepare a small fire in your grill and cook the figs for a moment or so on each side—just enough to warm the figs and give them a smoky flavor. They should remain firm. Spoon or pipe the mascarpone onto the cut sides of the figs, dividing it evenly. Cut the prosciutto into sixteen 1-inch-wide strips. Wrap around the figs. Place on plates or a serving platter. Slice the mint into very thin strips (chiffonade) and sprinkle over the figs.

HOT SMOKING

Smoking, like salting, is one of the oldest ways of preserving food. There are two methods of smoking, one hot, the other cold. The cold smoking method requires longer periods of salting, or brining, and gives the food a smoky flavor without cooking. Temperatures rarely rise above 100°. Hot smoking actually cooks what is being smoked, with considerably hotter temperatures ranging from 200° to 350°.

To hot-smoke meats or fish, you'll need a smoker or covered kettle-type grill, some kosher salt, cracked black pepper, mesquite or brick charcoal, and wood chips that have been soaked overnight in water. It is very important to soak the chips for a long period of time—at least 8 hours. When added to the hot fire, the soaked chips create smoke and steam. While the smoke adds flavor, the steam keeps the food moist and juicy.

Begin by seasoning the outside of the meat or fish with the salt and pepper. If you are smoking fish, leave the skin on. Let the meat or fish sit in the refrigerator for 1 hour.

Prepare your smoker or grill. Make sure the ashes are cleaned out of the bottom of the grill so the air will draw well. Prepare a small charcoal fire. If you are using a kettle-style grill, make the fire on one side of the grill so you can place the food to be smoked on the other side. When the fire has burned down to embers, place a handful of the wet wood chips on the hot coals. It is very important that the fire be small so that the meat or fish will cook slowly and take on the smoke aromas. If it is too large, the meat will cook too quickly and not take on much of the smoky flavor.

Place the seasoned meat or fish on the grill of the smoker or kettle. Fish should be skin down. Place pork on the grill bone side down. In a kettle-type grill, place the top so that the vent holes are over the food. That way, the smoke will be drawn from the fire over the food. Cook slowly, adding more wood chips as needed to keep a steady, slow stream of smoke.

Cook until the meat or fish reaches an internal temperature of 140° (145° for pork). Cooking times will vary depending on the type of smoker, but approximate times are as follows:

Many things will affect the cooking times. The farther the food is from the grill, the more heat will be needed. I have both a medium and a large kettle-type grill, and the grill on the large one is about an inch farther from the fire than the medium one. So I build the fire a little larger. The larger volume of air in the bigger one also requires a bit more cooking time. In the medium grill, I build a pile of glowing embers about 6 inches in diameter and 3 inches tall. You are going to have to experiment with your grill; keep track of what you are doing and you will soon discover the perfect method for your own situation.

You can also use brines to flavor meat or fish before smoking. Common brines start with salt and water and can include brown sugar, granulated sugar, onions, garlic, chiles, citrus, vinegar, celery, and apples. My rule of thumb is if the brine tastes really strong—a real sweet-sour mouth puckerer—it will usually be great. Experiment with different combinations and lengths of brining time.

Fish fillets (with skin)	$1/2$ to 1 hour, depending on the thickness
A 3- to 4-pound chicken	2 to 3 hours
Duck breast	30 minutes
2-inch pork chops	1 to 2 hours

Chanterelle Toasts
with Parmesan Shards

The first chanterelles begin arriving in California in July, and they last throughout the summer and fall. Scientists have not yet been able to cultivate chanterelles, so we are at the mercy of the seasons and good foragers for our supply of the wild fungi. You can use other mushrooms for this finger food, but I find chanterelle and hedgehog mushrooms to be the best.

1 baguette

2 tablespoons olive oil

MUSHROOM TOPPING

1 pound chanterelle mushrooms

2 tablespoons olive oil

Kosher salt and freshly ground pepper

1 teaspoon minced shallot

1/2 teaspoon minced garlic

2 tablespoons Madeira

2 tablespoons sherry

1/4 cup heavy whipping cream

1 teaspoon chopped fresh thyme

1 teaspoon chopped fresh parsley

2 tablespoons Parmesan shards (page 209)

MAKES 20 TOASTS

🍶 WINE NOTES

A perfect contrast to rich mushrooms and heavy cream is a brut Champagne or sparkling wine. The fruity, nutty, and toasty elements in the sparkling wine, along with its crisp acidity, cleanse the palate, urging you on to further revelry.

To prepare the toasts: Preheat the broiler. Slice the baguette thinly on an angle so that you end up with pieces about 2 inches long. Brush one side of each slice with olive oil, and toast the oiled sides under the broiler until golden brown.

To prepare the topping: Clean the chanterelles of any dirt, twigs, or stems. Try to avoid washing them if you can, as they absorb water quickly, which dilutes their flavor. Cut the mushrooms into 1/2-inch dice. In a sauté pan over high heat, heat the olive oil until almost smoking. Add the chanterelles, season with salt and pepper, and cook until golden brown, stirring often.

Lower the heat to medium, and add the shallot and garlic. Cook for about a minute, stirring constantly. Add the Madeira and sherry and stir over medium heat to scrape up the browned bits from the bottom of the pan. Flame off the alcohol, as described on page 209. Add the cream and cook for a few minutes at high heat, until thickened. Add the thyme and parsley.

To serve, spoon the topping onto the toasts and top with Parmesan shards.

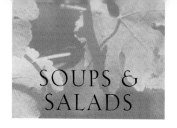

Garden Gazpacho
with Basil Pesto

SERVES 4

🐾 WINE NOTES

This soup is chock-full of raw vegetables, which can be a difficult wine match. Sauvignon Blanc has a strong, distinct varietal character that will equal the distinct flavors in the gazpacho. Because of its good acid content, a chilled Pinot Gris will also complement the vegetable medley.

I developed this recipe to incorporate many of the fresh ingredients coming from our garden in the summer, when it seems to be overflowing. When harvested in the cooler morning hours and then made into a chilled soup, the Garden Gazpacho provides a refreshing meal at lunch or a starter for a summer supper. If you would like a gazpacho with more bite, add more Tabasco and lemon juice. Serve with toasted focaccia wedges or pita toasts, brushed with olive oil, lightly salted, and sprinkled with fresh rosemary.

The pesto recipe makes more than needed for the soup—you might use the rest in a pasta with lamb or as a spread on a lamb sandwich. If you store it in a small jar with about $1/4$ inch of olive oil floated on top, it will last for 2 to 3 months in your refrigerator. —CW

6 large ripe tomatoes, peeled, seeded, and diced (1-inch dice) (page 209)

3 lemon cucumbers, peeled, seeded, and diced (1-inch dice)

1 tablespoon minced shallot

3 celery stalks, peeled and diced ($1/8$-inch dice), approximately 1 cup

2 carrots, peeled and diced ($1/8$-inch dice), approximately 1 cup

2 cloves garlic, pressed

1 teaspoon chopped fresh lemon thyme

1 teaspoon chopped fresh chervil

2 tablespoons chopped fresh basil

2 drops Tabasco sauce, or more to taste

2 tablespoons lemon juice, or more to taste

1 cup chicken stock, or more if needed (page 206)

1 cup salt-free tomato-based vegetable juice, more if needed

Kosher salt and freshly ground pepper

$1/2$ green bell pepper, seeded and diced ($1/4$-inch dice)

1 yellow bell pepper, seeded and diced ($1/4$-inch dice)

BASIL PESTO

3 to 4 cups loosely packed fresh basil leaves

5 cloves garlic, peeled

1 cup freshly grated Parmesan cheese

1 1/2 to 2 cups extra-virgin olive oil

3/4 cup pine nuts, toasted (page 210)

Kosher salt and freshly ground pepper

GARNISH

1 cup sour cream

1/2 cup Basil Pesto

4 basil leaves

This recipe is prepared in a food processor or blender. If your food processor bowl is not large enough to make this recipe in one batch, split the ingredients into two batches and combine in a large soup tureen after purée-ing. Chill before serving.

To prepare the gazpacho: Place the tomatoes, cucumbers, shallot, celery, carrots, garlic, herbs, Tabasco sauce, and lemon juice in a blender or food processor and purée. Add enough of the chicken stock and tomato juice to aid in puréeing the mixture. If you are using a food processor, process with the metal blade for about 30 seconds. The consistency of the soup will be somewhat chunky, containing small pieces of the different-colored vegetables. Don't purée to a smooth texture. Add more chicken stock or tomato juice, depending on how thick or thin you prefer your soup. The amount of stock and juice you use will also depend on the amount of liquid contained in the vegetables. Add salt and pepper to taste. Stir in the red and yellow bell peppers. Chill for at least 1 hour before serving.

To prepare the pesto: Place the basil, garlic, and Parmesan in a food processor fitted with the metal blade. Purée while slowly adding about 1 cup of the olive oil. When smooth, add the pine nuts, season with salt and pepper, and add the remaining oil, if necessary. The mixture should be smooth with coarse bits of pine nuts and no excess oil.

To serve, garnish the soup in the soup tureen with a dollop each of the sour cream and pesto. Surround the dollops with basil leaves. Pass the remainder of the sour cream and pesto in small bowls.

Melon and Sparkling Wine Soup with Mint Cream and Mango Purée

Choose melons that look ripe, without any green coloring (unless they are a green variety). The stem should be slightly soft but not mushy, and should smell of sweet fruit. With ripe melons you won't need to add any sugar. The acidity of the Champagne and lime balances the sweetness of the melon and mango. I like serving this soup with the same wine I used to prepare it. The soup can be served either at the beginning of a meal, in the middle as a palate cleanser, or at the end of a meal for a light dessert.

1 large ripe melon such as honeydew, crenshaw, or ambrosia,
    peeled, seeded, and cut into 1-inch dice (a 4-pound melon
    yields about 4 cups of purée)

1 mango, peeled and pitted

1 cup Champagne or sparkling wine

Simple syrup to taste (page 200; optional)

MINT CREAM

1/4 cup fresh mint leaves

1/4 cup crème fraîche or sour cream (page 199)

1 teaspoon lime juice

1 teaspoon water

Place the melon in a food processor fitted with the metal blade and process until smooth. Strain out any large pieces. Place in a bowl. Process the mango separately until smooth, and strain. Chill the melon and mango purées. Depending on the ripeness of your fruit, you may need to sweeten your purées to taste. I prefer to use simple syrup, as it blends in quickly.

To prepare the Mint Cream: Boil a couple of cups of water and add the mint leaves, reserving several for garnish, for about 10 seconds. Remove the mint quickly and dry. Purée with the crème fraîche, lime juice, and water in a mini-chopper or blender.

Just before serving, add the Champagne to the melon purée. Divide the melon purée among 4 bowls. With a spoon, drizzle the mango purée in one direction on top of the melon purée. You don't want to blend the two purées completely. Drizzle with mint cream in the other direction. Cut the reserved mint leaves into very thin strips and sprinkle on top. Serve immediately.

SERVES 4

❧ WINE NOTES

This refreshing soup needs an equally refreshing chilled wine. An obvious choice would be to serve the same Champagne or sparkling wine that you used to prepare the soup. With other wines, the challenge would be to match the level of sweetness found in the melon with an off-dry wine such as a Johannisberg Riesling. Some Chardonnays grown in warmer regions exhibit ripe melon characteristics, and these would be nice as well; go for a light-bodied wine with little or no oak aging.

Corn and Smoked Chicken Chowder
with Jalapeño–Cilantro Butter

SERVES 8

❧ WINE NOTES

The ripe fruit flavors from grapes grown in a warmer region, with some barrel aging, yields a full-bodied Chardonnay, which would complement this recipe. The toasty character of a barrel-fermented Pinot Blanc, aged in oak, would also pair well with this chowder.

Melissa Rossi (the chef my children call "Mom") prepared a corn chowder similar to this one years ago for me. I added the smoked chicken and jalapeño-cilantro butter to give it a little more oomph. Cooking the cobs in the chowder adds a deeper corn flavor. You can make a great vegetarian version of this soup by omitting the chicken and bacon and using vegetable stock.

Half a 3 1/2- to 4-pound chicken

Kosher salt and freshly ground pepper

1 1/2 slices thick bacon, diced

1/2 large onion, diced

3 tablespoons flour

8 cups chicken stock, cold (page 206)

2 bay leaves

1 tablespoon whole black peppercorns

Kernels from 8 ears of sweet corn (reserve the cobs)

3 large russet potatoes, peeled, cut in 1/2-inch dice, and reserved in water

4 cups heavy whipping cream

JALAPEÑO-CILANTRO BUTTER

1 cup loosely packed fresh cilantro leaves, about 1 bunch

1/2 cup unsalted butter, at room temperature

1 tablespoon lemon juice

1 teaspoon finely chopped lemon zest

2 cloves garlic, minced

2 jalapeño peppers, roasted, peeled, seeded, and diced (page 210)

Kosher salt and freshly ground pepper

To smoke the chicken: Season the chicken under the skin with salt and pepper. Smoke as described on page 62 until an internal temperature of 140° is reached, approximately 2 hours.

To prepare the Jalapeño-Cilantro Butter: While the chicken is smoking, lightly chop the cilantro. Combine with the butter, lemon juice, finely chopped lemon zest, garlic, and jalapeños. Season to taste with salt and pepper. Serve at room temperature.

To prepare the chowder: When the chicken is cool, remove the meat from the bones, and shred it with your fingers. Set aside.

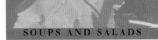

Place an 8-quart nonreactive stockpot over medium heat. Add the bacon and sauté, stirring often, until most of the fat has rendered and the bacon is golden brown. If your bacon does not render enough fat for frying the onion, add enough olive oil to total about 1 tablespoon. Add the onion and cook until translucent, approximately 10 minutes.

Slowly blend in the flour and cook for a few minutes, stirring constantly. Whisk in the chicken stock, a little at a time. Make sure to mix in the stock thoroughly each time before you add more, to avoid lumps.

Place the chicken bones, bay leaves, and peppercorns in a large piece of cheesecloth and tie closed. Add the reserved corncobs and the cheesecloth bag. Bring to a boil, stirring often. Reduce the heat to a simmer and cook for about 90 minutes, until the corn flavor is fairly strong.

Remove the cobs and lightly scrape any liquid on the cobs back into the soup. Remove the bag. Drain the potatoes and add to the soup, cooking for about 5 minutes, or until the potatoes are still slightly crunchy. Add the corn kernels, smoked chicken, and cream and bring to a boil. Be careful not to scorch. Season with salt and pepper to taste.

Serve with a dollop of the room-temperature Jalapeño-Cilantro Butter.

Kimball's Caesar Salad

SERVES 4

♨ WINE NOTES

Kimball's Caesar Salad has been one of our signature menu items at the restaurant, which has given me the opportunity to do a lot of testing with similar or contrasting wine pairings. My favorite pairing is one of our reserve Chardonnays—Riva Ranch. It is entirely barrel fermented, lush with tropical fruit, and complexity and richness are added through malolactic fermentation. Look for a Chardonnay that will complement the richness and intensity of the dressing.

What makes this Kimball's Caesar Salad? The secret is in the dressing—a classic balance of acidity, garlic, and anchovies, but I add puréed sundried tomatoes for a little extra body and balance. It is by far the best-selling salad in our restaurant and never comes off the menu.

2 heads romaine lettuce

1/4 cup olive oil

4 cloves garlic, sliced

1 cup rustic bread, preferably *pain levain,* hand-torn into 1/2-inch pieces

Kosher salt and freshly ground pepper

1/2 cup shaved Parmesan cheese, for garnish

DRESSING

3 egg yolks

1 tablespoon Chardonnay vinegar or white wine vinegar

1 tablespoon lemon juice

1 tablespoon Dijon mustard

1 tablespoon puréed anchovies

1 tablespoon minced garlic

2 teaspoons Worcestershire sauce

1 teaspoon Tabasco sauce

1 cup olive oil

1 tablespoon puréed sundried tomatoes in oil

1/4 teaspoon kosher salt

Freshly ground pepper

Remove and discard the tough outer leaves and any discolored leaves from the romaine. Twist the stem end to remove it, separating the romaine into individual leaves. Clean the whole leaves in very cold water and spin dry in a salad spinner. Reserve in the refrigerator.

To prepare the croutons: In a small pan over medium heat, heat the olive oil and sliced garlic until warm. Remove from the heat and let steep for 1 hour.

Preheat the oven to 350°.

Strain the garlic from the oil. Toss the bread in the garlic-flavored oil, coating thoroughly. Season with salt and pepper. Place on a baking sheet and bake in the preheated oven for about 15 minutes, turning once halfway through. The croutons should be a light golden brown. Set aside to cool.

To prepare the dressing: In a blender, process the egg yolks, vinegar, lemon juice, and Dijon mustard. In a small bowl, mash the anchovy and garlic together with a fork. Add half of the anchovy-garlic mixture to the egg mixture, then add the Worcestershire and Tabasco sauces. With a hand mixer or whisk, blend together. Slowly add the olive oil in a very thin stream, as you would to make mayonnaise. Thin with water if it gets too thick. Add the sundried tomatoes. Slowly add more anchovy-garlic mixture to taste. Taste for salt and pepper. There should be a good balance between the acid, anchovy, garlic, and sundried tomatoes. Always taste the results on a piece of romaine lettuce dipped in the dressing.

To serve, toss the lettuce and croutons separately in the dressing. You will achieve the best results if you toss the romaine with your hands, coating each leaf evenly. The dressing is fairly thick. On each plate, arrange about half a head of whole romaine leaves, with larger leaves on the bottom and smaller ones on the top, similar to the way they grew on the head. Garnish with the Parmesan and the croutons.

Heirloom Tomato Salad
with Balsamic–Cabernet Vinaigrette, Roasted Onions, Blue Cheese, and Opal Basil

SERVES 4

❧ WINE NOTES

This is my favorite summer salad at the restaurant. The elements that make this dish a challenge are the sweetness of the very ripe tomatoes along with the acid. A wonderful pairing would have the same elements. I have tried numerous wines and have found several that work extremely well, all light reds such as Pinot Noir, Merlot, and Sangiovese. These wines have forward fruit and ample acid, much like an heirloom tomato.

Each year I look forward to the delights of tomato season, which usually begins in July in California and runs until the first frost in October or November. We buy tomatoes for the restaurant from Dan Marciel, who owns a small farm in Livermore. The first chef arriving in the morning calls Dan, usually around 6:00 A.M., and orders what we need for the day. Dan then picks it fresh daily. The wonderful thing about this salad is how it changes, depending on which tomato varieties are the ripest that day.

BALSAMIC-CABERNET VINAIGRETTE

2 cloves garlic, thinly sliced

4 teaspoons balsamic vinegar

4 teaspoons cabernet vinegar (or a good-quality red wine vinegar)

1/2 cup extra-virgin olive oil

Kosher salt and freshly ground pepper

2 red torpedo onions (you can substitute regular red onions)

1 basket mixed small tomatoes such as Sweet 100s,
    Green Grape, or red and yellow plum

8 large heirloom tomatoes, such as Brandywine, Golden Queen,
    or Zebra

4 ounces blue cheese, crumbled

1/2 bunch opal (Thai) basil

4 slices crusty whole-wheat sourdough bread (or something similar)

Extra-virgin olive oil for brushing on the bread

1 clove garlic, peeled

To prepare the vinaigrette: In a shallow bowl, combine the garlic and the two vinegars. Slowly whisk in the olive oil. Season with salt and pepper to taste.

To prepare the onions: Preheat the oven to 350°. Cut the onions in quarters, root to stem, keeping the outside skin attached. Toss the onions with half of the vinaigrette and a little salt and pepper. Place cut side down on a baking sheet. Roast in the oven for 10 to 15 minutes, until the layers of the onion start to open up and the onion is cooked through but still a little firm. If you use red onions, you may have to increase the roasting time a bit. Remove from the oven and cool. Remove the tough and papery outer layers. Trim off the root. Combine with the mixed small tomatoes and remaining vinaigrette.

To assemble the salad: Core and trim the bottom of the large heirloom tomatoes and cut in half widthwise. Arrange on 4 plates, alternating tomatoes and colors. Place the roasted onions and small tomatoes around the larger tomatoes, and drizzle the vinaigrette remaining in the bottom of the bowl over the large tomatoes. Divide the crumbled blue cheese among the 4 plates.

Slice the basil leaves into thin strips and scatter over the salads.

Brush each slice of bread with olive oil and grill or toast until golden brown. Rub each slice with the whole garlic clove. Cut the bread slices in half diagonally, placing 2 halves on each plate. Serve immediately.

THE FOOD CHAIN

Our commitment to using the freshest ingredients demands that we buy our produce as locally as possible. This makes the restaurant an active participant in what I call our "food chain"—a network of interdependent suppliers of the most wonderful products of Mother Nature. The links in this network that are available to many home chefs are the local farmers' markets. These days they are everywhere. The Internet lists almost two thousand such markets, in virtually every state in the union. These markets are wonderful sources for culinary delights.

Another link in my food chain is the restaurant's direct connection with the small farmers. We are lucky enough to be close to these growers who can be more responsive to the growing patterns of their crops. They pick their fruits and vegetables only when ripe, assuring that the mother plant gives all of the nutrients that result in the finest flavor. Nothing can replace that; an early pick never gets these flavor enhancers. A lot of produce is bred for mechanical harvesting, shipping, and storage; flavor is not the highest priority.

The home chef benefits from our contact with the small farmers. For example, we buy tomatoes for an appetizer from a small grower in our area, Dan Marciel. He has a space at the local farmers' market as well. In the course of doing business with Dan, we talk about the availability of the highly rated heirloom tomatoes—those very flavorful older varieties no longer planted by commercial growers. Because of our interest and commitment, Dan plants some heirloom tomatoes. These tomatoes show up simultaneously on our menu and in Dan's booth at the farmers' market. He has also added some wonderful French pumpkins to his pumpkin patch at our request, and these too have made their way to the farmers' market.

An outstanding source for produce and another link in my food chain is Green Leaf, a Bay Area produce distributor. Referring to themselves as agents of Mother Nature, they are absolutely committed to supplying the finest produce to restaurants and caterers, mostly in the Bay Area. Green Leaf works with an incredible network of small growers, from small family farmers in the Salinas Valley to back-to-the-landers in the Sierra foothills.

A wonderful aspect of working with Green Leaf is their two-way street. Not only do they supply produce to restaurants and caterers, but Green Leaf will seek out or develop a grower for a chef's special request. Frequently, that grower will end up selling it in the farmers' markets as well.

But, as Dan Marciel says, bringing these specialty items to farmers' markets hasn't been an easy sale. In the case of the heirloom tomatoes, it took time to develop buyers savvy enough to realize that those oddly shaped, strangely colored, not-as-firm-as-commercial tomatoes were vine-ripened and had outstanding flavor. Many people were judging the heirloom varieties by the same standards they use in the large grocery store chains.

In our food chain, the local farmers' markets are an incredible two-way source of information and produce for chefs, restaurateurs, and home chefs. Support the small growers so we all can benefit from their efforts in the chain.—KJ

Pizza with Pesto, Corn, Vine-Ripened Tomatoes, and Fresh Mozzarella

MAKES FOUR 12-INCH PIZZAS

🏶 WINE NOTES

Zinfandel grapes are widely grown throughout California, and their flavor characteristics change depending on the climate. Those planted in warmer regions will be fuller-bodied and will demonstrate the more condensed, fruity flavors of jams, while cooler regions and vineyard sites produce lighter, crisper wines with delicate flavors of cherry and berry. A tasty "cooler-region" Zinfandel, with berry flavors and moderate tannins, would be a wonderful fit for these pizzas.

Cooks in restaurant kitchens are always making food for their own meals that the public never sees. We almost always make something simple to be eaten standing up. One day we were fooling around in the kitchen with some leftovers from the night before and developed this recipe. It's colorful, light, flavorful, and easy to make. Try to find fresh mozzarella. The flavor and texture are very mild and not at all stringy, like most commercial mozzarella.

PESTO

1 cup loosely packed fresh basil leaves

1/2 cup loosely packed fresh parsley leaves

1 jalapeño, roasted, peeled, and seeded (page 210)

2 tablespoons minced garlic

1/4 cup grated Parmesan cheese

2 tablespoons toasted pine nuts (page 210)

1/2 cup olive oil

Kosher salt and freshly ground pepper

Pizza dough (page 203)

1/2 cup fresh corn kernels

4 large vine-ripened tomatoes, thinly sliced

4 (4-ounce) balls fresh mozzarella (1 pound in all), thinly sliced

Prepare the oven for pizza, as described on page 204. Preheat to 550°.

To prepare the pesto: Place the basil, parsley, jalapeño, garlic, Parmesan, and pine nuts in a blender or food processor, along with half of the oil. Purée. With the motor running, slowly add the remaining oil. Season with salt and pepper to taste.

Divide the pizza dough into fourths and shape each into a 12-inch round, as described on page 204. Spread 2 tablespoons of pesto onto each pizza. Sprinkle the corn over the pesto, dividing it among the 4 pizzas. Arrange the tomatoes and mozzarella on the pizzas, alternating slices. Bake until the edges and bottom are golden brown, 10 to 12 minutes. Drizzle with the remaining pesto. Cut and serve.

Calzone with Teleme Cheese, Smoked Pork, and Chile Salsa

MAKES 4 CALZONES

≈ WINE NOTES

A medium-bodied, slightly sweet white wine will counteract the heat from the chiles and balance the weight of the cheese. Try a Johannisberg Riesling or a Gewürztraminer. Even a rosé will complement this recipe's flavors.

Teleme is a wonderful soft, creamy cheese traditionally coated with rice flour to preserve it. You can substitute other soft cheeses in this calzone, but it's well worth searching for the real thing.

You can easily turn this into a vegetarian calzone by replacing the pork with summer vegetables such as zucchini, squash, and eggplant. Sauté them in a little olive oil before adding to the cheese mixture. For a spicier version, include the seeds of the chiles—that's where the heat is!

1 pound pork butt or shoulder

1 pound Teleme cheese, cubed

2 cups ricotta cheese (to make your own, see page 200)

Kosher salt and freshly ground pepper

2 Anaheim chiles, roasted, peeled, seeded, and sliced lengthwise (page 210)

2 pasilla chiles, roasted, peeled, seeded, and sliced lengthwise

1 jalapeño chile, roasted, peeled, seeded, and sliced lengthwise

1 cup peeled, seeded, and diced fresh tomatoes (page 209)

1 tablespoon minced garlic

1 tablespoon coarsely chopped fresh cilantro leaves

1 teaspoon lime juice

1/2 recipe pizza dough (page 203)

Smoke the pork as described on page 62. When it has cooled, dice the meat into small pieces.

Prepare the oven for pizza, as described on page 204. Preheat to 550°.

To prepare the filling: In a bowl, mix the diced pork with the two cheeses. Season with salt and pepper. Set aside.

In another bowl, combine the three types of chiles, tomatoes, garlic, cilantro, and lime juice.

To make the calzones, divide the dough into fourths and shape into 4 individual rounds. Divide the pork-cheese filling among the dough rounds, placing the filling on half of each round. Top the filling on each round with one-fourth of the chile-tomato mixture. Moisten the edges with water, and fold each round in half, covering the filling. Press the edges to seal. Bake in the oven until golden brown, 8 to 10 minutes. Serve immediately.

Grilled Pizza with Figs, Goat Cheese, and Pancetta

My grandparents had both Mission and Kadota fig trees in their orchard, which they generously shared with family and friends. My mother and I absolutely love figs and found many uses for them, from hors d'oeuvres to desserts. The combination of the figs and pancetta is reminiscent of an Italian favorite—figs and prosciutto. Either variety of fig will work, or try combining them. Grilling this pizza adds a nice smoky flavor, but if you prefer to bake the pizza in your oven, see page 204 for how to do it. —CW

3 cups quartered fresh figs

2 tablespoons lemon juice

8 slices pancetta

$^1/_2$ recipe pizza dough (page 203)

Olive oil

1 cup crumbled goat cheese

$^1/_4$ cup toasted pine nuts (page 210)

4 sprigs fresh basil, for garnish

In a small bowl, combine the figs and lemon juice and toss lightly.

Cut the pancetta into $^1/_4$-inch pieces. In a frying pan over medium heat, sauté until crisp, approximately 10 minutes. Remove from the pan with a slotted spoon and drain on a paper towel.

As described in the sidebar on page 25, prepare your grill by arranging the coals on one side, so there will be a hot and a cool side.

Divide the dough into fourths, and shape each into an 8- to 10-inch round; brush with olive oil.

Gather the figs, pancetta, goat cheese, and pine nuts close to the grill. Place a round of dough over the hot side of the grill until it has browned. It will cook very quickly; don't let it burn. Flip it over, move it to the cool side, and add the toppings. Scoot it back toward the heat to melt the cheese and warm the toppings. Watch it carefully! Garnish the center of the pizza with basil, and serve immediately. Repeat with the remaining dough rounds.

MAKES FOUR 8- TO 10-INCH PIZZAS

✵ WINE NOTES

Try a nicely chilled Gewürztraminer or Johannisberg Riesling with this pizza. Look for an off-dry wine to play off the sweet figs and goat cheese. A medium-bodied red wine, such as a Zinfandel, will balance the fruitiness of the figs, the acid and creaminess of the goat cheese, and the salt of the pancetta.

Linguine with Tomato-Basil Purée, Halibut, Pattypan Squash, and Garlic

SERVES 4

🐟 WINE NOTES

The dominant flavors in this recipe are found in the purée, so I would match the wine to the tomato and basil instead of to the halibut and squash. A medium-bodied red (a full-bodied red would overwhelm the halibut) with hints of mintiness, herbal tones and full, mouth-filling fruit would be a tasty selection—such as Zinfandel, Barbera, or Gamay.

After a winter of canned tomatoes, there is nothing like the real thing fresh from the garden. You can use any tomato for this recipe, but Romas (plum tomatoes) tend to hold up the best for a sauce. I don't serve fresh Parmesan with a fish pasta like this, because I find that the cheese overpowers the fish. Thin strips of basil and even toasted bread crumbs are a great garnish. This recipe also can be prepared using other seafoods.

TOMATO-BASIL PURÉE

2 tablespoons olive oil

1/2 cup sliced onion

2 tablespoons minced garlic

1 pasilla chile, roasted, peeled, and chopped, or
    1 jalapeño prepared the same way (page 210)

5 pounds Roma tomatoes, peeled and seeded (page 209)

1/4 cup fresh basil leaves

2 tablespoons olive oil

1 cup diced green pattypan squash (1/2-inch dice)

1 cup diced yellow pattypan squash (1/2-inch dice)

Kosher salt and freshly ground pepper

1 pound fresh linguine

1 pound halibut fillet, cut into 1-inch cubes

To prepare the Tomato-Basil Purée: In a 3-quart sauté pan over medium heat, heat the olive oil. Add the onion and cook over low heat until softened, about 15 minutes. Add the garlic and cook for a minute, stirring constantly. Add the chile and tomatoes. Bring to a simmer, and simmer for 30 minutes. Remove from the heat and purée in a food processor with the basil leaves. Return the purée to the sauté pan and set aside.

To prepare the pasta and finish the sauce: Heat a large pot of water to cook the linguine.

In a sauté pan over high heat, heat the olive oil. Add the squash, season with salt and pepper, and cook until lightly golden, stirring often. Add to the Tomato-Basil Purée.

Slowly heat the purée over low heat.

When the pasta water boils, add the linguine and cook until tender, about 7 minutes.

At the same time that you add the pasta to the water, add the halibut to the purée and cook until just done, about 5 minutes.

To serve, drain the pasta and toss with the sauce. Add salt and pepper to taste and serve immediately.

Grilled Pork Tenderloins Marinated in Merlot and Molasses

This dish is the result of a day I spent in the kitchen trying to create a white meat recipe that would pair well with our Merlot. It's typical of how my family looks at selecting or creating new recipes. We know what wine we want to feature and then decide on the menu. Most cooks match the wine to the food! —CW

MARINADE

2/3 cup molasses

2 cups Merlot

1/2 cup balsamic vinegar

4 large cloves garlic, sliced

3 tablespoons lemon juice

1/2 teaspoon ground cinnamon

1 tablespoon grated fresh ginger

1 teaspoon ground nutmeg

1 teaspoon paprika

1 teaspoon kosher salt

2 or 3 pork tenderloins, or 1 boneless pork loin
(2 to 2 1/2 pounds), well trimmed

In a small bowl, combine the marinade ingredients and mix well. Place the pork in a large, nonreactive bowl and cover with the marinade. Set aside in the refrigerator for at least 3 hours (it can marinate overnight).

Prepare a medium-sized fire in your grill. Remove the pork from the marinade and place on the grill over hot, glowing coals until cooked through, turning to cook it evenly, 20 to 25 minutes for the loin, 12 to 15 minutes for the tenderloins, or until a meat thermometer registers 140°. Let the pork rest for approximately 10 minutes before cutting it into thin slices. Serve warm or at room temperature.

SERVES 6

❧ WINE NOTES

Serve Merlot! With the Merlot in the marinade, the pork is already carrying some of the wine flavors. The molasses and the grilling add a sweetness and weight to the pork that help transform it into a fuller-flavored white meat.

Grilled Colorado Lamb Loin Chops with Spicy Couscous and Grilled Ratatouille

August and early September is the ideal time to make ratatouille. All of the summer vegetables are in their glory, and combining them seems so natural. Grilling the vegetables, which caramelizes the surface, adds a little smokiness and sweetness. This is a great meal for a barbecue or picnic. Prepare the couscous and marinate the meat and vegetables in advance.

8 Colorado lamb chops, 1 1/2 inches thick

MARINADE

8 cloves garlic, thinly sliced

Leaves from 1/2 bunch mint, coarsely chopped (about 40 leaves)

SPICY COUSCOUS

3 cups water

2 cups couscous

2 tablespoons extra-virgin olive oil

1 jalapeño pepper, roasted, peeled, seeded, and diced (page 210)

1/4 teaspoon ground cayenne pepper

Kosher salt

GRILLED RATATOUILLE

2 tablespoons balsamic vinegar

2 tablespoons olive oil

1 zucchini, cut in half lengthwise

1 yellow or sunburst squash, cut in half lengthwise

1 small eggplant (about 3/4 pound), peeled and cut into quarters lengthwise

1 red bell pepper, cut into quarters and seeds, stems, and inner ribs removed

1 yellow bell pepper, cut into quarters and seeds, stems, and inner ribs removed

Kosher salt and freshly ground pepper

1 tablespoon minced garlic

2 vine-ripened tomatoes, peeled, seeded, and diced (page 209)

1 teaspoon minced capers

2 tablespoons small fresh mint leaves for garnish

2 tablespoons small fresh basil leaves for garnish

SERVES 4

WINE NOTES

Since childhood, marinated and grilled lamb chops have been one of my favorite foods. It is easy to find a red wine that works with this wine-friendly dish. Pinot Noir and Cabernet Franc are obvious choices.

81

To marinate the lamb chops: Rub each chop with approximately 1 clove of garlic and 5 coarsely chopped mint leaves, leaving half of the mixture sticking to the top of the chop and half to the bottom. Place the lamb chops in a nonreactive baking dish and let marinate for at least 1 hour in the refrigerator.

To prepare the couscous: In a saucepan, bring the water to a boil. Add the couscous, return to a boil, then lower to a simmer. Cover and cook for 5 minutes over low heat. Remove from the heat and let stand for 10 to 15 minutes. Add the olive oil, jalapeño, cayenne, and salt, and fluff with a fork to mix and separate the grains. Set aside in a warm place.

To prepare the ratatouille: Prepare a medium fire in your barbecue.

In a bowl, whisk together the balsamic vinegar and olive oil. Toss the zucchini, squash, eggplant, and bell peppers in the mixture. Season with salt and pepper.

When the coals are ready, wipe the cleaned grill with olive oil and set in place. Lay the vegetables on the grill and cook on both sides until light golden brown. Cool.

Cut the vegetables into 1/2-inch dice and toss together with the garlic, tomatoes, and capers. Season to taste with salt and pepper. Set aside and serve at room temperature or reheat in a sauté pan before serving.

To grill the lamb chops: Remove the chops from the marinade and season with salt and pepper. On the same grill as used for the vegetables, grill the chops for 6 to 7 minutes per side for medium doneness.

To serve, divide the room-temperature couscous among 4 plates, placing it in the middle. Surround it with the ratatouille. Top with 2 lamb chops per plate. Sprinkle with the mint and basil leaves.

ADDING FLAVOR INTENSITY

Preserving fruits and vegetables by drying them is part of our national tradition. Many a frontier settler survived the winter eating nothing but apple pies made from dried apples that had been stored for the winter. But drying fruits and vegetables is also a great way to add intensity to the flavors in your recipes.

Slow oven drying reduces the amount of liquid, giving the ingredients a higher concentration of flavor. It also can make use of flavors that might otherwise go to waste. When you peel fruits such as apples, pears, or peaches, lay the peels on parchment paper on a baking sheet and place them in a barely warm oven (150°) overnight. The skins dry out and become crispy. I then like to pulverize them in a spice grinder (similar to a coffee grinder but used only for spices) until they're reduced to a powder. Dried mushrooms can also be ground. You can dust a plate with this powder for decoration; add it to a dish for extra flavor; use it as a coating, alone or in combination with other coating ingredients; or combine it with oil or simple syrup to make an accompanying sauce. See New Potato, Leek, and Fennel Soup with Apple Oil (page 16) and Pan-Roasted Sea Bass with Porcini Crust and Mushroom-Leek Ragout (page 187) for examples of using these techniques.

Slices of fruits such as toma-

toes, apples, and pineapple can be dried in the same manner—slowly dehydrating them in the oven. Dried apples and pineapples can be used as a garnish for sweet or savory dishes. I love dried tomatoes for sauces and especially relishes because of the intense flavor and dry texture. As an ingredient in pizza toppings, they add flavor without a lot of liquid, which can make a pizza crust soggy. Try the Pizza with Oven-Dried Tomatoes, Goat Cheese, and Duck Sausage (page 168) or Halibut Poached in Fennel Broth with Dried Tomato Relish (page 42). And don't forget chiles. They can be oven-dried, pulverized, and combined with other powders to add flavor and heat to coatings and sauces. Dried tomato skins can be pulverized and used as a garnish on non-tomato-based pizzas. Experiment in your own kitchen with produce as it comes into season.

Long, slow cooking of sauces, stocks, and braises is another way to concentrate flavors, giving depth to the final dish. Reducing stocks and sauces does much the same thing that drying does by eliminating water and extracting the essence of the ingredients. When preparing stocks, you can also oven-roast some of the ingredients, such as vegetables and bones, before adding them to the liquid. This, too, deepens and intensifies the flavors. Even wines can be reduced to intensify flavor in sauces.

When you slowly reduce stocks and sauces, the flavors become more rounded and well-integrated. If you reduce them quickly, the resulting flavors will be sharper and out of balance, possibly even bitter. I always say you get fast flavor from fast reductions and slow flavors from slow reductions. —KJ

Fried Chicken with Buttermilk and Cornmeal Crust and Twice–Cooked Green and Yellow Wax Beans with Balsamic Vinegar

SERVES 4

🐎 WINE NOTES

To add a clean, refreshing taste to most fried foods, I prefer a wine with good acidity or a sparkling wine. Try a cooler-region Chardonnay with little or no oak flavor or a non-herbal-style Sauvignon Blanc with acidity and fruit.

My kids have to have this chicken at least once a week. If you can, begin marinating the chicken in the morning for your evening meal. The salt penetrates the chicken and the buttermilk breaks down the fibers, making the bird more flavorful and tender.

Twice-cooking the beans is a technique borrowed from the Chinese kitchen. It gives the beans a sweeter edge that is balanced by the acidity in the balsamic vinegar. This dish is great served with roasted potatoes.

1 chicken, cut up

Kosher salt and freshly ground pepper

$^3/_4$ cup buttermilk

1 cup flour

$^1/_2$ cup cornmeal

2 tablespoons ground chile powder

1 tablespoon kosher salt

TWICE-COOKED BEANS

1 cup fresh Blue Lake green beans

1 cup fresh yellow wax beans

2 cups peanut oil

1 tablespoon balsamic vinegar

Kosher salt and freshly ground pepper

Season the chicken with salt and pepper. Let rest in the refrigerator for 1 hour. Add the buttermilk to the chicken and marinate in the refrigerator for at least another hour (all day if you can).

To prepare the beans: Bring a pot of salted water to a boil. Remove the stem ends of the beans, add to the boiling water, and cook for 2 minutes. Drain and blot dry.

In a 12-inch nonstick frying pan over medium-high heat, heat the oil to about 350°. Add the beans and cook until light golden brown. Remove from the oil, drain on a paper towel, and toss with the balsamic vinegar. Season to taste with salt and pepper. Keep warm in a heated oven. The oil will also be used to fry the chicken.

To prepare the chicken: In a paper bag, combine the flour, cornmeal, chile, and salt. Remove the chicken from the buttermilk, leaving a bit on to keep the skin moist. Piece by piece, place the chicken in the paper bag, hold the top closed, and shake the bag for a few seconds. Remove each piece as it is coated, and set aside.

Place all of the chicken in the same hot oil you used for the beans, making sure the temperature is about 350°. If the oil isn't hot enough, the coating will fall off. The oil should come halfway up the chicken. You may have to cook the chicken in batches or use 2 frying pans. Lower the heat to medium-low and cover the pan. Cook until golden brown on the first side, about 12 minutes. Turn the chicken over and continue cooking, covered, for about 12 more minutes. Covering the chicken keeps it moist and prevents the oil from spattering.

When the chicken is golden on both sides, drain it on paper towels and reserve in a warm oven. When done, it will register an internal temperature of 155° on an instant-read thermometer. If necessary, repeat the process with the remaining chicken. Serve immediately with the beans.

Grilled T-Bone Steaks with Corn, Tomato, and Chile Relish and Fresh Black-Eyed Peas with Pancetta and Leek

SERVES 4

Try to get the steaks thickly cut (about 2 inches), even if diners have to share them. They cook more evenly and remain juicier. I let the steaks rest for a few minutes before cutting them, which allows the juices that were forced to the center of the meat by the cooking heat to flow back. If you can't find fresh black-eyed peas, dried peas can be substituted. I don't soak them overnight; add a little extra liquid when cooking them. I like to wilt spinach or chard in the peas for added flavor and texture.

2 T-bone steaks, 2 inches thick
2 tablespoons sliced garlic
2 tablespoons extra-virgin olive oil
Kosher salt and freshly ground pepper

CORN, TOMATO, AND CHILE RELISH

1 cup fresh corn kernels
1 cup seeded, cored, vine-ripened tomatoes ($1/4$-inch dice)
1 jalapeño pepper, seeded and finely diced
1 teaspoon minced garlic
2 teaspoons lime juice
1 tablespoon extra-virgin olive oil
Kosher salt and freshly ground pepper

BLACK-EYED PEAS WITH PANCETTA AND LEEK

2 tablespoons minced pancetta
$1/2$ cup minced leek, white part only
1 teaspoon minced garlic
2 cups fresh, shucked black-eyed peas or dried black-eyed peas
4 cups chicken stock (6 cups if using dried peas) (page 206)
1 bay leaf

To marinate the steaks: Rub the meat with the sliced garlic. Drizzle the olive oil over the steaks and rub it in. Season with salt and pepper. Set aside in the refrigerator until ready to cook.

To prepare the relish: Combine the corn, tomatoes, jalapeño, garlic, lime juice, and olive oil. Season with salt and pepper. Serve at room temperature.

To prepare the black-eyed peas: Heat a saucepan over medium heat, add the pancetta, and cook until crispy, stirring often. Remove the pancetta and set aside on paper towels, leaving the fat in the pan. If the pancetta doesn't render enough fat, add olive oil to total 1 tablespoon of fat. Add the leek and cook until soft, about 5 minutes. Add the garlic and cook for a minute, stirring often. Add the peas, stock, and bay leaf. Bring to a simmer and cook until the peas are tender, about 30 minutes for fresh peas, 1 hour for dried peas. Remove the bay leaf and add the reserved pancetta. Taste for seasoning.

To grill the steaks: Prepare a medium-sized fire in your grill. Cook the steaks to the desired doneness, approximately 10 minutes per side for medium-rare. Let the steaks rest for 5 minutes and then trim off the bone.

To serve, divide the black-eyed peas equally among 4 plates. Slice the steaks at an angle and fan them out on top of the peas. Garnish with the relish.

Pan-Seared Pacific Salmon with Basil–Goat Cheese Sauce and Vegetable Tian

SERVES 4

❧ WINE NOTES

Central Coast or Carneros Pinot Noirs pair well with salmon—grilled, roasted, or poached. In this recipe, though, I would steer away from the red wine and go to a rich, full-bodied Chardonnay because of the wonderful basil–goat cheese sauce. This is an example of the sauce and side dishes having more of an influence on the wine selection than the main event.

I love to use the tail portion of the salmon for this dish. Because the tail is the part of the fish that gets the most exercise, it has a meatier flavor and firmer texture. It also cooks faster because it's thinner. As an added bonus, it's cheaper than fillets or steaks in many fish markets, and it also has no bones.

VEGETABLE TIAN

1 zucchini, sliced as thinly as possible

Kosher salt and freshly ground pepper

1 tablespoon minced garlic

1/4 cup shredded Parmesan cheese

1 red bell pepper, roasted, peeled, and cut
  into julienne (page 210)

2 Anaheim chiles, roasted, peeled, seeded,
  and cut into julienne (page 210)

1 summer squash, sliced as thinly as possible

2 tomatoes, thinly sliced

1 cup vegetable stock, reduced to 1/4 cup

BASIL–GOAT CHEESE SAUCE

1/4 cup fresh basil leaves, loosely packed (reserve stems)

1/2 cup heavy whipping cream

1/4 cup mild fresh goat cheese (such as Laura Chanel)

4 (6-ounce) salmon fillets, preferably Pacific salmon

2 tablespoons olive oil

To prepare the tian: Preheat the oven to 350°. Arrange the zucchini on the bottom of a 1 1/2-quart baking dish. Season with salt and pepper and sprinkle lightly with garlic and Parmesan. Repeat the layering with the pepper and chiles, the summer squash, and finally the tomato, lightly sprinkling with garlic and Parmesan between each layer. Pour the reduced vegetable stock over the top. Sprinkle the top with Parmesan cheese. Bake until golden brown on top, about 30 minutes. Remove from the oven and let rest for 10 minutes.

While the tian is baking, prepare the Basil–Goat Cheese Sauce: In a non-reactive saucepan, combine the basil stems and cream and bring to a simmer. Cook at a low simmer for about 20 minutes. Remove from the heat and let steep for another 5 minutes. Strain the stems out and transfer the cream to a blender or food processor. Add the basil leaves and goat cheese and purée until smooth. Keep warm on the top of the stove.

To prepare the salmon: Leave the oven at 350°. Season the salmon with salt and pepper. In an ovenproof frying pan over high heat, heat the olive oil. When almost smoking, add the salmon, skin side down. Lower the heat slightly and cook until golden brown, about 4 minutes. Turn to the other side and place in the oven. Cook until done, about 5 minutes. Remove from the oven and drain on paper towels.

To serve, cut the tian and divide among 4 plates. If the tian has a little extra liquid, serve it with a slotted spoon, letting the extra juice drain from each serving. Place a piece of salmon on each plate and spoon the Basil–Goat Cheese Sauce over the fish. Serve immediately.

Rhode Island Clams
Steamed in Sauvignon Blanc with Gravenstein Apples, Shallots, and Chervil

This recipe was inspired by a summer vacation trip to Mendocino County on the Northern California coast. My buddies at Monterey Fish gave me a big bag of clams to take with me. Along the way in Sonoma, we bought some Gravenstein apples as well as a few bottles of Sauvignon Blanc. That day, my family enjoyed the clams cooked in a pan over a covered mesquite grill. The barbecue added a wonderful smokiness to the clams. Be sure to have a large loaf of bread on hand to sop up the broth.

SERVES 4

❧ WINE NOTES

This is an easy match: After preparing the clams and enjoying a glass myself during the process, I would serve the remainder of the bottle of Sauvignon Blanc. This very versatile white wine has one of the broadest flavor spectrums, exhibiting hints of herbs, citrus, melon, apple, green olive, green bean, nuts, oak, and honey. Many of these are the same flavors found in this broth.

4 pounds clams

1 Gravenstein apple (or substitute Granny Smith or pippin), peeled, cored, and cut into 1/4-inch dice

2 tablespoons diced shallot

1/4 cup diced fennel bulb (reserve some tops for garnish)

1 cup Sauvignon Blanc

Kosher salt

2 tablespoons chopped fresh chervil

Wash the outsides of the clams in cold water, scrubbing with a scrub pad. In a large pot over high heat, combine half of the apple with the shallot, fennel, and wine and bring to a boil. Add the clams, cover, and cook, shaking every minute or so, until the clams fully open. This may take 10 to 15 minutes. Do not eat clams that do not fully open. Salt the liquid to taste. Add the remaining apple and chervil and toss. Divide the clams and liquid among 4 bowls. Garnish with fennel tops and serve immediately.

Pan-Fried Sand Dabs with Crispy Potatoes and Summer Vegetable Ragout

SERVES 4

❧ WINE NOTES

While the fish is delicate, the vegetables and potatoes need a wine that will hold its own. A lighter-style Sauvignon Blanc (stainless steel fermented, no oak) or an austere, crisp Chardonnay (again, stainless steel fermented) are both fine choices.

This is a great way to cook sand dabs. In our markets, the sand dabs come with the head and tail removed but not boned. They stay moist and keep their shape, making them very easy to fillet after cooking. If you can't find sand dabs in your market, try substituting a firm sole.

SUMMER VEGETABLE RAGOUT

1 tablespoon olive oil

1 yellow summer squash, cut into wedges

1 sunburst squash, cut into wedges

1 tablespoon minced garlic

2 ears corn, kernels cut off of the cob

2 tomatoes, peeled, seeded, and diced

1/4 cup basil leaves, cut into thin strips

Kosher salt and freshly ground pepper

CRISPY POTATOES

4 russet potatoes, peeled and cut into fine julienne

2 cups peanut oil

1 cup all-purpose flour

1/2 teaspoon ground cayenne pepper

4 sand dabs

2 tablespoons olive oil

To prepare the ragout: In a sauté pan over medium-high heat, heat the olive oil. When hot, add the squashes and cook, shaking occasionally, until golden brown. Remove from the heat and add the garlic and corn. Stir together for a few minutes off the heat, and then add the tomatoes. Toss the basil with the vegetables. Season with salt and pepper. Set aside.

To prepare the potatoes: Rinse the potatoes in water several times, until the water runs clear. In a high-sided sauté pan over medium-high heat, heat the peanut oil to about 350°. Add the potatoes, frying only as many as will fill one layer. When golden brown, transfer to a paper towel–lined plate and season with salt. Continue cooking in batches. Serve at room temperature.

Combine the flour and cayenne. Season the sand dabs with salt and pepper and dredge in the flour, coating all sides. In a nonstick frying pan over medium-high heat, heat 2 tablespoons olive oil. Add the fish and cook both sides until golden brown, 4 to 5 minutes per side.

Serve immediately with the ragout and potatoes on the side.

ADJUSTING RECIPES TO COMPLEMENT WINE

Flavor is extremely subjective, making wine and food pairing very personal. There is not one right answer to a particular pairing of food with wine; it depends on individual taste preferences. Throughout the wine notes, I have tried to make recommendations with a consideration for personal taste. However, just as there are several wines that will pair with a particular dish, so too are there ways to adjust recipes to complement preferred wines.

When I prepare a meal or develop a recipe, my general approach begins with the wine—the opposite of what most chefs do. I do this because I want my choice of wine to taste as it was meant to, not be pushed out of balance by the food with which it is served. Kimball uses this same approach when preparing our Winemaker's Dinners, which showcase a particular selection of a vintner's wines. The key to matching wine with food is balance; a good balance allows the wine to taste genuine.

A number of principles will help you adjust recipes to make them more compatible with a wine, allowing the wine to taste true to itself.

Ingredients with an acidic base, such as vinegar, will cause a wine to taste thin or bitter. To alter the recipe, particularly one for a dressing to be used with a salad or appetizer, try using citrus (lemons or limes) in the dressing instead of vinegar. This will reduce the sour component, making the wine appear less thin. In fact, when cit-rus juice is used in place of the vinegar in a vinaigrette, the acid in the wine will create a balance with the oil. Another possible adjustment for a dressing is to add a touch of honey to counteract the acid. Or try substituting a bit of the wine to be served in place of the vinegar. This too will reduce the acid component and allow the wine to be true to itself.

Other perplexing wine and food pairings are those with artichokes and asparagus, because these vegetables contain cynarin, a type of organic acid. Anything eaten after a food that contains cynarin will taste sweet. A dry wine with a high acid content will help to balance this effect. The dressing or sauce served with the artichoke or asparagus can also affect the wine flavor, often making the pairing work better. Adjusting the sauce by adding acid such as citrus juice enhances the pairing.

Sweetness in a recipe will cause a dry wine to taste bitter, sour, or thin. The same principle used to pair wine with desserts applies here: Make sure the wine is as sweet as or sweeter than the dish. Also, the fruit flavors in a wine will be overpowered by sweet ingredients in a dish. If serving a dry wine with a recipe containing fresh or dried fruit, be careful that the fruit used has a lower sugar content than the wine. When

making a sauce with fruit, it is also possible to remove the fruit after cooking, leaving the flavor but taking away the sweetness. Another possibility is to add a squeeze of lemon juice to the fruit—the sweet-sour principle—which helps counterbalance the sugar. The Grilled Jumbo Prawns Marinated in Ginger, White Wine, and Lemon with Mango-Mint Salsa (page 44) is an example of a balanced pairing of a dry wine having some fruit flavors with the lemon and lime juice in the salsa and marinade.

Generally, the salty and sour flavors in food cause a wine to taste perceptibly less dry and bring out the fruit characteristics, making it seem less bitter and tannic. Conversely, the sweet and savory tastes in food enhance the wine's flavors, making them stronger. The wine will appear less sweet and less fruity. These foods will also make the wine perceptibly more bitter and tannic in nature as well as more acidic. Too much salt in any dish will take away the fruitiness in wines, especially reds, making them seem more astringent.

By keeping these basic principles in mind, we have developed recipes at our restaurant that are wine friendly, meaning that they are in proper balance. When paired with wine, the wine is a true reflection of itself and is not altered by the dish. —CW

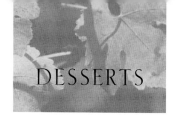

DESSERTS

Nectarine and Blueberry Crisp
with White Chocolate Sauce

SERVES 6

When I see nectarines, I think of late-harvest Rieslings because they have hints of the same flavors. However, the addition of blueberries and white chocolate requires a more intense wine. White port fills the bill. This port, which is made from white grapes, is drier than a red-grape port and should be enjoyed while still young. Serve slightly chilled.

For those who are not great bakers but love desserts made with the fresh fruits of summer, this dessert is perfect. Try peaches, plums, berries, or pears for variety. Add just enough sugar to balance the sweetness of the fruit. The cooked fruit will make a wonderful chunky "sauce" at the bottom of the baking dish. Nectarines are not the easiest fruit to slice because their stones don't seem to loosen as they ripen. I usually slice them toward the center against the stone, as though separating the sections of an orange with a knife. A great twist on the white chocolate sauce is to thin it with a little milk and churn it in an ice cream maker for white chocolate ice cream.

WHITE CHOCOLATE SAUCE

2 ounces white chocolate

1/2 recipe crème anglaise (page 199)

6 nectarines, sliced (about 6 cups)

1 cup blueberries

1/2 cup granulated sugar

1 tablespoon grated fresh ginger

1 tablespoon all-purpose flour

1 teaspoon vanilla extract

1 cup old-fashioned oats

1/2 cup all-purpose flour

1/2 cup brown sugar

1/4 cup sliced almonds

1/2 cup unsalted butter, cut into pieces

1/2 teaspoon ground cinnamon

To prepare the White Chocolate Sauce: In a metal bowl over a hot water bath, melt the white chocolate. Blend the crème anglaise and melted chocolate together while the crème anglaise is still hot. Strain and cool.

To prepare the crisp: Preheat the oven to 375°. In a bowl, combine the nectarines, blueberries, sugar, ginger, flour, and vanilla. Mix thoroughly and place in a 1 1/2-quart baking dish.

In another bowl, blend together the oats, flour, brown sugar, and almonds. Add the butter and cinnamon and work in with your fingers until the butter is blended. Sprinkle on top of the fruit. Bake in the preheated oven for about 30 minutes. Let cool or serve warm. Spoon the White Chocolate Sauce over each serving.

Chocolate-Hazelnut Soufflé Cake
with Strawberry and Raspberry Compote

This light chocolate cake is very versatile. Serve it hot, as individual soufflés, or cooked, cooled, and sliced as usual. You can also make it a day ahead for a special occasion.

Sugar for dusting pan

8 ounces bittersweet chocolate

1 cup heavy whipping cream

1 tablespoon espresso or very strong coffee

1/2 cup finely ground hazelnuts

8 large eggs, separated, plus 4 egg whites

6 tablespoons granulated sugar

STRAWBERRY AND RASPBERRY COMPOTE

2 cups strawberries, hulled and cut into fourths

1 cup raspberries

2 tablespoons granulated sugar (optional)

To prepare the soufflé cake: Preheat the oven to 375°. Butter a 9-inch springform pan with 3-inch sides and dust with sugar.

Melt the chocolate over simmering water in a double boiler. Blend the cream into the melted chocolate. Remove from the heat and stir in the espresso, hazelnuts, and egg yolks.

Beat the 12 egg whites to soft peaks while slowly adding the sugar. Whisk one-third of the egg whites into the chocolate mixture. Fold in the remaining egg whites carefully.

Pour the batter into the springform pan and bake until set, 25 to 30 minutes. Place on a rack to cool.

To prepare the compote: In a food processor, purée half of the strawberries and raspberries together. Strain out the seeds through a coarse sieve and discard. Add the remaining berries to the purée. Add sugar if needed—this will depend on the ripeness of the berries.

To serve, after the cake has cooled, slip a knife around the edge of the cake and remove the springform. Slice, spoon some of the berry compote over each slice, and serve.

SERVES 8 TO 12

WINE NOTES

Here is an opportunity for a classic pairing—port with chocolate and nuts. The strawberry and raspberry flavors mirror the fruit of the port. Because of the aging process, ports often have a nutty character as well as the same weight, texture, and percentage of sugar as chocolate.

Strawberries, Raspberries, and Olallieberries Marinated in Red Wine and Lemon Zest with Lemon Butter Wafers

CANDIED LEMON PEEL:
MAKES 10 GENEROUS SERVINGS

LEMON BUTTER WAFERS:
MAKES 3 DOZEN COOKIES

MARINATED BERRIES:
MAKES 4 SERVINGS

🐾 WINE NOTES

Serve with the same Zinfandel or Cabernet Sauvignon that you used in preparing the berries. Be careful not to add too much sugar to the berries, as you don't want the dessert to be sweeter than the wine, which will make the wine taste flat.

This happens to be one of my favorite berry desserts because all of the ingredients are grown here in the Livermore Valley. Strawberries are abundant in my garden during the summer, as long as my son has not been eating them straight off the bush. Mint and basil grow like weeds, and I always enjoy their flavor and freshness. Down the country road from us is Joan and Wanda's, a fruit and vegetable stand where you can pick your own olallieberries—another fun family outing.

The Lemon Butter Wafers were inspired by my grandmother Bess and my great-aunt Edith, who loved to make candied citrus peel, often with my help. Lemon was always my favorite, and it certainly adds a nice texture to these wafers. The candied citrus peel needs to steep overnight, so start it the day before. If you prefer, you can cut the candied citrus peel recipe in half, but my general cooking philosophy is "If you're in for a dime, you're in for a dollar." It will keep well in an airtight jar for up to three months, and there are many uses for it. The cookies will keep for two weeks in an airtight container. —CW

CANDIED LEMON PEEL

12 large lemons, or 4 lemons, 4 oranges, and 2 grapefruit

2/3 cup granulated sugar

1/3 cup water

Sugar for coating peels

LEMON BUTTER WAFERS

1/4 cup unsalted butter, at room temperature

1 1/2 cups granulated sugar

1 large egg

4 to 5 teaspoons finely chopped lemon zest

2/3 cup all-purpose flour

1/4 teaspoon baking soda

Pinch of kosher salt

2 tablespoons finely chopped Candied Lemon Peel

BERRIES MARINATED IN RED WINE AND LEMON ZEST

1 pint strawberries, sliced

1 pint raspberries

1 pint olallieberries (or blackberries)

2 to 4 tablespoons granulated sugar, or to taste

1 cup dry red wine, such as Zinfandel or Cabernet Sauvignon

1 teaspoon lemon juice

$1/4$ teaspoon ground cinnamon

2 teaspoons finely chopped lemon zest

4 fresh basil leaves, for garnish

4 fresh mint leaves, for garnish

To prepare the Candied Lemon Peel: Using a vegetable peeler, remove the lemon peels and cut into $1/8$-inch julienne. Each strip should be approximately $1^1/2$ inches long. In a saucepan, bring 4 cups of water to a boil. Add the julienned peels, lower the heat, and simmer for 6 to 8 minutes. Remove from the heat, drain, and plunge into cold water. Drain again.

In another saucepan, combine the sugar and water and bring to a simmer. Add the citrus peel and simmer 15 to 20 minutes. Remove from the heat, and let steep overnight. Remove the peel from the syrup, and let dry on waxed paper (this will take a couple of hours); then toss in sugar to coat. Store in an airtight container.

To prepare the berries: In a bowl, toss the berries with sugar. The amount will vary depending on the ripeness of the fruit and your taste. Set aside for 2 hours at room temperature, or for up to 6 hours in the refrigerator, which allows the berries to create a syrup.

An hour before serving, divide the berries and syrup into 4 goblets or dessert bowls. In a small bowl, combine the wine, lemon juice, cinnamon, and finely chopped lemon zest. Divide evenly among the goblets and toss lightly, then set aside.

To prepare the Lemon Butter Wafers: In the bowl of an electric mixer fitted with a paddle attachment, cream the butter and 1 cup of the sugar until light and fluffy, about 5 minutes, frequently scraping down the sides of the bowl. Add the egg and mix at high speed until combined. Add the finely chopped lemon zest and continue to mix.

Sift the flour, baking soda, and salt together and add to the butter-egg mixture. Mix at medium-low speed until combined, about 30 seconds. Remove from the bowl and wrap in plastic wrap. Chill until firm, about 30 minutes (or overnight if you want to prepare the cookies in advance).

Preheat the oven to 350°. Lightly grease 2 baking sheets.

Pour the remaining $1/2$ cup sugar into a bowl. Remove the dough from the refrigerator and slice into thirds. Keep one-third of the dough out and the other two pieces chilled in the refrigerator. Slice the dough into approximately twelve 1-inch pieces, and shape into balls. Drop each ball into the bowl of sugar, and coat completely. The sugar will prevent the dough from sticking to your hands.

Place the sugared balls on the baking sheets, spaced $2^1/2$ inches apart.

Gently flatten the balls to a $1/4$-inch thickness. Place 2 or 3 pieces of the chopped Candied Lemon Peel on each cookie. Bake the cookies until golden, 7 to 10 minutes. Remove from the baking sheet immediately. Transfer to a wire rack or waxed paper to cool.

Repeat the process with the remaining dough.

Before serving, garnish each goblet of berries with a basil leaf and a mint leaf, tucking into the berries. Accompany with Lemon Butter Wafers.

KIMBALL'S PICNICS

My perspective on what you can and cannot do for a picnic is undoubtedly quite different from the normal, everyday experience. I once prepared a picnic in the middle of Yosemite Valley with smoked trout toasts, grilled duck and asparagus, potato gratin, and Pinot Noir in real wineglasses. Of course, this was a very special occasion, but it demonstrates what you can do with planning. That's the key—knowing what can be done ahead and what can be done on-site. (Coincidentally, these are the same rules for successful catering.) For my Yosemite outing, the components for the toasts—the smoked trout, crème fraîche, and baguette toasts—were done ahead and then assembled there. I cooked the potato gratin in my hotel room in a toaster oven I brought with me, then wrapped the gratin in towels and placed it in a cooler to keep hot. The duck and asparagus were cooked on a grill at the picnic site. Now this was a real picnic, with a view of Half Dome to boot!

These days, there is a wonderful range of equipment—from soft coolers and ice packs to plastic plates, dinnerware, and glasses—that makes it much easier to do delicious picnic food. The presentation can be rustic or refined or very close to what you would do at home.

If your picnic site includes a grill or you can bring a portable barbecue, try these suggestions. I always make a fire with a hot spot on one side and a cooler area on the other. The grill can be used much as you would use the stove top in your home kitchen. You can heat sauces and warm vegetables in pans on the cooler side. Meats

can be marinated beforehand, placed in heavy-duty plastic storage bags, and cooked on the grill when you get there. I love potatoes, onions, and garlic with a little olive oil and herbs wrapped in two layers of aluminum foil and cooked directly in the hot coals. I also love grilled vegetables. The heat caramelizes the sugars, giving them a distinctive sweetness. If you plan to have a salad, assemble it beforehand and toss it with the dressing on-site.

If you don't have access to a grill, plan the menu with cold or room-temperature dishes in mind. Poached salmon made the night before and served with a simple salad is incredible. Many of the items normally served as starters work great for picnics, such as smoked salmon rillettes (page 59) and grilled figs with mascarpone (page 60). Bring all of the prepared ingredients with you and do the final assembly at the picnic site.

By keeping the menu simple and the food in components ready for the final assembly, you can have wonderful meals in places you never dreamed of.—KJ

CAROLYN'S PICNICS

These days, almost any food can make up a picnic. The main factors are the age of the picnickers, the location, and how quickly you want to go. On one end of the spectrum is a bottle of wine, a loaf of bread, and a chunk of cheese. Then there is Kimball's birthday dinner in Yosemite, complete with glassware. My family does impromptu picnics where we fill up the saddlebags, throw them on the horses, and set out through the foothills looking for the perfect spot to eat.

Our annual kite-flying picnic has become a favorite family outing. In the late spring, the winds pick up, blowing from the San Francisco Bay through our valley toward the warmer Central Valley. This weather pattern makes the Livermore Valley not only a great grape-growing region but also a terrific spot for flying kites. Usually three or four families come, kites in hand, some store-bought, some homemade. We supply extra kites, individual picnic baskets packed with surprises for each family, and large bowls of salads and beverages for all to share. Each basket has a variety of sandwiches, homemade potato and vegetable chips, fresh seasonal fruit, a selection of cheeses, and some kind of dessert and cookies. There's juice for the kids and, of course, a choice of wines for the adults.

We try to keep the sandwiches pretty straightforward for the little people, but the big people enjoy pushing the limits on the type of bread—walnut, sundried tomato, rosemary, onion-olive, focaccia, or sourdough—and the filling. Instead of lettuce, we've used roasted peppers or balsamic onions, or perhaps arugula, radicchio, onion sprouts, curly watercress—even pea sprouts. Try mint pesto on a lamb sandwich. Aioli made with sundried tomatoes or an olive tapenade also makes a good spread. The kids often enjoy "aram" sandwiches, rolled up with turkey, roast beef, ham, or cheese. Sliced in rounds, these sandwiches are often traded for favorites.

I bring a variety of salads. One is made by quartering new potatoes, tossing them with olive oil, whole garlic cloves, and a cup of freshly chopped herbs, such as rosemary, tarragon, basil, lemon thyme, and chives, and then roasting all in the oven. Just before it's served, squeeze lemon juice over the potatoes.

Another potato salad I do involves tossing quartered onions with balsamic vinegar, olive oil, and salt and roasting them until they're still fairly crunchy. They come out very sweet. I mix them with boiled potatoes, olives, and capers, and dress the salad with a vinaigrette dressing.

A pasta salad, not prepared with mayonnaise, is easy and good for a warm outing. Take rotini, the little corkscrew pasta, and toss with fresh basil pesto, green peas, and finely chopped red bell pepper. Sprinkle in toasted pine nuts. It has a delightful crunch and texture.

At our picnic, each family opens its own basket and then the horse-trading begins—much as we used to do as kids during lunch at school! —CW

Cinnamon Apple Napoleons
with Berry Purées and Ricotta Cream

SERVES 6

🏮 WINE NOTES

To offer a contrast to the rich fruitiness of this dessert, I would pair it with a demi-sec sparkling wine—remember, this is a sweeter Champagne. The opposite approach, of matching the dessert's sweetness and texture, could also work well; if you want to do this, try a late-harvest Muscat.

Shortly after the U.S. embargo of Vietnam was lifted, I prepared this dish at the Hotel Sofitel Metropole, a French-run hotel in Hanoi. As Wente was the first California wine to be sold in Vietnam after the war, I wanted to showcase our wine by preparing a dish that used traditional French techniques with a California twist. In this dessert, the ricotta offsets the pastry cream, making the whole dish a little less sweet than a normal napoleon. Look in your grocer's freezer case for puff pastry if you don't want to make it yourself.

RICOTTA CREAM

¹/2 recipe pastry cream (page 199), flavored with 1 vanilla bean

1¹/2 cups fresh ricotta, about 8 ounces (to make your own, see page 200)

BERRY PURÉES

1¹/2 cups raspberries (a 6-ounce container)

1¹/2 cups blackberries (a 6-ounce container)

5 tablespoons simple syrup (page 200, optional)

3 Gravenstein, Granny Smith, or pippin apples, peeled, cored, and thinly sliced horizontally, forming circles

¹/4 cup granulated sugar

1 teaspoon ground cinnamon

2 tablespoons butter

1 pound puff pastry, homemade (page 202) or store-bought

Confectioners' sugar, for dusting

To prepare the Ricotta Cream: Prepare the pastry cream, flavoring it with the vanilla bean. Refrigerate until cool. Just before assembling the dessert, mix the pastry cream and the fresh ricotta together.

To prepare the Berry Purées: Purée the raspberries and blackberries separately in a food processor. Keeping them separate, strain each of the purées through a coarse sieve, discarding the seeds. Depending on the ripeness of the berries, add simple syrup until the desired sweetness is reached. I use about 3 tablespoons for the raspberries and 2 tablespoons for the blackberries. This yields about ¹/2 cup of each of the purées. Set aside.

To prepare the napoleons: Preheat the oven to 350°. In a bowl, toss the apples with the sugar and cinnamon. Spread out on a baking sheet and dot with the butter. Bake for about 10 minutes; the apples should still be slightly crisp. Set aside to cool.

Set the oven at 400°. Roll out the puff pastry until it is the size of a baking sheet, approximately 12 by 10 inches, and $1/2$ inch thick. Chill in the freezer for 15 minutes.

Cut the dough into thirds lengthwise, making three 12 by $3^1/_2$-inch strips. Arrange the strips on 2 baking sheets lined with parchment paper. Prick the dough thoroughly with a fork to prevent it from rising much. This makes the cooked pastry flaky and crisp. Place the dough in the freezer for 15 minutes.

Remove the dough from the freezer, and place another baking sheet on top of the dough to prevent it from rising. Place it in the oven and bake for about 15 minutes. Remove the baking sheet from the top and continue to cook until golden brown, approximately 15 minutes.

If the bottom of your oven runs on the hot side, place another baking sheet under the first to prevent the bottom of the dough from browning too much. This is especially troublesome in gas ovens. Check it halfway through, and use a fork to prick any bubbles that may have formed. Remove from the oven and cool.

To assemble the napoleons, place one strip of puff pastry on a cold baking sheet. Spread it with a $1/2$-inch layer of Ricotta Cream. Arrange half of the apple slices on top of the cream. Spread another $1/2$-inch layer of Ricotta Cream on top. Add another piece of puff pastry and repeat the layering of cream, apples, and cream. Top with the third piece of pastry. Smooth the sides with a spatula. Refrigerate for at least an hour, then cut into 6 pieces.

To serve, drizzle the berry purées in a crisscross pattern across each plate and place a napoleon in the center. Dust the tops with confectioners' sugar.

AUTUMN

Smoked Salmon and Buckwheat Galette
with Lemon Mascarpone Cream

MAKES 16 TO 20 APPETIZERS

The inspiration for this dish is the wonderful buckwheat crepes made throughout Brittany in northern France. When I make them at home for my kids, we fill the cooked crepes with ham, cheese, and a raw egg. We then fry them in a little butter and serve with a simple salad. This version makes an elegant passed hors d'oeuvre that can easily be made ahead of time. If serving as a first course, place several on a plate with some greens. Although the caviar is wonderful as a garnish, the galette can survive quite well without it!

BUCKWHEAT CREPES
1/4 cup buckwheat flour
2 tablespoons all-purpose flour
1/4 teaspoon kosher salt
1/4 cup plus 3 tablespoons milk
1 tablespoon unsalted butter, melted

1/2 cup mascarpone (reserve 1 tablespoon for garnish)
2 tablespoons finely chopped lemon zest
2 tablespoons minced chervil leaves
   (reserve 1/2 teaspoon for garnish)
2 tablespoons snipped chives
   (reserve 1/2 teaspoon for garnish)
1/2 pound thinly sliced smoked salmon
2 ounces caviar (optional)

To prepare the crepes: In a bowl, combine the buckwheat flour, all-purpose flour, and salt. Slowly add the milk, whisking out any lumps that occur. You may need to strain through a fine-mesh sieve. Whisk in the butter.

Heat a large nonstick or cast-iron crepe pan over high heat. If you do not have a crepe pan, use a large nonstick frying pan. Pour 3 tablespoons of the batter into the pan and tilt the pan around until the batter forms a thin layer, about 8 inches in diameter. A metal spatula can also be used to spread out the batter. (In Brittany they use an implement called a crepe paddle.) Cook until golden brown on the first side. Flip and cook for about another 10 seconds. Remove from the pan and cool. Repeat with the remaining batter. This recipe should make at least four 8-inch crepes

To prepare the galette: In a small bowl, combine the mascarpone with the finely chopped lemon zest. Using half of the lemon mascarpone, spread a thin layer on 3 of the 4 crepes, dividing it evenly. (Save the best crepe for the top!) Sprinkle the chervil and chives evenly over these 3 crepes. Divide the smoked salmon into 3 portions and cover each of the mascarpone-spread crepes completely. Using the remaining mascarpone, spread another thin layer on top of the smoked salmon. Stack the three crepes one on top of another. Place the fourth crepe on top. Refrigerate for at least 30 minutes.

To serve, cut the galette into 16 to 20 wedges and top each piece with a dab of the reserved mascarpone and a little caviar. Sprinkle with the reserved chopped chervil and chives.

Jean Wente's Chicken Liver Pâté with Toasted Walnuts

MAKES 3/4 TO 1 CUP

This recipe is one of my mother's solutions to finding sack upon sack of fresh walnuts from our walnut trees on our doorstep. We were always creating recipes to use walnuts and, of course, we were always thinking in terms of dishes to enjoy with wine. This is one of my favorite hors d'oeuvre recipes, developed with two wines in mind, our *méthode champenoise* Brut and our Johannisberg Riesling. —CW

1/2 pound chicken livers, membranes trimmed away

1 tablespoon sherry or port

1/2 cup unsalted butter, at room temperature

1/4 cup finely minced (not ground) toasted walnuts (page 210)

1 teaspoon kosher salt

1/8 teaspoon ground cloves

1/4 teaspoon ground nutmeg

1 teaspoon dry mustard

2 tablespoons chopped scallion

WINE NOTES

Chicken livers have a sweetness to them that pairs well with Johannisberg Riesling. The Riesling should have a slight residual sugar, making it light to medium in body. If it comes from the Central Coast appellation, the wine will be assured of good acidity—essential to counterbalance the rich, buttery pâté. A brut sparkling wine is also an excellent choice because of its acidity and effervescence providing a contrast to the rich pâté.

In a medium-sized saucepan, barely cover the chicken livers with water. Bring to a boil, reduce to a simmer, cover, and cook for 15 to 20 minutes, until cooked through. Remove from the heat and drain off the water. Place the livers in a blender or food processor, add the sherry, and purée. Add the butter and continue to blend. Add the walnuts, salt, cloves, nutmeg, mustard, and scallion and blend thoroughly. Check the seasonings, adding mustard or nutmeg to taste. Pack into a crock-type container, cover, and refrigerate.

To serve, take the pâté out of the refrigerator about an hour before serving and remove it from the crock. It will soften to a spreadable consistency. Spread the pâté on thinly sliced baguette rounds or water biscuits.

Smoked Muscovy Duck Breast Toasts
with Heirloom Tomato
and Hedgehog Mushroom Relish

MAKES 20 TOASTS

🐾 **WINE NOTES**

This recipe has three intense, rich flavor components—duck, tomato, and mushrooms. All together, they need a full-bodied wine with good intensity such as a Pinot Noir or a Zinfandel. I liken duck more to meat than poultry because of its rich and dense texture. Smoking the duck adds additional richness that necessitates a big wine—lots of fruit, ample tannin, and a fair amount of toasty oak character.

The best time to cook this dish is in early fall when there is a wonderful convergence of the last tomatoes of the summer (before the first frost) and the game and wild mushrooms that are so reminiscent of fall. Slowly roasting the tomatoes intensifies the sweet tomato flavors while lowering the acid, making them more wine friendly. Other types of duck can be substituted for the Muscovy.

**1 duck breast (6 to 8 ounces), bone and skin on
  (or purchase a smoked duck breast and skip the smoking step)**
Kosher salt and freshly ground pepper
1 baguette
1 tablespoon olive oil

HEIRLOOM TOMATO AND HEDGEHOG MUSHROOM RELISH
2 Brandywine or other heirloom tomatoes (about 12 ounces each)
2 cloves garlic, sliced very thin
1 tablespoon balsamic vinegar
1/4 pound hedgehog mushrooms or other wild mushrooms
1 tablespoon olive oil
1 teaspoon chopped fresh tarragon leaves
Whole tarragon leaves for garnish (optional)

To prepare the duck breast: Season the duck with salt and pepper and smoke, following the directions in the smoking sidebar on page 62. Cool, remove the skin and bones, and slice thinly. Set aside.

To prepare the toasts: Preheat the broiler. Slice the baguette thinly on an angle so that you end up with pieces about 2 inches long. Brush one side of each piece with olive oil. Toast the oiled sides under the broiler until golden brown.

To prepare the relish: Preheat the oven to 300°. Core the tomatoes and slice in half. Arrange the sliced garlic on top of the tomatoes and drizzle with the balsamic vinegar. Season lightly with salt and pepper. Place on a baking sheet and bake for 1 hour to dry out. Remove from the oven and cool. Scoop the flesh and seeds out of the tomatoes and discard the skin. Coarsely chop the tomato pulp and place it in a sieve, catching the juice in a bowl. In a small saucepan, reduce the juice over low heat until thick. Cool and stir back into the tomato pulp.

With a brush or clean towel, remove any dirt or twigs from the mushrooms. Trim the stems and cut the mushrooms into bite-sized pieces. Heat the olive oil in a sauté pan over high heat. Add the mushrooms, season with salt and pepper, and cook, shaking often, until light golden brown. Cool and add to the tomatoes, along with the chopped tarragon.

To serve, place a slice of duck breast on each toast and top with the relish. You can garnish each with a leaf of tarragon if you wish.

Baked Baby Yukon Gold Potatoes Filled with Butternut Squash and Goat Cheese

MAKES 20 APPETIZERS

🍇 **WINE NOTES**

Following the old rule of thumb of beginning with lighter wines and serving progressively more full-bodied wines through the meal makes sparkling wines or dry to medium-dry, light-bodied white wines the first choice for serving with starters or appetizers. The reason for beginning with these styles of wine is that they have a refreshing quality that stimulates the appetite. The carbonation in a sparkling wine also teases and pleases the palate. Try a brut sparkling wine or a Johannisberg Riesling as your apéritif with these tasty hors d'oeuvres.

I first served this dish at a reception for the American Institute of Wine and Food in Seattle at artist Dale Chihouli's glass studio. These are great vegetarian, one-bite hors d'oeuvres. You could also use the filling for ravioli, or as a side dish for a holiday meal. It's possible to substitute many different types of squashes. Among the best are acorn, blue hubbard, and Danish. You could also use a Sugar Pie pumpkin. If you use pumpkin, be sure to buy an eating type rather than a decorating type. The jack-o'-lantern pumpkins have very little flavor.

10 creamer-sized (1 1/2 inch in diameter) Yukon Gold potatoes, cut in half

2 tablespoons extra-virgin olive oil

Kosher salt and freshly ground pepper

1/2 small butternut squash (cut lengthwise)

1/2 red onion, skin removed

2 tablespoons peeled, sliced fresh ginger

4 ounces mild goat cheese, about 1/2 cup

2 tablespoons freshly grated Parmesan cheese

Lemon juice to taste

1 cup peanut oil, for frying

20 sage leaves, for garnish

To prepare the potatoes: Preheat the oven to 350°. Slice just a bit off the rounded end of each cut potato half so it will sit flat. With a melon baller, scoop some of the potato out of each cut side, forming a shell. Discard the inner, scooped-out portion of the potatoes or save for another use. Toss the potato shells with 1 tablespoon of the olive oil. Season with salt and pepper to taste. Put them on a baking sheet with the rounded ends up and place in the oven. Bake until cooked through, 20 to 25 minutes. They should be tender when pierced with a sharp knife.

To prepare the filling: While the potatoes are baking, season the cut side of the butternut squash with salt and pepper and rub with the remaining 1 tablespoon olive oil. Put the red onion in the cavity of the squash and the sliced ginger on the cut surface. Turn the squash over on a baking sheet so that the cut surface with the ginger slices rests on the sheet. Place in the oven and bake until tender, about 25 minutes. Cool.

When the squash has cooled, remove the red onion and ginger and chop finely. Scoop the pulp from the inside of the squash and place in a bowl. Mash gently. Add the chopped red onion–ginger mixture, goat cheese, and Parmesan. Season, adding salt, pepper, and lemon juice as needed.

Fill the insides of the cooked potato shells with the squash filling. Return to the oven for 5 to 10 minutes to warm through.

To prepare the garnish: Heat the peanut oil to 350° in a saucepan. Fry the sage, 5 or 6 leaves at a time, for 30 seconds, until crisp. Drain on a paper towel.

To serve, garnish the filled potatoes with the crisped sage leaves.

SERVES 4 TO 6

This straightforward soup with its broth-like consistency and chicken and noodles calls for a fairly simple wine, such as a Pinot Blanc or a dry Chenin Blanc. Both of these wines can be light to medium-bodied with varietal characteristics that complement the ingredients. The lesson to be learned here is that the wine needs to be slightly fuller in body than the soup broth. If you plan to thicken the broth, it will require a weightier wine. Adding more vegetables adds more texture, so again you will need a heartier wine. You could even move into a red wine such as a Merlot or Sangiovese.

Real Homemade Chicken Noodle Soup

Why buy store-bought soup when it is so easy to make yourself? Although it does take some cooking time, there is very little actual preparation time involved, and the results are fantastic. Rice, wild rice, and various pasta shapes can be substituted for the noodles. If you like hot food, spice it up with some chiles. You can also add other vegetables, such as potatoes, parsnips, squash, chiles, tomatoes, and so on.

1 whole chicken (3 to 3 1/2 pounds)
6 carrots, diced
1 onion, diced
2 stalks celery, strings removed and diced
4 bay leaves
4 stems parsley, leaves removed and reserved
5 cloves garlic, peeled
4 cups chicken stock (page 206)
1/4 pound dry egg noodles
Kosher salt and freshly ground pepper

In a large pot, combine the chicken, carrots, onion, celery, bay leaves, parsley stems, and garlic. Add the chicken stock and enough water to cover, and bring to a simmer. Cook slowly at a low simmer until the chicken is falling off the bone, about 1 1/2 hours. Skim the fat off the top as it renders. Remove the chicken and let cool.

Strain the stock and set aside the herbs and vegetables. Return the stock to medium-high heat and reduce by one-third, approximately 30 minutes. Continue to skim fat off as necessary.

Remove the meat from the chicken bones and add to the reduced stock. Remove the bay leaves and parsley stems from the vegetables and discard. Return the vegetables to the stock.

Bring a pot of salted water to a boil. Cook the noodles. Drain and add to the soup.

To serve, coarsely chop the parsley leaves. Season the soup with salt and pepper to taste. Serve immediately in bowls, garnished with the parsley.

VARIATIONS

To make this more like a stew, thicken the stock with flour or cornstarch dissolved in water. You could serve this over rice or inside a burrito with beans and rice.

Watercress Soup

The Livermore Valley is surrounded by Northern California's Coastal Range. Many of its arroyos and creeks cut their way through the valley, draining into several main streams. When the rains come during the fall and winter months, watercress thrives in most of their waters. I grew up near two such creeks—one running past my parents' house and the other passing right by my grandparents' back door.

My grandmother not only made watercress soup and watercress sandwiches but also used it in a purée to add a peppery flavor to other soups and sauces. This is a recipe I have updated from my grandmother's recipe file. It is tasty served either hot or chilled. —CW

1/4 cup unsalted butter

3 cups sliced and minced leeks, white part only

3 tablespoons flour

5 cups hot water

4 cups peeled, diced white potatoes (about 3 potatoes)

2 tablespoons kosher salt

1 1/2 teaspoons to 1 tablespoon freshly ground pepper, as needed

2 bunches watercress (the gathered stems of each bunch should be 1 to 1 1/2 inches in diameter)

1 cup heavy whipping cream or sour cream

3 tablespoons lemon juice, more or less as needed

Sour cream, for garnish

3 tablespoons minced chives or fresh parsley leaves, for garnish

To prepare the soup base: In a 4-quart saucepan over medium heat, melt the butter. Add the leeks and sauté for 5 minutes, being careful not to brown them. Sprinkle the flour over the leek and butter mixture and continue to stir for another 2 minutes. Again, be careful not to brown the flour mixture. Remove from the heat and gradually whisk in 1 cup of the hot water, blending the mixture thoroughly. Add the remaining 4 cups hot water and the diced potatoes, salt, and pepper. Bring to a boil, reduce the heat, and simmer for 30 minutes.

To make the soup: While the soup base is simmering, pull the large leaves off the watercress and set aside on a paper towel. To avoid bitterness, remove the largest stems from the bunches and discard. Coarsely chop the remaining leaves and stems; you should have about 2 cups chopped watercress.

When the soup base has simmered for 30 minutes, add the chopped watercress and simmer for 5 minutes. Purée the entire mixture in a food processor or blender until smooth. Return to the stove and add the cream,

SERVES 6

☙ WINE NOTES

A Sauvignon Blanc contrasts nicely with the peppery base of this soup. Or to match the soup's creaminess, try a medium-bodied, barrel-fermented Chardonnay.

lemon juice, and reserved whole leaves. Adjust the lemon juice and seasoning to taste. Warm thoroughly but do not boil. (If you are serving the soup cold, set aside to chill.)

To serve, ladle into bowls and garnish with a dollop of the sour cream and a sprinkling of minced chives.

EPICUREAN ALCHEMY

As I watch many cooks approach recipes with slavish adherence to ingredient lists and instructions, I can't help but think that they are stifled by their rigidity. I look at food preparation as alchemy, the ancient system of quasi-scientific methods that were used to turn baser elements into gold. My epicurean alchemy is made up of a collection of solid techniques that I use to transform the simple flavors of the best, freshest ingredients into what I hope are "golden" meals. While these techniques need to be applied with discipline, the techniques and ingredients I use are wide open to interpretation and creativity. I like to think that there is something intangible, magical, even mystical about how certain combinations come together—a little more of this here and a little more of that there. It is definitely an organic process.

Within my personal alchemical system of techniques, some apply to the savory side of cooking, some to the baking of breads, pastries, and desserts—the opposite sides of the kitchen spectrum. Baking requires more adherence to the recipe and its specific techniques to ensure the same results; a lot of chemistry is involved. While some variations are possible, the formulas are more exact. And when it doesn't work, the results seem to be more disastrous. On the other hand, savory cooking has many paths to the same result. There is a bit of alchemy involved, and it is easier to save your creation if you take a wrong turn.

To figure out which ingredients, flavorings, and techniques to use in a dish, consider the basic components or ingredients. Think about what might be substituted, and don't be afraid to take a risk. I try to imagine what the final balance of flavors and textures of all of the components might feel like in my mouth. The balance of sweet and sour, bitter and sweet; crispy, soft, or chewy textures; and rich or lean flavors all play a part in the composition of a dish. This is how great dishes are discovered and created. One of the goals of this cookbook is to pass on the information and confidence you need to use a recipe as a guideline, not a rule. Get inspired!

Look for ways to expand your skills. If a recipe comes out very well every time you make it, that's fantastic. If you find another way to make it, you are starting to build a repertoire. That is what we are looking for. And when you find a new technique, remember how you did it. That is what technique is about. It is the hardest thing to learn because it requires discipline to be consistent.

Learn some simple techniques that you can use to change and improve a dish. (See "Adding Flavor Intensity," page 83.) Understanding the effects of different techniques helps you to put them to use again in the future. Talk to other people, read magazines and cookbooks, watch cooking shows. Discover new ideas. By cooking all over the world, I pick up different techniques, depending on the ingredients, the facilities, and the utensils I have to use.

Expose your palate to new flavors and aromas. Go to different restaurants. Order menu items you think you won't like. Taste foods as you are preparing them. It's important that you do this with all of the ingredients involved. Lettuces and dressings are a prime example. If you don't taste the dressing or vinaigrette with the lettuce that you are going to serve it with, you won't know if the dressing or vinaigrette is in balance, particularly with a Caesar salad. (The romaine contains a lot of water that will dilute the dressing.)

Develop a memory bank of flavors and flavor combinations, including wines. Remember pairings that you particularly enjoyed and why. What did a wine taste like, what was the consistency, did it have a lingering aftertaste? Sometimes I remember flavors and try to re-create them. Carolyn sees pictures of recipes and tries to make them taste like what she imagines them to be. When I think of a dish, I start tasting it. Without having made anything, I get sensations on my palate.

My favorite way of planning a meal is to go to the market and pick out what looks best, trying to keep focused on what is in season (produce at the height of the season is usually the cheapest and the tastiest). I look for ingredients that I can play with. I go without preconceived notions of what I am going to prepare. By stirring up my imagination and my memory bank of flavors with what's available at the market, I know I'll cook up something interesting to eat and fun to share.—KJ

Watercress, Radicchio, and Gorgonzola Salad with Walnut Vinaigrette

SERVES 6

❧ WINE NOTES

Johannisberg Riesling, a noble grape variety originating in Germany, is widely planted throughout the coastal regions of California. Also known as White Riesling, it exhibits good acid with floral, peach, and pear aromas. It can be made either dry or off-dry, the latter of which tends to be slightly fuller and richer. This wine would be an excellent accompaniment to the wonderful sweetness and richness in this salad. If you prefer a red, try a Pinot Noir.

Grapes are not the only harvest in the Livermore Valley. During the fall months, our ranch yields walnuts, pears, apples, olives, and watercress. The refreshing change offered by this autumn salad is inspired by many of our homegrown ingredients. You can substitute apples for the pears and olive oil for the walnut oil. Watercress can be picked or purchased a couple of days in advance. To keep it fresh, rinse the leaves in cold water, place the stems in a glass of water, cover with plastic wrap or a plastic bag, and refrigerate. To add flavor to unripened pears, sauté them in the vinaigrette for 3 to 4 minutes, or until warmed through. Look for a fresh Gorgonzola, which is creamier in texture and harder to crumble. If you can't find it, use an aged one. —CW

WALNUT VINAIGRETTE

3 tablespoons lemon juice

2 teaspoons Dijon mustard

$3/4$ cup fresh walnut oil (or extra-virgin olive oil)

Kosher salt and freshly ground pepper

2 bunches watercress (the gathered stems of each bunch should be $1 1/2$ inches in diameter)

1 medium head radicchio, torn into $1/2$-inch-wide pieces

Tender inner leaves from 2 heads butter lettuce, torn into 2-inch pieces

$1/2$ cup toasted walnut halves (page 210)

8 ounces crumbled sweet Gorgonzola

2 ripe Bartlett pears, halved, cored, and cut lengthwise into $1/8$-inch wedges

Kosher salt and freshly ground pepper

To prepare the vinaigrette: In a small bowl, whisk together the lemon juice and mustard. Continue to whisk while slowly drizzling in the walnut oil. Season to taste with coarsely ground salt and pepper.

To prepare the salad: Remove the leaves and tips from the watercress, discarding the tough stems. Combine the watercress, radicchio, and butter lettuce in a large bowl. Drizzle with the vinaigrette and toss lightly. Add the crumbled cheese, toasted walnuts, and pear wedges. Season with salt and pepper. Toss again gently and serve.

Belgian Endive and Radicchio Salad with Butter Pear Dressing, Goat Cheese, and Hazelnuts

The sweetness of the dressing in this salad helps to tame the bitterness often associated with endive and radicchio. French Butter pears are a heritage variety grown near us in the Sacramento Delta by Pettigrew Farms. The flavor is rich, buttery, and lusciously sweet. They have a very limited season and require gentle handling. If you cannot locate these pears in your area, use a pear such as Comice or Bosc, but make sure that it is ripe and juicy.

BUTTER PEAR DRESSING

2 French Butter pears, 1 cut into julienne for garnish

1 tablespoon Dijon mustard

1 egg yolk

2 tablespoons sherry vinegar

2 tablespoons apple cider vinegar

1/2 cup olive oil

1 tablespoon maple syrup, more as needed

4 heads Belgian endive

1 head radicchio

4 to 5 ounces mild goat cheese (about 1/3 cup)

2 tablespoons toasted, skinned, chopped hazelnuts (page 210)

To prepare the dressing: Peel one of the pears and cut into quarters. Remove the core. Place in a food processor with the mustard, egg yolk, and sherry and cider vinegars. Process until smooth. Slowly add the olive oil. Remove from the processor and place in a mixing bowl. Whisk in the maple syrup, a little at a time. You may need more or less than 1 tablespoon of maple syrup, depending on the sweetness of the pears. The dressing should have a good balance between sweet and sour.

To prepare the lettuces: Remove any bruised or wilted leaves from the outside of the endive and radicchio, and trim the root ends. Cut the endive into quarters lengthwise and remove the core. Cut the radicchio into quarters, remove the core, and cut the remaining radicchio into thin strips.

To serve, toss the endive and radicchio with the dressing. Divide among 4 plates and top with the goat cheese, hazelnuts, and julienned pear.

SERVES 4

WINE NOTES

Pairing wines with dishes containing a vinaigrette can be difficult because the sour component of the vinaigrette often clashes with the wine. In this dish, that tendency is diminished with the use of two milder vinegars plus the hint of sweetness in the dressing. I would look to pair the wine with the bitter component of the radicchio that Kimball mentions. Keep it youthful, simple, and light, such as a light red Napa Gamay, Gamay Beaujolais, or Sangiovese.

Steamed Artichokes with Aioli and Sundried Tomato Bread Salad

SERVES 4

ꙮ WINE NOTES

Kimball's recommendation of a crisp, acidic Sauvignon Blanc is perfect, matching the weight and textures found in the dish. The crispness of the wine also counterbalances the effects of the cynarin contained in the artichokes, which distorts the perception of sweetness on your palate. If you were to serve a fruitier style wine, the cynarin would make it appear overly sweet.

In Tuscany, no stale bread ever goes to waste. It's used in soups and coatings and is the basis for this wonderful bread salad. I prefer cooking the artichokes upside down with just a little water so that they retain their flavor without getting waterlogged. The cynarin in the artichoke fools your palate into thinking that any wine served with artichokes tastes sweeter than it actually is. Crisp, acidic Sauvignon Blanc goes well with artichokes.

4 medium artichokes

1 lemon, cut in half

Bouquet garni with 2 bay leaves and 1 teaspoon
   whole black peppercorns (page 211)

Aioli (page 207)

Parsley sprigs, for garnish

VINAIGRETTE

1 teaspoon balsamic vinegar

$1/2$ teaspoon Dijon mustard

$1/2$ teaspoon minced shallot

1 tablespoon extra-virgin olive oil

SUNDRIED TOMATO BREAD SALAD

4 cups cubed day-old rustic sourdough whole-wheat bread
   ($3/4$-inch cubes)

$1/4$ cup olive oil

Kosher salt and freshly ground pepper

$1/2$ teaspoon minced garlic

1 tablespoon sherry vinegar

2 tablespoons plus $1^1/2$ teaspoons extra-virgin olive oil

2 teaspoons capers, coarsely chopped

1 tablespoon plus $1^1/2$ teaspoons julienned sundried tomatoes
   packed in oil

$1/4$ cup finely diced red onion

12 kalamata olives, pitted and coarsely chopped

1 tablespoon chopped parsley leaves

To prepare the artichokes: Trim the bottom of each artichoke with a sharp knife. Cut the top off so it will be able to stand on its "head." With scissors, trim off the thorny ends of the leaves. To prevent discoloration after trimming each artichoke, rub it with the cut surface of a lemon half and place it in a bowl filled with water until ready to cook. Place the bouquet garni in the bottom of a large pot, add the artichokes upside down—the stem end pointing up—and add 1 1/2 inches of water. Bring to a boil, lower to a slight simmer, and cover. Cook until the hearts are tender when pierced with a sharp knife and the leaves pull away easily from the heart, approximately 40 minutes. Remove from the water and drain upside down.

Carefully remove the thin, small inner leaves of the artichoke, keeping the outer leaves intact. Using a tablespoon, carefully scoop out the fuzzy inner choke from the artichoke.

Prepare a vinaigrette by combining the balsamic vinegar, mustard, and shallots in a small bowl. Slowly whisk in the olive oil.

Turn the artichokes right side up so that the heart is on the bottom, and place them in a shallow dish. Drizzle the vinaigrette between the leaves and on the inside of the artichokes. Chill in the refrigerator for a couple of hours.

To prepare the bread salad: Preheat the oven to 350°. In a bowl, toss the cubed bread with the 1/4 cup olive oil and season with salt and pepper. Place on a baking sheet and toast in the oven until light golden brown, about 15 minutes, turning once halfway through. Remove from the oven and transfer to a large bowl to prevent further cooking. Cool to room temperature.

In a bowl, combine the garlic, sherry vinegar, extra-virgin olive oil, capers, sundried tomatoes, red onion, olives, and chopped parsley. Season with salt and pepper to taste.

To serve, spoon one-fourth of the aioli inside each artichoke and place each one in the middle of a plate. Toss the toasted bread cubes with the sundried tomato mixture, and surround each artichoke with one-fourth of the mixture. Garnish each plate with sprigs of parsley.

SERVES 4 GENEROUSLY

Braising is a cooking method that actually deepens the flavor of a meat recipe. A younger, aggressive red wine such as a Syrah or Barbera will enhance the variety of flavors in this dish.

Braised Rabbit Ragout with Butternut Squash, Currants, and Spinach Pappardelle

Braising the rabbit allows you to use every little bit and makes this usually lean meat succulent. I like to season the rabbit at least 2 hours before cooking. This allows the seasoning to penetrate the muscles. This ragout is even better made the day before and then reheated. The meat absorbs a lot of the wonderful braising liquid while sitting in it overnight. If you want to shorten the preparation time, buy fresh spinach pappardelle.

> 1 whole rabbit (2 1/2 to 3 pounds)
> Kosher salt and freshly ground pepper
> 2 tablespoons olive oil
> 1 cup diced carrot
> 1 large onion, diced (about 1 cup)
> 2 shallots, peeled
> 1 cup red wine
> Bouquet garni with 2 sprigs each of sage, thyme, and parsley (page 211)
> 1 (8-ounce) can whole tomatoes in juice
> 1 tablespoon sherry vinegar
> 1 butternut squash, peeled and diced (about 2 cups)
>
> SPINACH PAPPARDELLE
> 1/2 pound fresh spinach, about 5 cups loosely packed (about 1/2 cup cooked spinach)
> 2 cups all-purpose flour
> 1 large egg
>
> 1/2 cup toasted bread crumbs
> 1 teaspoon finely chopped lemon zest
> 1 teaspoon finely chopped orange zest
> 1 teaspoon lemon juice
> 1 teaspoon orange juice
> 1/2 cup currants

To braise the rabbit: Trim the legs off of the rabbit and cut the loin in half. Season the rabbit with salt and pepper and set aside in the refrigerator.

In a roasting pan or nonreactive, ovenproof pan with a tight-fitting lid (you could use aluminum foil to cover, as well) heat 1 tablespoon of the olive oil over medium heat. Add the carrot, onion, and shallot and cook, stirring often, until lightly golden brown, approximately 8 minutes. Add the rabbit and sauté until browned, another 8 to 10 minutes.

Preheat the oven to 350°.

Add the wine to the pan and stir over medium heat, scraping up the browned bits from the bottom. Add the bouquet garni, tomatoes, and juice. Add water to cover, 4 to 5 cups, and bring to a simmer. Cover, place in the oven, and cook about 30 minutes. Lower the heat to 300° and cook for an hour, or until the rabbit is very tender and falling off the bone.

Toss the remaining tablespoon of olive oil and the sherry vinegar with the squash, season with salt and pepper, and place on a baking sheet. Roast until tender, about 15 minutes. Set aside.

To prepare the pappardelle: In a pot of boiling, salted water, blanch the spinach until just wilted. Drain and quickly plunge into ice water. Drain again, place in a clean kitchen towel, and wring out until dry.

Place a large pot of salted water on the stove and bring to a boil.

In a food processor or a mixer with a paddle attachment, combine the spinach and flour and purée until well incorporated. Place this green flour on a clean work surface and make a well in the center. Crack the egg into the well and whisk thoroughly with a fork. Using the fork, slowly work the flour into the egg. Knead with your hands until the dough just comes together. Don't force the flour into the dough; blend in only as much flour as the liquid will absorb. Depending on how dry your spinach is, you may need to use more flour than called for in the recipe.

Flatten the dough into a large, thick pancake shape and wrap in plastic wrap. Let rest for 30 minutes. To shape, roll out by hand or with a pasta machine until $1/16$ inch thick. (For instructions, see page 202.) Dust liberally with flour. Cut by hand into wide noodles, about $5/8$ inch wide.

Cook the pasta in the boiling water until done, approximately 5 minutes.

To assemble the ragout: Remove the rabbit from the oven and strain the rabbit, vegetables, and herbs from the stock. Discard the herbs. Cool the rabbit, remove the meat from the bone, and reserve the meat in the refrigerator.

Place the vegetables and stock back into the pot and purée with a hand blender, or use a food processor, food mill, or blender. Bring the puréed mixture to a simmer and cook for about 15 minutes, or until slightly thickened. Taste for seasoning.

Season the bread crumbs by combining them with the lemon and orange zest.

To serve, add the rabbit and squash to the purée and warm thoroughly. Add the lemon and orange juice. Toss with the spinach pappardelle. Adjust salt and pepper. Divide among 4 plates and garnish with the currants and seasoned bread crumbs.

Linguine with Fennel, Dungeness Crab, and Meyer Lemon Cream

SERVES 4

🍶 WINE NOTES

In keeping with Kimball's thoughts, when you're picking up the ingredients on the way home from a busy day, pick up a bottle of wine as well. I recommend a Chardonnay with an obvious fruitiness, modest complexity, a smoothness on your palate, some amount of oakiness, and a crisp finish. This style of Chardonnay is one of the easiest to find in California and is moderately priced. With the crab and linguine, this wine is a straightforward match.

This is an easy pasta to make on those busy nights when you want something quick. Other shellfish such as shrimp, crayfish, or lobster can be substituted for the crab. You can also experiment with other citrus such as tangerines, limes, and even grapefruit.

MEYER LEMON CREAM

1 tablespoon minced shallot

1 cup white wine

1 tablespoon fennel seeds

1 teaspoon white peppercorns

2 cups heavy whipping cream

1/4 cup finely chopped Meyer lemon zest

Kosher salt and freshly ground white pepper

2 bulbs fennel (reserve tops for garnish)

1 cup julienned leeks, white part only

2 tablespoons olive oil

1 pound linguine, fresh or dried

4 Meyer lemons, peeled and segmented

2 cups Dungeness crabmeat (approximately 1 pound)

1 tablespoon sliced chives, for garnish

To prepare the lemon cream: Place the shallot, white wine, fennel seeds, and peppercorns in a nonreactive saucepan. Bring to a simmer and lower the heat to keep the mixture at a bare simmer. Reduce the liquid until there is very little left, about 1 tablespoon. Watch carefully. Add the cream and return to a simmer. Cook at a low simmer for 30 minutes. Strain through a fine-mesh sieve, add the finely chopped lemon zest, and season with salt and white pepper to taste. Set aside in a warm place.

To prepare the linguine: Place a large pot of salted water on the stove and bring to a boil.

Cut the fennel bulbs in half from root to top. Remove the core and slice the remainder of the bulbs thinly with the grain. A mandoline or a sharp, thin-bladed knife works best.

In a large sauté pan over medium heat, heat the olive oil and add the fennel and leek. Cook until translucent, approximately 10 minutes. Remove from the heat.

Add the linguine to the boiling water. When almost done, add the lemon cream to the leek and fennel mixture, and gently warm together.

When the pasta is cooked, drain and add to the cream mixture, along with the crabmeat and lemon segments. Toss together and taste for seasoning.

To serve, divide among 4 plates and garnish with chives and fennel tops.

Calzone with Winter Squash, Ham, and Ricotta

I use kabocha squash in this recipe, but virtually any winter squash available in your area can be used, such as delicata, hubbard, acorn, and sugar pumpkin. Cook them in the same manner as the kabocha; the cooking time will vary depending on which squash you use. Be sure that the squash is very tender before removing it from the oven. This will ensure a clean, sweet flavor.

1 kabocha squash, about 3 pounds

1 tablespoon olive oil

Kosher salt and freshly ground pepper

$^1/_2$ recipe pizza dough (page 203)

1 teaspoon minced garlic

1 cup ricotta cheese (to make your own, see page 200)

$^1/_2$ teaspoon finely chopped fresh rosemary

$^1/_2$ cup finely grated Parmesan cheese

$^1/_4$ pound Black Forest ham, diced

1 tablespoon lemon juice

MAKES 4 CALZONE

☙ WINE NOTES

When selecting wines for calzone or pizza, focus on the accompanying ingredients to determine your wine options. In this case, the ham, cheese, squash, and herbs point toward a soft, medium-bodied red wine such as Merlot or Zinfandel.

Preheat the oven to 350°. Cut the squash in half and remove the seeds. Rub the inside flesh of the squash with olive oil and season with salt and pepper. Place cut side down on a baking sheet and roast in the oven for 30 minutes, or until a sharp knife easily pierces the squash. Cool.

Prepare the oven for pizza, preheat the oven to 550°, and shape the dough into 4 rounds, as described on page 204.

Remove the flesh of the squash with a spoon, being careful to not scoop out any of the skin. Place in a bowl, and mash with a fork. Combine with the garlic, ricotta, rosemary, Parmesan, ham, and lemon juice. Taste for seasoning, adding lemon juice, salt, and pepper if necessary.

Place a quarter of the filling on half of each round of dough. Moisten the edges with water. Fold the dough over, enclosing the filling, and seal the edges. Bake in the oven until golden brown, about 10 minutes. Remove from the oven and brush lightly with olive oil. Serve immediately.

Pizza with Roasted Peppers, Chiles, Garlic, Chorizo, and Dry–Aged Jack Cheese

MAKES FOUR 12- TO
14-INCH PIZZAS

🌾 WINE NOTES

The major flavor component in this pizza is the chorizo, so select a medium-bodied to full-bodied red wine. Zinfandel or Cabernet Sauvignon are ideal with this more rustic, heavily spiced pizza. If you really like heat and you added the chile seeds to your filling, the high alcohol content of these wines will enhance the heat. If you want to diminish the effect, try a lighter, fruitier wine with a lower alcohol content, such as a Barbera or a rosé made from cabernet sauvignon or sangiovese grapes.

You can purchase chorizo to use for this recipe, but I prefer to make my own. Most store-bought chorizo contains strange parts of the pig seldom seen at the butcher's, such as cheeks, jowls, and trotters. With this recipe you know what you are eating. Note that you need to make the chorizo 24 hours ahead of time. If you would like a spicier pizza, include the seeds from the poblano chile.

CHORIZO

1 pound ground pork
2 1/4 teaspoons kosher salt
1/2 teaspoon freshly ground pepper
2 teaspoons paprika
1/2 teaspoon ground cumin
1/2 teaspoon ground coriander seed
1/2 teaspoon granulated sugar
1/4 cup red wine
1 1/4 teaspoons minced garlic
1 1/4 teaspoons crushed red pepper flakes
1 1/4 teaspoons cayenne pepper
1 jalapeño with seeds, minced
1 teaspoon dried oregano
1/2 teaspoon chile powder

1 whole head garlic
1 tablespoon extra-virgin olive oil
Kosher salt and freshly ground pepper
1 red bell pepper, roasted, peeled, and thinly sliced (page 210)
1 yellow bell pepper, roasted, peeled, and thinly sliced
1 poblano chile, roasted, peeled, seeded, and thinly sliced
1 jalapeño, roasted, peeled, seeded, and thinly sliced
Pizza dough (page 203)
1 cup grated dry-aged Jack cheese

To prepare the chorizo: In a nonreactive bowl, blend the pork, salt, pepper, paprika, cumin, coriander, sugar, wine, garlic, pepper flakes, cayenne, jalapeño, oregano, and chile powder thoroughly and let marinate for 24 hours.

To make the pizza: Preheat the oven to 300°. Cut the top off of the garlic, place in a small, ovenproof baking dish, drizzle with the olive oil, and season with salt and pepper. Pour $1/4$ inch of water into the baking dish, cover, and place in the oven. Cook for 1 hour, or until soft. Remove from the oven and cool.

Prepare the oven for pizza and preheat to 550° as described on page 204. Separate the cloves of the garlic and remove the skins. Combine with the peppers and chiles.

Sauté the chorizo over medium heat until cooked through, about 5 minutes.

Shape the pizza dough into 4 rounds. Divide the pepper mixture among the 4 dough rounds. Break the chorizo into little pieces and divide among the dough rounds. Top with the cheese and place in the oven. Bake until golden brown, 8 to 10 minutes. Serve piping hot.

Roast Pork Loin with Spicy Applesauce and Braised Red Cabbage

SERVES 4

☙ WINE NOTES

A medium-bodied, slightly off-dry Johannisberg Riesling would be a delicious match. The wonderful fruits found in the recipe—figs and apples—are flavors and aromas found in the Johannisberg riesling grape. This wine originates in Germany and is now referred to in California as White Riesling. It develops best in the cooler appellations. The wine usually has good acidity, which will help cleanse the palate of the fattiness in the pork.

Applesauce is the ultimate comfort food and extremely easy to make. Because the balance of acid and sweetness in apples varies widely, the amount of sugar in the applesauce should be used as a guideline, not an absolute. The amount of sugar in the cabbage can vary as well, depending on your preference for sweet versus tart. I add the sugar in a little at a time, tasting as I go, until there is an even balance of sweet and sour in both the applesauce and the braised red cabbage. The cabbage and applesauce are also wonderful accompaniments to sausages.

ROAST PORK LOIN

1/2 cup dried figs

1/4 cup Madeira

1 pork loin roast (2 pounds)

Kosher salt and freshly ground pepper

12 to 15 red creamer-sized
   (1 1/2 inches in diameter) potatoes, cut in half

SPICY APPLESAUCE

3 pippin apples, peeled and cut into 1-inch dice
   (about 3 1/2 cups)

1/8 teaspoon cayenne

1 cup apple cider or juice

2 teaspoons granulated sugar

1/4 teaspoon ground cinnamon

BRAISED RED CABBAGE

2 slices bacon, diced

$^1/_2$ cup thinly sliced yellow onions

$^1/_2$ cup thinly sliced carrots

1 small head red cabbage, thinly sliced (about 6 cups)

$^1/_2$ cup brown sugar

$^3/_4$ cup red wine vinegar

1 teaspoon caraway seeds

1 bay leaf

Kosher salt and freshly ground pepper

To prepare the pork loin: Soak the figs in the Madeira overnight.

Preheat the oven to 350°. Butterfly the pork loin (or have your butcher do this for you), and season the inside with salt and pepper. Lay the Madeira-soaked figs down the center of the pork loin, roll the loin around the figs to encase them, and tie with butcher's twine. Season the outside with salt and pepper. Place in a roasting pan and surround with the potatoes. Roast in the oven for 1 hour, or until the internal temperature of the pork reaches 145° when checked with an instant-read thermometer.

Remove the pork from the oven and let rest for 10 minutes.

To prepare the applesauce: In a nonreactive saucepan, combine the apples, cayenne, apple cider, sugar, and cinnamon. Bring to a boil and lower the heat to a simmer. Cook for 20 to 25 minutes, until the apples are soft and tender. Purée in a food processor. Set aside.

To prepare the cabbage: In a large sauté pan or small stockpot over medium heat, sauté the bacon until lightly browned, about 5 minutes. Add the onion and carrot to the pan and cook, uncovered, until the onion is transparent, about 10 minutes, stirring occasionally. Add the cabbage, sugar, vinegar, caraway seeds, and bay leaf. Reduce the heat to low and cook, covered, until tender, approximately 30 minutes. Check for seasoning.

To serve, make a small bed of the braised cabbage on each plate. Slice the pork loin and place one or two pieces on the cabbage. Serve the applesauce over the pork or on the side. Surround with the potatoes.

Roast Chicken with
Pear and Cornbread Stuffing

SERVES 4

🦌 WINE NOTES

A full-bodied Chardonnay that has undergone malolactic fermentation would complement the flavors in this recipe. The cooking method adds some rich moistness to the chicken, while the sour cream and buttermilk in the cornbread add richness to the stuffing. The creamy texture of the Chardonnay would be pleasing with this dish.

This cornbread recipe will make about twice as much as you need for the stuffing, but it is delicious by itself. My son Taylor devours it for breakfast drizzled with lavender honey. The stuffing recipe can easily be doubled for use in a Thanksgiving turkey. It's also great combined with fresh oysters instead of pears for a holiday side dish.

CORNBREAD

1/2 cup flour

1/2 cup cornmeal

1/2 teaspoon kosher salt

2 teaspoons granulated sugar

2 teaspoons baking powder

2 eggs

1/4 cup plus 2 tablespoons buttermilk

1/4 cup sour cream

3 tablespoons melted butter

CORNBREAD STUFFING

1 tablespoon olive oil

1/2 cup diced carrot

1/2 cup diced onion

2 very ripe pears, peeled, cored, and cut into 1/2-inch dice (about 2 cups)

2 cups cubed cornbread (1/2-inch cubes)

1 tablespoon chopped fresh sage leaves

1/2 cup chicken stock (page 206)

Kosher salt and freshly ground pepper

1 roasting chicken (31/2 to 4 pounds)

Olive oil for seasoning

To prepare the cornbread: Preheat the oven to 350°. In a mixing bowl, combine the flour, cornmeal, salt, sugar, and baking powder. In another bowl, whisk the eggs. Blend in the buttermilk, sour cream, and melted butter. Combine the wet and dry ingredients with a few quick strokes. You only need to break up the largest lumps! Pour into a buttered 8 by 4 by 2-inch loaf pan and place in the oven. Bake until golden brown, about 30 minutes. Cool.

To prepare the stuffing: In a sauté pan over medium heat, heat the olive oil. Add the carrot and onion. Cook until lightly golden brown, about 15 minutes. Add the pear and toss together. Remove from the heat and combine with the cornbread, sage, and chicken stock. Season to taste with salt and pepper.

To roast the chicken: Preheat the oven to 400°. Wash the chicken thoroughly inside and out and pat dry with a towel. Season the inside of the chicken with salt and pepper and fill with the stuffing. Tie the legs together. Rub the outside of the chicken with olive oil and season with salt and pepper. Place on a rack in a roasting pan (I use a ceramic oval baking dish) with an inch of hot water in the bottom of the pan. This will keep the bird moist while it roasts. Place in the oven. Reduce the heat to 350° and roast for about 1 hour and 15 minutes, or until the juices run clear when you poke a thigh with a sharp knife. (Getting the oven good and hot before adding the bird allows the fat on the skin to begin basting the bird right away.) Because the inside cavity is filled, the bird will have to cook entirely from the outside in. This may take a little longer.

To serve, remove the stuffing from the chicken and divide among 4 plates. Carve the breast meat and legs off of the chicken. Place a serving of chicken on top of the stuffing. Serve immediately.

Grilled Skewered Squabs
with Apple Cider Sauce and
Lemon Sweet Potatoes

SERVES 4

I think of squab as a fuller-flavored meat, like duck. Pinot Noir or Zinfandel has the perfect body and flavor spectrum. The spicy nature of both of these wines will further complement the grilled squab. When served with spinach or chard, the addition of the bitter component may require a slightly "bigger" wine—such as a Cabernet Sauvignon—to balance the tannins to the greens.

I first skewered squab this way for the groundbreaking ceremony for Opus One Winery in my previous incarnation as executive chef for Paula Le Duc Catering. Any rustic skewer will work, but vine cuttings add a distinctive touch. Soaking the skewers in water before cooking prevents them from burning on the grill. This dish is great served with sautéed greens such as spinach, chard, or frisée. You can have your butcher bone the squab, but make sure you get the bones for the sauce.

4 squabs

$1/4$ cup apple cider vinegar

$1/4$ cup honey

$1/2$ cup apple cider

4 5-inch-long skewers, preferably grapevine cuttings, soaked in water for 2 hours

2 cups chicken stock (page 206)

2 tablespoons butter, cut into small pieces

LEMON SWEET POTATOES

3 large sweet potatoes (yields 3 to 4 cups purée)

3 tablespoons lemon juice

2 tablespoons finely chopped lemon zest

$1/4$ cup extra-virgin olive oil

Kosher salt and freshly ground pepper

To prepare the squab: Preheat the oven to 350°. With a sharp boning knife, cut the squabs along each side of the breastbone to the bone. Continue following the breastbone with the knife, cutting along the wishbone and through the wing bone joint, detaching the wing bone. Cut along the backbone and detach the thigh from the carcass. You should now have 2 halves of squab completely boned, except for the wing and leg bones, which are still attached. Trim any loose skin. Set the bones aside.

In a nonreactive baking dish, combine the vinegar, honey, and $1/4$ cup of the cider. Place the squab breasts and thighs in this marinade with the skin side up. Don't marinate the skin because the honey in the marinade will burn when you cook it. Marinate for 2 hours.

To make the sauce: While the squab is marinating, place the squab bones in a roasting pan and roast until golden brown, 20 to 30 minutes.

In a saucepan, combine the roasted bones and the chicken stock. Add the remaining $1/4$ cup apple cider to the roasting pan and stir over medium heat, scraping up the browned bits from the bottom of the pan. Add to the stock, bring the stock to a simmer, and slowly reduce by half, about 30 minutes. Strain the sauce and reserve.

To prepare the sweet potatoes: Preheat the oven to 350°. Place the sweet potatoes on a baking sheet and roast in the oven for about 1 hour, or until tender when pierced with a sharp knife. Cut the sweet potatoes in half and scoop out the meat with a spoon. Place in a bowl and mash with a fork or potato masher. Add the lemon juice, zest, and olive oil and season with salt and pepper. Place in a heatproof bowl over a pot of simmering water to keep warm.

When you are ready to begin cooking the squab, make a medium-sized fire in your grill. Thread the squab pieces onto the skewers, placing all of the parts of one squab on a skewer, like matching bookends. Season with salt and pepper. Place the skewered squab on the grill, skin side down. Cook until still rare inside, 6 to 7 minutes per side, turning once. The squab should take about 12 to 15 minutes to cook and have an internal temperature of 120° when done.

To serve, warm the sauce over medium heat and swirl in the butter, a few pieces at a time. Divide the sweet potatoes among 4 plates. Top with a grilled squab, and spoon some of the cider sauce over the squab. Serve immediately.

Filets of Beef Stuffed with Roast Garlic and Herbs and Wrapped in Pancetta with Potato–Butternut Squash Gratin

SERVES 4

❧ WINE NOTES

Fine cuts of meat such as filet mignon pair wonderfully with complex or aged red wines. Complexity in wines refers to the variety of aromas and range of bouquets as well as to the layers of flavor. Aged red wines tend to lighten in color, soften in tannins, and marry in flavors to create a better developed wine, one that is "well-knit." Cabernet Sauvignon or Merlot are wines that have complexity and can age nicely, providing the right complement to Kimball's filets.

This potato gratin can be made any time of the year by substituting other ingredients for the butternut squash. Experiment with wild mushrooms, roasted garlic or shallots, sweet potatoes, or even truffles. Because of the richness of the beef and gratin, I like to serve lightly sautéed greens or a simple salad with this meal. It is important that the potatoes and squash be very thinly sliced. If you don't have a mandoline, carefully slice the potatoes thinly by hand. Thick potatoes will throw off the cooking time, and the dish won't be as creamy as it should be.

ROAST GARLIC

2 whole heads garlic

Kosher salt and freshly ground pepper

1¹/₂ teaspoons extra-virgin olive oil

POTATO–BUTTERNUT SQUASH GRATIN

¹/₂ small butternut squash, peeled and thinly sliced (about 1¹/₂ cups)

1 cup heavy whipping cream

1 teaspoon minced garlic

¹/₂ teaspoon minced fresh thyme leaves

1 teaspoon kosher salt

Freshly ground pepper

3 russet potatoes, peeled and thinly sliced (about 4 cups)

2 tablespoons freshly grated Parmesan cheese

1 teaspoon chopped fresh tarragon leaves

1 teaspoon chopped fresh parsley leaves

4 filets of beef (6 ounces each)

4 thin slices pancetta

Kosher salt and freshly ground pepper

Olive oil for sautéing

To roast the garlic: Preheat the oven to 300°. Trim the tops off of the garlic heads, exposing the tops of the cloves. Place the garlic in an ovenproof pan, cut side up, filled with $1/2$ inch of water. Season lightly with salt and pepper and drizzle lightly with extra-virgin olive oil. Cover with a lid and roast for about 1 hour, or until the garlic cloves are soft. Cool.

To prepare the gratin: Preheat the oven to 350°. Check to make sure that you didn't leave any of the green part of the skin on the squash when you peeled it, as it will taste bitter. In a large bowl, combine the cream, garlic, and thyme and season with the salt and pepper.

Mix the potatoes thoroughly with the seasoned cream. After the potatoes have been added, I always check the cream to test for saltiness. Potatoes vary a lot in waxiness and water content and they love to absorb salt, so the amount of salt used to flavor the cream will vary. (A way to "fix" a dish that is too salty is to add potatoes.) Place half of the potatoes in the bottom of a $1^1/_2$-quart baking dish. Layer the butternut squash on top of the potatoes. Cover with the remaining potatoes. Pour any cream left over the top layer of potatoes. Sprinkle the Parmesan evenly on top. Bake, uncovered, for about 1 hour, or until a sharp knife easily pierces the gratin.

To prepare the filets: While the gratin is baking, separate the cloves of the roasted garlic, and peel them. Combine the whole roasted cloves with the tarragon and the parsley. Divide the garlic-herb mixture into 4 portions.

Make an incision on the side of each filet. Slip your finger inside and wiggle it around until a pocket is formed. Stuff one portion of the garlic-herb mixture into the pocket of each filet. Wrap a piece of pancetta around the side of each filet, covering the incision and leaving the top and bottom unwrapped. Tie the pancetta in place with butcher's twine.

Five minutes before the gratin is ready to come out of the oven, start cooking the filets. Season the filets with salt and pepper. In a sauté pan over high heat, heat a little olive oil until almost smoking. Sear the outside of each filet until golden brown. When you have removed the gratin from the oven, raise the temperature to 400°. Put the filets on a rack in a roasting pan and place in the oven. For medium-rare, cook for approximately 15 minutes, or until the internal temperature reaches 120°. Remove the filets from the oven, and take off the string.

To serve, place a filet on each plate and serve the gratin.

Turkey Ballottine with Prosciutto, Sage, and Roasted Root Vegetables

SERVES 8 TO 10

❧ WINE NOTES

To satisfy everyone's taste, it is traditional to serve both red and white wine at the Wente family Thanksgiving dinner. More importantly, it is not necessarily the turkey that you are trying to pair with the wine. The other side dishes, gravies, and stuffing may have the stronger flavors and intensity with which the wine needs to be paired. For a white wine, we usually serve a Sauvignon Blanc–Sémillon blend or a full-bodied Chardonnay—both providing enough flavor and weight. We generally tend toward a light to medium-bodied red wine with nice acid, balanced tannins, and rich fruit, such as a Pinot Noir or Merlot. Whatever you choose, remember that there is no one right answer to a melting pot of traditions and flavors.

The most difficult task of the Thanksgiving dinner is cooking the turkey. One part comes out perfectly while the other is dry, and it always takes so darned long. This recipe allows you to cook the turkey in about an hour and a half. The meat remains moist and evenly cooked. If you want to have dark meat too, you can use the whole turkey and roll it up in the same manner as the breast. It will take a little longer to cook, however. A rule of thumb to remember when cooking large pieces of meat or poultry is that the larger the piece you are cooking, the longer you cook it and the lower the cooking temperature. If you are having lots of guests and still want to prepare a traditional bird, cook one turkey the traditional way and add a few ballottines for ease of serving…and oven space.

> **1 boneless breast from a 10-pound turkey (about 6 pounds)**
> **Kosher salt and ground Szechuan peppercorns**
> **1 tablespoon chopped fresh sage leaves**
> **1 tablespoon chopped fresh parsley leaves**
> **12 very thin slices prosciutto**
>
> **ROASTED ROOT VEGETABLES**
> **2 red onions, peeled and quartered**
>   **(or 16 cipollini, if available, peeled and left whole)**
> **4 carrots, peeled and cut in half lengthwise**
> **2 turnips, peeled and cut in sixths**
> **4 parsnips, peeled and cut in half lengthwise**
> **2 tablespoons olive oil**
> **2 tablespoons apple cider vinegar**

To prepare the ballottine: Preheat the oven to 375°. Lay out the turkey breast on a flat surface with the skin side down. Pull the fillet (the piece that is loosely attached to the center of the breast on the opposite side from the skin) toward the middle of the breast so that it lays flat. Split open the large end of the turkey breast, while still keeping it attached to the rest of the breast, and lay next to the fillets. You should have a turkey breast that is roughly rectangular. Cover with plastic wrap and pound with a mallet until the surface is even and flat.

Season the flattened breast with kosher salt and Szechuan peppercorns. Sprinkle the surface with the chopped herbs. Cover with the prosciutto. Starting with the end closest to you, roll tightly into a cylinder and tie every 2 inches with butcher's twine. Season the outside with kosher salt and Szechuan peppercorns. Place in a roasting pan and bake for about 1^1/$_2$ hours, or until an internal temperature of 140° is reached.

To prepare the roasted vegetables: Toss the onions, carrots, turnips, and parsnips in the oil and vinegar. After the ballottine has been cooking for 45 minutes, add the vegetables to the roasting pan.

When the ballottine and vegetables are cooked, remove them from the oven. Let the turkey rest for 20 minutes, loosely covered with aluminum foil.

To serve, remove the strings from the turkey (scissors work best for this), slice, and serve with the roasted vegetables.

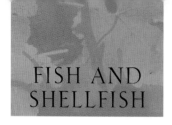

Seared Day Boat Scallops with Citrus-Scented Risotto and Mizuna

SERVES 4

🍷 WINE NOTES

Try a light to medium-bodied Chardonnay with hints of citrus and crisp apple and a buttery finish. The acid notes from the citrus and apple will pair nicely with the scallops and the creaminess of the risotto.

True day boat scallops are caught by fishing boats that return to port daily and dry-pack their scallops without adding water or preservatives. A common practice among scallop packers is to add as much as 25 percent water and a preservative called sodium tripolyphosphate. This prolongs the shelf life of the scallops but greatly diminishes their flavor. They also do not brown as nicely when sautéed. Most good fish markets carry day boat scallops. If you can't find mizuna, try spinach, arugula, or spicy mustard greens.

The best rice for risotto comes from the Po Valley in the Veneto region of Italy. The most well known is arborio, but you can make excellent risotto with vialone nano, baldo, and especially carnaroli rice. My favorite is carnaroli because of its short grain, firm texture, and high starch content. It makes the creamiest risotto while keeping the individual grains of rice firm and separate. Try to use stocks with little or no salt to keep the risotto from becoming overly salty during the long cooking.

1 tablespoon finely chopped lemon zest

1 tablespoon minced tangerine zest

1 tablespoon minced grapefruit zest

1 pound dry-pack day boat scallops

1 tablespoon extra-virgin olive oil

Kosher salt and freshly ground pepper

2 tablespoons olive oil

CITRUS-SCENTED RISOTTO

4 cups chicken stock (page 206), more if needed

1 tablespoon olive oil

1 tablespoon minced shallot

$1/2$ cup peeled, diced turnip

1 cup carnaroli or arborio rice

1 tablespoon lemon juice

1 tablespoon tangerine juice

1 tablespoon grapefruit juice

$1/2$ pound whole mizuna

To marinate the scallops: In a bowl, combine half the lemon, tangerine, and grapefruit zest. Add the scallops and the 1 tablespoon extra-virgin olive oil and toss gently. Marinate in the refrigerator for 30 minutes.

To prepare the risotto: In a saucepan, bring the stock to a boil. In a thick-bottomed pot over medium heat, heat the olive oil. Add the shallot and turnip and cook until translucent, about 5 minutes. Add the rice and cook, stirring often, until the rice is coated with the oil and starting to change color but is not brown. It should just start sticking to the bottom of the pot and make a little squealing sound. Season with a little salt. Add enough of the boiling stock to cover the rice by about $1/2$ inch. Once you start adding liquid, the risotto usually takes from 30 to 40 minutes to complete. Cook over medium-low heat, stirring often with a wooden spoon, until most of the stock is absorbed. Continue to add stock, stirring until it is nearly all absorbed. The rice should always be barely covered by stock and barely simmering. Taste as you go in order to prepare it to your preferred texture. I like mine with a little bite, but still cooked through. You need to add enough stock in the final phases of cooking so that a nice, medium-thick sauce is formed. Add the lemon, tangerine, and grapefruit juices. When the risotto is finished to your liking, stir in the remaining lemon, tangerine, and grapefruit zest.

To cook the scallops: About 5 minutes before the risotto is done, remove the scallops from the marinade and season with salt and pepper. In a sauté pan over high heat, heat the 2 tablespoons olive oil until very hot but not smoking. Add the scallops and cook on both sides until golden brown, 3 to 4 minutes per side.

To serve, stir the mizuna into the risotto. Divide among 4 bowls and top with the seared scallops.

"JUST ASK THE FISH MAN!"

In addition to supplying us with wonderful fresh ingredients, our vendors are also a source of information and new ideas. I always encourage home cooks to use their local merchants in the same way. The phrases that our grandmothers often used, "Just ask the butcher" or "Just ask the fish man" are as applicable today. Good suppliers are brimming with feedback from their sources plus their own experiences in their business and are more than willing to pass it on to you. Get to know these people—a personal relationship with a quality supplier will definitely help your culinary efforts.

The family-run Monterey Fish Market, a wholesale operation on Pier 33 in San Francisco and a retail storefront in Berkeley, is a perfect example. Over twenty years, they have built up a network of small, local fishermen, mostly day boat fishers, who are dedicated to providing the highest-quality fish and shellfish. Through the wholesale part of their operation, Tom Worthington and Paul Johnson fill the wide variety of requests they receive from chefs throughout the Bay Area with the freshest seasonal catch. Unlike the large, commercial fishing vessels, which stay out at sea for long periods of time and process and freeze each day's catch, the smaller day boats deliver their catch dockside daily, assuring fresher, higher-quality seafood for the consumer. Tom and Paul have a sixth sense when it comes to discerning the subtle differences in the day's catch, always searching for the last catch of the day. Tom says you could spend a day with him as he explained the differences in quality, such as a certain crispness to an edge, but there's more that can't be described. Somehow, he says, he just knows. It's the experience that I count on from him.

Monterey Fish Market's network of cottage industry fishers and suppliers around the world runs the gamut. There is the Boone family in North Carolina, who supply turtle-free shrimp by using nets that allow sea turtles to swim out the back. The absolutely best crabmeat in the world comes from MDI Shellfish near Bar

Harbor, Maine. David Smith, the owner, takes an immense amount of care in his efforts, and it is reflected in the quality of his crabmeat. Tom made contact with David through a company in Boston similar to Tom's. These are just a few of the connections made in Tom's and Paul's ongoing and ever-changing worldwide search.

Tom and Paul have seen a lot of change in the industry during their twenty-year history. One reason is the demand placed on the industry by culinary professionals for new and different tastes. Fish that ten years ago were viewed as trash fish are now on your table and in the finest restaurants. Trends in types of fish and in preparation techniques, such as blackened fish, have put pressure on suppliers. The present demand for fresh sardines hasn't been seen since the 1920s. Another influence that has really changed the game is transportation. These days, fresh fish can be flown almost anywhere in the world. Of course, the shipping costs are reflected in the price.

Tom figures that about 70 percent of the catch they sell is fished from the wild. The ability of these fish to roam the seas freely, feeding on a variety of sources, gives them superior flavor and texture. The remaining 30 percent is farm raised, using either aquaculture or mariculture. In aquaculture, the

environment, feed, health, and breeding of the fish are all controlled. The number of fish in the closed tanks is high, which necessitates the use of antibiotics. The color and flavor of the fish is controlled by the type of feed, which usually lacks variety. In mariculture, the only element that is controlled is the environment. There is no feeding or use of antibiotics. An example is an oyster farm, where the depth and location of the oysters is controlled, usually for ease in harvesting.

When asked what advice he would give the home cook, Tom has a quick and simple reply. "Don't be married to the type of fish called for in your recipe. Tell your fishmonger what you are doing, what type of fish you are using, how you are preparing it, and what ingredients you are using. Then be open to suggestions for a similar fish that is fresh that day. Use the best ingredients possible, what's in season. And if you don't know what's in season, just ask!"—KJ

Grilled Swordfish with Fall Herb Pesto and Cranberry Bean Stew

Cranberry beans are rather large, very meaty, and quite delicious. The bright, red-and-white streaked color adds a dramatic look to a dish. The key to cooking any dried bean is to presoak them in water and then cook very slowly. The slow cooking allows the beans to stay tender without breaking apart. Never add salt until the beans are cooked; this keeps the beans tender. You can substitute any big, meaty bean if you can't find cranberry beans. Scarlet runners would be good. You want to use a bean that will hold together and have some texture. Cranberry beans are very versatile—try them with chicken, lamb shanks, pork, or even steak.

FALL HERB PESTO
Leaves from 4 sprigs oregano (reserve stems for stew)
Leaves from 4 sprigs sage (reserve stems for stew)
Leaves from 4 sprigs parsley (reserve stems for stew)
1 tablespoon minced garlic
1 teaspoon finely chopped roasted hazelnuts (page 210)
1/2 cup olive oil
1 tablespoon grated aged Jack cheese
Kosher salt and freshly ground pepper

CRANBERRY BEAN STEW
1 cup dried cranberry beans, soaked in 4 times their volume of water (4 cups) for at least 8 hours
4 cups vegetable stock (page 205)
1/2 cup diced onion
1/2 cup diced carrot
1/2 cup diced fennel
2 tablespoons sliced garlic
Kosher salt and freshly ground pepper
2 cups thinly sliced savoy cabbage

4 (5-ounce) swordfish fillets
Olive oil for seasoning

To prepare the pesto: Place the oregano, sage, and parsley leaves in a blender or mini-chopper with the garlic, hazelnuts, and oil. Process until smooth. Add the cheese and season with salt and pepper to taste. Set aside.

To prepare the stew: Drain the water from the beans. In a pot, combine the beans, stock, onion, carrot, fennel, and garlic. Bring to a boil and lower the heat to a simmer. Tie the reserved oregano, sage, and parsley stems together with kitchen string and add to the beans. Cook until tender, about 1 hour. Season with salt and pepper. Remove the herb stems from the beans. Set aside.

To prepare the swordfish: Prepare a medium fire in your grill, or heat a cast-iron stovetop grill. Season the swordfish with salt and pepper. Rub with olive oil. Cook for 3 to 4 minutes per side, depending on the thickness of the swordfish. It should still be a little rare inside.

To serve, return the bean stew to a simmer. Add the cabbage and cook until just done, 1 to 2 minutes. Ladle the stew into large bowls, top with a grilled swordfish fillet, and drizzle with the herb pesto.

SUSTAINABLE AGRICULTURE

My grandfather always said that good wine came from good grapes and good grapes came from good soil. Since his time, the methods used to cultivate good soil have changed drastically. Throughout the 1950s and 1960s, farming practices were heavily influenced by a glowing view of technology. Millions of dollars of chemical fertilizers and soil amendments were used, as well as huge networks of aluminum pipe and irrigation systems. Over the past twenty years, we have dramatically revised our farming practices, exclusively employing the concepts of sustainable agriculture and organic farming in the cultivation of our 3,000 acres of vineyards as well as the

restaurant gardens. It's ironic that we are shifting back to the farming techniques practiced by my grandfather.

Unlike conventional agriculture, which is dependent upon pesticides, synthetic fertilizers, and fossil fuels, sustainable agriculture promotes healthy soils and systems through the development of alternative farming techniques. We look at the grapevines as part of a whole ecosystem, not just the monoculture of the traditional California vineyard. Because we are trying to foster an ecological balance, we manage the space between the vines just as carefully as we do the vines themselves. By cultivating native grasses and other beneficial plantings, we can promote the growth of organisms and natural systems that control pest infestations and promote healthy soil and vines that are naturally stronger and more resistant to pests and diseases. We have also planted fruit trees in the vineyards to encourage natural predators of leaf pests.

(continued on page 141)

139

Tuna Niçoise with Heirloom Tomatoes, Green and Yellow Beans, Roasted Potatoes, Olive Mayonnaise, and Garden Herbs

SERVES 4

🍂 WINE NOTES

This recipe is a challenge to pair with wine. Many of the ingredients are a difficult match or not particularly compatible with wine, such as vinegar, beans, and olives. Sauvignon Blanc again comes to the fore as having many of the same harmonic flavors in its spectrum, along with good acid. A Pinot Grigio also has good acidity to balance the dressing and fruitiness that will stand up to the vegetables. Both of these wines are excellent with tuna and will contrast with it nicely. To complement the flavors, try a slightly chilled, light to medium-bodied Pinot Noir.

Fresh tuna and good tomatoes elevate this dish from the ordinary to the exquisite. I like to make this salad in late summer through early fall, when the tomatoes and beans are at their peak.

1 pound whole Yukon Gold creamer-sized
   (1¹/₂ inches diameter) potatoes

2 tablespoons olive oil

Kosher salt and freshly ground pepper

1 teaspoon lemon juice

1 teaspoon finely chopped lemon zest

¹/₂ pound yellow wax beans

¹/₂ pound Blue Lake beans (or other green beans)

2 tablespoons extra-virgin olive oil

VINAIGRETTE

2 tablespoons red wine vinegar

1 teaspoon minced shallot

¹/₂ teaspoon Dijon mustard

2 tablespoons extra-virgin olive oil

2 tablespoons olive oil

4 (5-ounce) portions fresh ahi tuna

2 tablespoons olive oil

4 large heirloom tomatoes such as Brandywine, Marvel Stripe,
   or Evergreen, cored and cut into wedges

¹/₂ pound organic mixed salad greens

Basic Mayonnaise (page 207)

2 tablespoons pitted, minced niçoise olives

To prepare the potatoes: Preheat the oven to 350°. Warm a baking sheet in the oven while it is preheating. This helps prevent the potatoes from sticking to the sheet. In a bowl, toss the potatoes in the olive oil, season with salt and pepper, and place on the warmed baking sheet. Roast for 30 to 40 minutes, or until tender when pierced with a knife. Turn potatoes with a spatula halfway through the cooking time. Remove from the oven and toss with the lemon juice and finely chopped lemon zest. Set aside.

To prepare the beans: Bring a large pot of highly salted water to a boil, using approximately 2 tablespoons salt per quart of water. Add the beans and cook until tender but still a little crisp, about 5 minutes. Drain and toss with extra-virgin olive oil. Set aside. Refrigerate them if you are not going to use them in the next 30 minutes.

To prepare the vinaigrette: In a bowl, combine the red wine vinegar, shallot, and mustard. Slowly add the oils.

To sauté the tuna: Season the tuna with salt and pepper. In a sauté pan over high heat, heat the 2 tablespoons of olive oil. When hot, add the tuna and cook for a few minutes on each side. Drain on paper towels.

Prepare the mayonnaise and mix in the olives.

To serve, toss the tomatoes and greens with the vinaigrette and divide among 4 plates. Arrange the potatoes and beans around the outsides of the plates. Place a piece of ahi on top of the greens and tomatoes. Top with some of the olive mayonnaise. Put the rest in a bowl on the table and pass it around.

MORE ABOUT SUSTAINABLE AGRICULTURE

(continued from page 139)

The native grasses and other beneficial plantings down the middle of our rows are plowed under near the vine rootstock, a technique called French plowing. This removes weed growth from under the vines. The shade from the vine canopy also discourages the growth of weeds close to the vines, which would compete for nutrients and moisture. The summer grasses are allowed to reseed themselves in the middle of the rows. Water usage is a very important political and economic issue in California, and we are working to reduce the amount of water needed by the vines. Adding organic matter to the coarse, gravelly soil dramatically increases water retention and reduces the need for irrigation by as much as 25 percent. The organic matter is added to the soil in two ways. Under state law, California cities are now required to pick up and separate lawn cuttings, brush, and other vegetation from ordinary waste materials. We are recycling green waste collected by the city of San Jose by putting it through a mulching process and tilling it directly into the vineyard soil. We also mix this green waste with grape pomace, the residual mixture of grape skins, stems, and seeds left over after pressing, and then compost it, breaking down the organic matter into a nutrient-rich organic plant food. Many wineries use their grape pomace, but we found that composting it with green waste greatly increases the available nutrients. These organic soil amendments strengthen the vines and their innate ability to fight pests.

In the words of Ralph Riva, our passionate head of agricultural operations, "We create 'living soil'—soil that nourishes itself. We consider ourselves stewards of the land, with our goal being to create vineyards that will not only endure, but improve over time. We seek to accomplish this in a way that preserves the viability of the land for future generations." —CW

Dungeness Crab Cakes
with Fried Caper and Lemon Aioli

SERVES 4

🦀 WINE NOTES

My fondest recollections of eating Dungeness crab are from the Tadich Grill, one of the oldest and most famous seafood eateries in San Francisco. The Tadich Grill is owned and operated by the Buich family, who have been Wente family friends for four generations. My grandfather and great-uncle told stories of delivering wine in large barrels known as puncheons from our Livermore Valley vineyards to the restaurant in San Francisco by horse and wagon. Once at the restaurant, they would roll the barrels down into the Tadich Grill basement below the street. This wine was a classic medium-bodied white with moderate fruit and a crisp, clean finish. Known as Grey Riesling, it would be chilled and served to the patrons with their seafood. Today, many native Californians tell me that their first wine experiences were with Wente Grey Riesling and they have pleasant memories of it served with seafood dishes. We no longer produce a Grey Riesling. I highly recommend a Sémillon–Sauvignon Blanc blend with these crab cakes.

Some of my best eating memories involve Dungeness crab, a good loaf of sourdough bread, and a crisp white wine. Eating a whole crab is messy but well worth the effort. This recipe makes it easy to enjoy the essence of the crab without all of the mess. You can use other types of crabmeat if Dungeness is not available. If you can only get frozen or "previously frozen" crab in your area, make sure that it is well drained before combining it with the other ingredients.

CRAB CAKES

1 pound fresh Dungeness crabmeat

1 Granny Smith apple, peeled, cored, and finely diced

1/4 cup chopped cilantro leaves

1 jalapeño, seeded and finely diced

1 egg

1 tablespoon lemon juice

1 teaspoon finely chopped lemon zest

About 1/2 cup fresh bread crumbs

Kosher salt and freshly ground pepper

2 tablespoons peanut oil, more as needed

Fried Caper and Lemon Aioli (page 208)

To prepare the crab cakes: Carefully run your hands through the crabmeat and remove any pieces of shell you find. Squeeze out as much liquid as you can from the crab.

In a bowl, combine the crab, apple, cilantro, jalapeño, egg, lemon juice, and finely chopped lemon zest. Add enough bread crumbs to bind the mixture. Season with salt and pepper to taste.

In a large frying pan over medium-high heat, heat the peanut oil until almost smoking and cook a small sample cake. Adjust the seasonings if necessary.

Divide the remaining crab mixture into 8 portions and form into cakes. Cook in the hot peanut oil until each side is golden brown, 4 to 5 minutes per side.

To serve, top each crab cake with a spoonful of the aioli and serve immediately.

Olive Oil, Late-Harvest Riesling, and Pear Cake

This cake was inspired by a wonderful olive oil and Sauternes cake made at Chez Panisse Restaurant in Berkeley. (The original recipe is in the *Chez Panisse Menu Cookbook*.) I first developed this recipe for a cooking class devoted to olive oil. Every recipe in the class featured olive oil in a different way. Try to find a fruity, spicy extra-virgin oil for this recipe. Of course, I highly recommend the Wente Vineyards Oro Fino. This cake is best the day it is made.

2 French Butter pears, peeled, cored, and diced

1 cup late-harvest Riesling

6 extra-large eggs, separated

3/4 cup granulated sugar

1 tablespoon plus 1 teaspoon finely chopped lemon zest

1 teaspoon kosher salt

1 1/2 cups sifted cake flour

1/2 cup extra-virgin olive oil

1/2 cup crème fraîche (page 199)

Sugar to taste

In a nonreactive saucepan over medium heat, combine the pears and the Riesling. Cook until soft, about 20 minutes. Cool and purée.

Preheat the oven to 375°. In a mixing bowl, combine the egg yolks and sugar, and beat until pale. Add the finely chopped lemon zest. In another bowl, combine the salt and flour. Slowly add the flour and pear-Riesling mixtures to the eggs and sugar, alternating between the two. Make sure that each addition is fully blended before adding the next. Beat in the olive oil.

Line the bottom of a 9-inch springform pan with parchment paper and liberally coat the sides with butter. In a shallow bowl, whip the egg whites to soft peaks. Gently fold them into the batter, a third at a time. Pour the batter into the springform pan, place in the oven, and bake for 15 minutes. Lower the temperature to 325° and cover the top of the cake with a round piece of parchment paper so that the top does not brown too much. Bake 15 to 20 minutes more, or until a toothpick comes out clean when pushed into the center of the cake. Turn the oven off and let the cake sit for another 15 minutes before removing it. Cool on a rack.

To serve, whip the crème fraîche with sugar to taste. Top each piece of cake with the sweetened crème fraîche. Serve immediately.

MAKES ONE 9-INCH CAKE

❧ WINE NOTES

In California we use the term "late harvest" to refer to a wine grape that has been picked late, giving it a higher sugar content, and then made into a sweet dessert-style wine. There are varying degrees of sweetness in a late-harvest wine. In this recipe, serve the wine you cooked with, because it will have the same degree of sweetness as the cake, creating a perfect balance.

OLIVE OIL

When I was a young girl, my daily walk to the school bus would take me down the dirt road that meandered through the vines between my grandparents' home and ours. The cool, shady part, flanked by a colonnade of gnarled olive trees, was always my favorite. Historically, my family has pressed the fruit of these trees, which were brought from France and Spain in the 1800s, in the French tradition—in keeping with the trees' heritage. The resulting olive oil was smooth and buttery. More recently, under the direction of Antonio Zaccheo, whose family has tended olive trees in Tuscany for 200 years, we have shifted to producing oils in the Tuscan tradition—very lively, spicy, and peppery, with flavors of fresh peas and

almonds. What I find amazing is that our primarily French trees can produce an olive oil in the peppery Tuscan tradition, all due to the growing, harvesting, and processing techniques. We have only two trees that are recognized as an Italian variety!

In the words of Antonio, we are practicing a bit of a paradigm shift when harvesting the olives for our artisanal oils. We harvest them by variety, picking only when the olives are at the level of ripeness we want. We may pick only one branch on a tree on a particular day. It seems simple enough, but a commercial grower wouldn't be able to take this much time. This also helps the tree by allowing it to have more energy to ripen the remaining fruit.

Antonio waits for a certain level of ripeness as the green olives mature to black. Selecting the harvesting times is very much an art. One year, our first harvest was on October 23. The final picking was December 4. Between these two dates, a total of eight days were selected as optimal for harvesting about 150 trees. The oil from the earlier, greener batches has a wonderful spicy, peppery flavor but a lower yield. Toward the end of the harvest, the flavor of the riper olives becomes more mellow and buttery, losing its spiciness. But it has much more body—and these riper olives have a much higher yield. The different harvestings are kept separately, and pressed separately, too. Then, in the early

spring, we taste the varied flavors of the pressings and decide on a final blend, producing a well-balanced, flavorful oil.

Just as there are wines that pair well with certain foods, there are olive oils that are appropriate for certain dishes. If you are going to sauté onions or lots of garlic in olive oil, don't waste the flavors of a finely produced oil. Use the best oils in a vinaigrette, and let the wonderful flavors of the olive oil stand on their own. Don't overdo the garlic or heavy herbs. If you are going to drizzle it over steamed vegetables, use the best oil you can find.

Think of it as salt and pepper—the final flavoring. In Antonio's words, "Try a baked potato with a finely flavored olive oil instead of butter. The taste will be right next to heaven. There is nothing more delicious." —CW

Antonio Zaccheo and Kimball tasting first pressings.

Red Wine–Poached Pears with Rum Raisin Ice Cream and Almond Tulip Cookies

SERVES 4

❧ WINE NOTES

I like to serve a wine similar to the one I used for poaching. If I used a Zinfandel, I would try to find a late-harvest Zinfandel with a good amount of residual sugar (around 5 to 10 percent) to serve. Another way to go is to cut back on the amount of sugar used in the poaching liquid, making the dish more wine friendly. This would allow you to serve a regular Zinfandel with this dessert.

The texture of the tulip cookie dough resembles a paste, and it can be shaped into many different forms. You can make shapes like grape leaves, stars, and strips by cutting a stencil of your design from very thin cardboard, placing the stencil on the baking sheet, and spreading the dough inside the stencil onto the pan. Remove the stencil before baking. The dough is also very malleable right out of the oven and can be formed into any shape you want. One-inch strips can be wrapped around dowels to form swirly sticks. If the cookie starts to stiffen before you have time to form it, pop it back into the oven for a few seconds and try again.

In this recipe, I use a peeler to remove the skin of the citrus when flavoring the poaching liquid. It is much easier to remove the pears from the liquid when little bits of zest are not clinging to them.

RED WINE–POACHED PEARS

3 cups plus 2 1/2 tablespoons red wine (1 bottle)

3 cups water

Juice and peel of 1 lemon

Juice and peel of 1 lime

Juice and peel of 1 orange

12 whole cloves

2 cinnamon sticks

1 cup granulated sugar

4 pears, peeled, cored, and cut in half

RUM RAISIN ICE CREAM

1 cup heavy whipping cream

1 cup rum, reduced to 1/3 cup

4 egg yolks

1/2 cup granulated sugar

1 cup milk

1 cup raisins

ALMOND TULIP COOKIES

5 tablespoons plus 1 1/2 teaspoons confectioners' sugar

2 egg whites

1/4 cup all-purpose flour

2 tablespoons unsalted butter, melted

2 tablespoons sliced toasted almonds (page 210)

To prepare the poached pears: In a nonreactive pan, combine the wine, water, citrus juice and strips of peel, cloves, and cinnamon sticks. Add the sugar and stir to dissolve it in the liquids. Add the pear halves, bring to a boil, remove from heat, and let stand until cool. Let the pears macerate in the liquid for at least a couple of hours.

If the pears are very ripe, they will overcook using this method. In this case, bring the pears to a boil in the liquid and remove them when they are still slightly crunchy. Chill the pears and the liquid separately. When chilled, recombine the pears and the liquid and let them sit for a couple of hours in the refrigerator.

To prepare the ice cream: In a nonreactive pot, bring the cream to a boil. Remove from the heat and add the rum. Let steep for 30 minutes. In another bowl, blend the egg yolks and sugar together until smooth. Continue as described in the ice cream recipe on page 199. Freeze in an ice cream machine. Halfway through the freezing, add the raisins.

To prepare the cookies: In a nonreactive mixing bowl, whisk the sugar and egg whites together until smooth. Add the flour and continue to mix until all of the flour has been blended in and the batter is smooth. Slowly blend in the melted butter. Chill.

Preheat the oven to 350°. On the back of a baking sheet, parchment paper, or a nonstick baking sheet, spread the batter out to form 4- to 5-inch circles. I use a small, thin offset spatula. Make the cookies as thin as you can. Sprinkle almonds on each cookie and bake for 6 to 7 minutes, or until very lightly browned. With an offset metal spatula, remove the cookies from the baking sheet and shape. The dough will be very pliable while it is warm, but you must be quick. I like to shape them into L shapes over a counter edge or a rolling pin. Cool. The cookies will harden and retain their shape.

This recipe makes more than enough batter. However, I always seem to overcook or break a few of these delicate cookies, so a little extra is helpful. You can keep any remaining dough for 1 week.

To serve, reduce 2 cups of poaching liquid down to $1/4$ cup in a nonreactive pot. You will use this as a sauce.

Pool a tablespoon of the sauce on each plate and lay a cookie in the sauce with the "leg" of the L in the air. Slice each pear half 5 or 6 times lengthwise, but don't cut all the way through the top (where the stem was), then fan it out with the top resting against the vertical side of the cookie. Place a scoop of ice cream next to the pear on the cookie.

Oatmeal Cookie Sandwich
with Sautéed Apples and Ice Cream

At the restaurant, we always have this cookie dough on hand for Carolyn and her mother, Jean. We start baking the cookies when we hear they have walked into the restaurant! The uncooked dough will keep quite well in the freezer if you have any left over. These cookies are chewy, not cakey.

OATMEAL COOKIES

1 1/4 cups brown sugar

1 cup granulated sugar

1 cup unsalted butter, at room temperature

2 eggs

1 tablespoon plus 1 teaspoon vanilla extract

1 1/2 cups all-purpose flour

1 teaspoon baking soda

1 teaspoon kosher salt

2 1/2 cups old-fashioned rolled oats

3/4 cup raisins

2 tablespoons butter

2 large Granny Smith apples, peeled, cored, and thinly sliced

2 tablespoons maple syrup

4 large scoops vanilla ice cream

To prepare the cookies: Cream the sugars and butter together until light and fluffy. Add the eggs and vanilla and mix until well blended. In another mixing bowl, sift together the flour, baking soda, and salt, then combine with the oats and raisins. Add the combined dry ingredients to the egg-butter mixture. Blend well. Place the dough on a piece of plastic wrap and roll the wrap around the dough. Form into a 2-inch cylinder. Tighten the wrap at the ends and refrigerate for 30 minutes.

Preheat the oven to 350°. Remove the dough from the refrigerator, unwrap, and slice into 1/2-inch-thick rounds. Place on a greased baking sheet about 2 inches apart and bake until golden brown, 8 to 10 minutes. Cool.

To prepare the apples: In a sauté pan over medium heat, warm the butter until it starts to bubble. Add the apples and cook for about 5 minutes, or until they just begin to soften. Stir often. Add the maple syrup and bring to a simmer. Remove from the heat.

To serve, place a cookie on each of 4 plates. Place a big scoop of ice cream on top of each cookie. Divide the apples among the plates, spooning them over the ice cream. Top with another cookie and serve immediately.

SERVES 4

WINE NOTES

I would recommend a sauterne-style dessert wine—a late-harvest wine made from a blend of sauvignon blanc and sémillon grapes. This wine would have a higher residual sugar content that would pair nicely with the flavors enhanced by the Granny Smith apples. Unlike most white wines, white dessert wines have the ability to age well past the vintage date on their bottles, some for 10 to 15 years.

Chocolate Pecan Tart
with Maple Cream

Our executive pastry chef, Chris Draa, made this recipe for me when he first
tried out for the job. I liked it so much I hired him. I buy my chocolate in
big blocks and coarsely chop it into 1/2-inch chunks. You can use different
nuts, such as almonds, hazelnuts, or walnuts, instead of the pecans, and you
can even use white chocolate instead of dark. This tart should be made the
day before serving to assure that the chunks of chocolate will harden. After
it has been made it also freezes well. You can make the filling and pie dough
4 to 5 days in advance.

1/4 recipe sweet pie dough (page 201)

TART FILLING

1 1/4 cups heavy whipping cream

1 cup plus 1 tablespoon granulated sugar

1/2 cup water

3/4 cup toasted pecans (page 210)

3/4 cup coarsely chopped semisweet chocolate
   (about 1/2-inch chunks)

2 large eggs

1 large egg yolk

1 tablespoon unsalted butter

1 teaspoon vanilla extract

1/2 cup heavy whipping cream

2 tablespoons maple syrup

To prepare the tart shell: Roll out the pie dough about 1/4 inch thick
and use it to line a 9-inch tart tin. Set aside in the refrigerator for at least
30 minutes.

When ready to bake the shell, preheat the oven to 350°. Remove it from
the refrigerator, line with parchment paper or waxed paper, and fill with
beans or rice. Bake the shell for 10 to 15 minutes, until blond in color. It
should be cooked through but not brown at all. (This is called blind baking.)
Remove from the oven and take out the beans. If you are going to proceed
with the recipe, leave the oven at 350°.

To prepare the tart filling: In a small saucepan, bring the cream to a
boil and set aside. This helps the blending of the cream into the caramel. If
the cream were cold, the caramel would seize up.

In a medium saucepan, dissolve the sugar in the water. This helps prevent lumps. Cook over medium-high heat until the color becomes a rich caramel hue. Remove from the heat and slowly add the heated cream, a little at a time. Be careful when first adding the cream as the mixture will bubble up. Return to the heat and cook, stirring continuously, for another 3 minutes. Remove from the heat and cool for 15 minutes.

Fill the baked shell with the pecans and chopped chocolate.

Add the eggs, egg yolk, butter, and vanilla to the caramel mixture, stirring in with a few quick strokes. Pour into the pie shell, covering the pecans and chocolate. Return to the 350° oven and bake until the caramel has set, about 30 minutes. Cool.

To serve, whip the cream and maple syrup together until it forms soft peaks. Serve each piece with a dollop of maple cream.

WINTER

STARTERS

WINE NOTES

Serve a light-bodied Pinot Noir with a nice fruity, floral character and ample acidity to balance the Tangelo-Currant Relish. A simple, straightforward Gamay with full, identifiable flavors, lighter alcohol, and clean acidity would also do nicely with this recipe.

Muscovy Duck Rillettes
with Tangelo-Currant Relish

Traditionally, rillettes have a fairly high proportion of fat to meat, with some pork fat added as well. This recipe adds in a bit of fat from the duck but relies on the reduced cooking stock for flavor and moistness.

> 2 duck leg-thighs, about 1 pound total
> Kosher salt and freshly ground pepper
> 2 sprigs fresh thyme
> 2 tablespoons tangelo juice
> 2 cups chicken stock (page 206)
> 1 teaspoon ground coriander
> 1/4 cup Madeira
>
> TANGELO-CURRANT RELISH
> 2 tangelos
> 1 tablespoon granulated sugar
> 1 tablespoon champagne vinegar
> 2 tablespoons dried currants
> 1 baguette
> Extra-virgin olive oil
> 1 tablespoon chopped fresh chervil leaves or fresh parsley leaves

To prepare the rillettes: Preheat the oven to 350°. Remove the skin and fat from the duck. In a small sauté pan over very low heat, cook (render) the skin and fat for about 1/2 hour. You will use a little of this fat for the rillettes.

While the skin and fat are rendering, season the duck with salt and pepper. Place in a small ovenproof pot or roasting pan with the thyme, tangelo juice, chicken stock, coriander, and Madeira. Bring to a simmer on top of the stove, cover, and place in the oven. Braise for 1 1/2 hours, until very tender.

Remove the meat from the liquid and cool. Strain the braising liquid into a saucepan. Bring to a simmer and cook at a low simmer until very thick and syrupy, about 1/2 hour. Cool.

Remove the duck meat from the bones. Shred it by pulling the meat apart into thin strips. Combine with the reduced braising liquid and 1 tablespoon of the rendered duck fat. Taste for seasoning.

To prepare the relish: Peel the tangelos and trim off the white skin, exposing the flesh. With a small paring knife, cut out the sections from each tangelo, leaving the membrane. Squeeze the remaining juice from the membrane. In a nonreactive saucepan, combine the juice, sugar, and vinegar.

Bring to a simmer and cook until slightly thickened, about 10 minutes. Combine with the tangelo segments and currants. Set aside.

Slice the baguette into $^1/_4$-inch rounds. Brush with extra-virgin olive oil and toast.

To serve, spoon a teaspoon of the duck mixture onto each toast. Top with a little tangelo-currant relish. Sprinkle with chopped chervil and serve.

Pacific Oysters on the Half Shell with Meyer Lemon–Fennel Seed Mignonette

Oysters, like most shellfish, are one of the blessings of fall and winter. I love the briny, juicy, fresh flavors washed down with a crisp white wine. The old saying that you should eat oysters only in months with an R in them still holds true. (I suppose some people may eat oysters flown in from the Southern Hemisphere in summer, but I find them a bit jet-lagged.) The main reason for eating oysters when it is cold outside has to do with the temperature of the water they grow in. When the waters become warm the oysters start to spawn, leading to a flabby taste and the increased possibility of food-borne illness in the oysters. When purchasing oysters, I always ask the fish purveyors what the best ones are that day because they usually have eaten them for breakfast. I like medium-sized oysters (about $2^1/_2$ to 3 inches long) with tightly closed shells.

MIGNONETTE

1 teaspoon Meyer lemon juice

$^1/_2$ teaspoon finely chopped Meyer lemon zest

$^1/_4$ teaspoon freshly cracked black pepper

$^1/_8$ teaspoon freshly cracked fennel seed

2 teaspoons Sauvignon Blanc

$^1/_2$ teaspoon minced shallot

1 teaspoon champagne vinegar

24 oysters, shucked (page 210)

To prepare the mignonette: Combine the lemon juice, finely chopped lemon zest, pepper, fennel seed, wine, shallot, and vinegar in a small bowl.

To serve, arrange the opened oysters on the half shell on a platter spread with cracked ice or rock salt. Place the mignonette in a small bowl in the center with a small spoon. I spoon some mignonette on the oyster and slurp it down.

SERVES 4

⅏ WINE NOTES

Many of California's white wine grape varieties were brought over from the great wine regions of France. Several of these French regions are along the coast or just inland, where seafood is an important part of their cuisine. These areas produce predominantly Sauvignon Blanc, Muscadet, and Chenin Blanc; all are exquisite paired with shellfish. Their lightness of character, snap of acidity, and clean flavor complement the simplicity of raw oysters. These same wine varietals in California can be relied upon as good pairings with our own Pacific oysters.

Wild Mushroom Flatbread with Prosciutto, Arugula, and Truffle Oil

MAKES 16 TO 20
HORS D'OEUVRES

☙ WINE NOTES

Because of the mushrooms and truffle oil, I immediately think of the distinctive earthiness of a Pinot Noir. The medium body and weight has a seriousness to it but is not too filling for a starter.

Yes, truffle oil is expensive, but you only need a little bit. It elevates the flavors of this flatbread to another level. If you cannot find wild mushrooms, try using portobellos. To clean most wild mushrooms (except morels), just brush the dirt and small twigs off of them with a clean towel or soft brush. Don't use water, as they are like little sponges and their flavor will be lost.

$^1/_2$ recipe pizza dough (page 203)

Extra-virgin olive oil

Kosher salt and freshly ground pepper

Crushed red pepper flakes

$^1/_4$ pound wild mushrooms (such as chanterelle, hedgehog, or porcini), thinly sliced

$^1/_4$ cup finely shredded Parmesan cheese

2 teaspoons white truffle oil, or as much as you can afford

1 teaspoon finely chopped lemon zest

1 teaspoon chopped fresh flat-leaf parsley

1 teaspoon chopped fresh oregano leaves

6 very thin slices prosciutto

ARUGULA

1 tablespoon lemon juice

1 teaspoon minced shallot

3 tablespoons extra-virgin olive oil

2 cups arugula

To make the flatbreads: Prepare the oven for pizza as described on page 204, and preheat to 550°.

On a floured surface, divide the dough into 2 pieces. Roll each piece out very thinly to approximately 12 to 14 inches in diameter. Drizzle with olive oil and sprinkle with salt, pepper, and chile flakes to taste. Spread the mushrooms evenly over the 2 pieces. Dust with shredded Parmesan.

Place the flatbreads on a baking sheet or pizza stone in the preheated oven. After a few minutes, use the tip of a sharp knife to burst any really large bubbles that have formed. Continue to bake until golden brown, 5 to 7 minutes longer. Remove from the oven.

To prepare the arugula: While the flatbread is baking, whisk together the lemon juice, shallot, and olive oil in a bowl. Add the arugula and toss.

To serve, drizzle the flatbreads with truffle oil and sprinkle with finely chopped lemon zest, parsley, and oregano. Cover the entire surface of the flatbreads with the sliced prosciutto. Cut into wedges. Arrange the arugula on top of the wedges. Serve immediately.

Mussels with Lemon–Fennel Butter

These mussels make a very quick, easy-to-do hors d'oeuvre. If you want to serve the mussels in bowls as a first course, you can simply add the Lemon-Fennel Butter to the cooking liquid after you have removed the mussels, reduce it a little, and then pour it back over the mussels. When selecting mussels, avoid those with broken shells. Smaller mussels are more tender and sweeter than the larger ones.

1 pound mussels (30 to 40)

1 tablespoon minced shallot

1/2 cup white wine

LEMON-FENNEL BUTTER

1 teaspoon olive oil

1 tablespoon finely diced fennel bulb (reserve tops for garnish)

2 tablespoons Pernod

1/2 teaspoon lemon juice

1/2 teaspoon finely chopped lemon zest

1/4 teaspoon ground fennel seed

1/4 cup unsalted butter, at room temperature

Kosher salt and freshly ground pepper

To prepare the mussels: Scrub the shells with a scrub pad and pull out the beard that the mussel uses to attach itself to rocks. Discard any mussels that don't stay closed when pressed shut.

In a pot large enough to hold all of the mussels, combine the shallot and wine. Bring to a boil and add the mussels. Cover and cook, shaking, until all of the mussels open, 5 to 7 minutes. Strain out the mussels and cool.

When cool, separate the two half shells of each mussel, put a mussel in one half, and place on a baking sheet. Set aside. Discard the unused shell halves.

To prepare the Lemon-Fennel Butter: In a small saucepan over high heat, heat the olive oil. Add the fennel and cook, stirring, for 1 minute. Add the Pernod and stir, scraping up the browned bits from the bottom of the pan. Flame off the alcohol, as described on page 209. Remove from the heat and cool.

Blend the fennel-Pernod mixture with the lemon juice, finely chopped lemon zest, fennel seed, and butter. Season to taste with salt and pepper.

To serve, preheat the broiler. Place a small dab of Lemon-Fennel Butter on each mussel. Broil until they just begin to sizzle. Top each with a small sprig of fennel and serve immediately.

SERVES 4

WINE NOTES

Of course, serve the wine in which you cooked the mussels. Kimball recommends a stainless steel–fermented dry white. A crisp, clean Chardonnay with no oak would pair well; one with some oakiness would be too overpowering for the mussels. Or try a brut sparkling wine, which has many of the same attributes but adds some effervescence.

Rosemary–Skewered Chicken Livers
on Crispy Polenta

SERVES 4

🎮 WINE NOTES

The polenta adds a soft, creamy texture but only a subtle flavor, so the wine pairing focuses on the rich and full-flavored chicken livers. Either a white or red wine will work. The white wine needs to be a rich, complex Chardonnay or Pinot Blanc. The red can be a medium-bodied wine, ripe in fruit with a hint of herbal character. Try a Merlot or Cabernet.

We always get a lot of requests for this dish in the restaurant, even when it's not listed on the daily menu. It's simple and satisfying—qualities of the best comfort foods. Other types of livers, such as duck, rabbit, and squab, also work well in this recipe.

8 chicken livers

1 tablespoon balsamic vinegar

1/4 cup olive oil

1 teaspoon minced garlic

1 recipe creamy polenta (page 204)

4 (5-inch-long) rosemary sprigs

2 cups chicken stock, reduced to 1 cup (page 206)

Kosher salt and freshly ground pepper

1 tablespoon chopped fresh flat-leaf parsley, for garnish (optional)

Clean the livers of any blood or connecting tissue. In a bowl, combine the livers, balsamic vinegar, 2 tablespoons of the olive oil, and garlic. Marinate in the refrigerator for at least 1 hour (longer if possible).

Prepare the polenta and put it into a 4 1/2 by 8 1/2-inch loaf pan. Cool until set.

Remove the leaves from the bottom half of the rosemary sprigs. Skewer the livers with the sprigs, placing 2 on each sprig. Set aside.

Make a small fire in your barbecue.

Cut the cooled polenta into 2 squares. Cut the squares in half, corner to corner, forming triangles.

In a sauté pan over medium-high heat, heat the remaining 2 tablespoons olive oil. Add the polenta, lower the heat to medium, and cook until golden brown. Turn and brown the second side.

Warm the reduced chicken stock.

When the fire is ready, season the chicken livers with salt and pepper to taste, and grill, turning once, until cooked through, 8 to 10 minutes total.

To serve, place a piece of polenta on each plate. Lean the skewered chicken livers on the polenta with the leafy end of the rosemary sprig sticking up. Spoon the reduced chicken stock over the livers and sprinkle with chopped parsley.

Flageolet Bean Soup
with Pancetta and Rosemary Oil

SERVES 4

WINE NOTES

When trying to imagine what wine you should select, think of the texture as well as the weight of the finished soup in your mouth. Since this soup has a thicker texture and more weight, choose a "richer" wine, such as a medium to full-bodied Chardonnay or a Meritage white wine (a blend of Sauvignon Blanc and Sémillon) that has been barrel aged.

Long cooking at low temperature is the key to good beans. I especially like flageolet beans because they get creamy without falling apart. Sort them by spreading on a baking sheet and removing any stones and discolored beans. Soak them overnight (or for at least 8 hours) in 4 times their volume of cold water. Discard any that float to the top. Always salt the beans when they are just about done cooking. This allows them to absorb the seasoning. If seasoned too early in the cooking process, beans tend to get tough. You can omit the pancetta and use vegetable stock to make a vegetarian soup. The crispy texture of the pancetta does add a nice texture, so you might try adding some fried julienned carrots instead.

2 tablespoons olive oil

1 cup diced carrot (1/4-inch dice)

1 cup diced onion (1/4-inch dice)

1 tablespoon thinly sliced sundried tomato (not packed in oil)

1 cup cleaned, thinly sliced leek, white part only

1/2 cup celery root (1/4-inch dice)

2 cups dried flageolet beans, soaked for 8 hours or overnight

4 cups chicken stock (or vegetable stock), more as needed (page 206)

4 sprigs rosemary

1/2 teaspoon black peppercorns

1 bay leaf

Kosher salt and freshly ground pepper

1/4 cup extra-virgin olive oil

1/2 pound pancetta (1/4-inch dice)

1/4 cup grated Parmigiano-Reggiano cheese

To prepare the soup: In a 4-quart stockpot over medium heat, heat the olive oil. Add the carrot and onion and cook for 10 minutes, stirring often. Do not brown. Add the sundried tomato, leek, and celery root and cook for another 5 minutes. Add the drained beans and chicken stock. Remove the leaves from the rosemary and reserve. Place the rosemary stems in a piece of cheesecloth with the peppercorns and bay leaf. Tie into a bag and add to the pot. Bring the mixture to a simmer and cook at a low simmer until the beans are tender, about 1 1/2 hours. You may need to add more stock, as these beans absorb a lot of liquid. The soup should be thick but not stewlike. Season with salt and pepper to taste.

To prepare the oil: While the soup is cooking, in a small sauté pan over medium heat, combine half of the rosemary leaves with the extra-virgin olive oil and heat until just warm. The leaves will start to sizzle. Remove from the heat and let steep for 1 to 2 hours. Strain. Finely chop the remaining rosemary leaves and add to the oil.

To prepare the pancetta: Heat a sauté pan over medium heat. Add the pancetta. Cook, stirring often, until crispy, about 10 minutes. Drain onto paper towels.

To serve, divide the soup among 4 bowls. Sprinkle some of the pancetta and Parmigiano-Reggiano over each bowl, and drizzle with rosemary oil.

Roasted Beet and Blood Orange Salad

When I was growing up, I never really liked beets. They came in cans and didn't have much flavor. I changed my mind when we started making this salad in the restaurant. The acid of the blood orange and vinegar is the perfect foil for the sweet beets. Be very careful when you work with beets, as the juice stains everything it touches. We use plastic hospital gloves to protect our hands and aprons to shield our clothes.

3 beets

4 blood oranges

1 tablespoon blood orange juice

1 tablespoon plus 1 teaspoon champagne vinegar

1 tablespoon extra-virgin olive oil

Kosher salt and freshly ground pepper

Whole leaves from 2 heads butter lettuce

SERVES 4

WINE NOTES

This is a challenging salad to pair with wine because of the sweetness in the beets. Blood oranges reduce the sweetness a bit, but you need a wine with some residual sugar, a good crispness, and the fruit of a red wine. Try a rosé for a pleasant surprise.

Preheat the oven to 350°.

Trim the tops from the beets and put the beets in a small roasting pan deep enough to hold them. Add 1/2 inch of water and cover with aluminum foil. Place in the oven and roast for about 1 hour, or until the beets are cooked through. Check by piercing with a sharp knife.

Remove from the oven and let cool for about 1/2 hour. Carefully peel in the sink to avoid staining your clothes. Cut each beet in half and then slice into half moons. Slice them right into a mixing bowl to spare your cutting board. Cut the skin off of the blood oranges and slice into 1/2-inch-thick circles. Remove any seeds you see. Combine the beets, oranges, orange juice, champagne vinegar, and extra-virgin olive oil. Season with salt and pepper to taste.

To serve, divide the lettuce leaves among 4 plates and serve the beet mixture on top. Drizzle with the liquid remaining in the bottom of the bowl.

Wild Mushroom Soup
with Sherry and Garlic Croutons

WINE NOTES

Here is an opportunity to serve either the wine that was used in the soup or the sherry. A dry sherry would be quite a nice touch; a full-bodied, oak-aged Chardonnay would also complement the texture and flavors.

Most types of mushroom will work for this dish. The cultivated types—champignon de Paris (the white mushroom you see everywhere), cremini, and portobello (a big cremini)—are widely available but have less flavor than wild varieties. Mycologists (mushroom experts) have to know where to pick wild mushrooms and the difference between the poisonous and safe varieties. The flavors of wild mushrooms elevate this soup above the ordinary. If you cannot get fresh wild mushrooms, you can use dried ones. Rehydrate them in hot water, pressing them down with a plate, until they plump up. The water that you used for soaking is full of flavor, but usually full of dirt as well. Strain it through a fine-meshed strainer or cheesecloth, and use it as part of the liquid in the soup.

1 whole head garlic

Kosher salt and freshly ground pepper

$1/2$ teaspoon extra-virgin olive oil

2 tablespoons olive oil

$1/2$ cup sliced onion

2 pounds cremini mushrooms, thinly sliced

2 pounds wild mushrooms (such as chanterelles, porcini, and so on), thinly sliced

1 tablespoon minced garlic

$1/2$ cup white wine

4 cups chicken stock (page 206)

Bouquet garni with a bay leaf and 2 sprigs of thyme (page 211)

$1/4$ cup sherry

$1/2$ cup heavy whipping cream

8 baguette slices

1 tablespoon minced chervil, for garnish

To roast the garlic: Preheat the oven to 300°. Cut the top off of the garlic head, exposing the cloves. Season lightly with salt and pepper and drizzle lightly with extra-virgin olive oil. Place in a small ovenproof pan filled with $1/2$ inch of water. Cover with a lid or foil and roast in the oven for about 1 hour, or until the garlic cloves are soft.

To prepare the soup: While the garlic is roasting, in a stockpot over medium-high heat, heat the olive oil. Add the onion and cook for 10 minutes, stirring often. Add the mushrooms and cook, covered, for another 10 minutes, stirring often. Remove $1/2$ cup of mushrooms from the pot and reserve for garnish. Add the minced garlic and cook, stirring, for 1 minute. Add the white wine and stir to scrape up the browned bits from the bottom of the pot. Simmer for 10 minutes. Add the chicken stock and bouquet garni and cook, uncovered, for 30 minutes. Remove and discard the bouquet garni and purée the soup.

In a small pot, flame the sherry as described on page 209, and add to the soup. Add the cream and bring back to a simmer, stirring often.

To prepare the croutons: Toast the baguette slices.

Separate and peel the roasted garlic cloves. Mash and spread onto the toasted baguette slices.

To serve, ladle the soup into 4 bowls. Top with 2 croutons per bowl and garnish with the reserved mushrooms and minced chervil. Serve immediately.

Pan-Seared Scallop Salad with Organic Greens, Champagne Vinaigrette, and Avocado-Lemon Mayonnaise

SERVES 4 AS A FIRST COURSE,
2 AS A MAIN COURSE

⁂ WINE NOTES

The scallops have a sweet rich-ness that is intensified by the addition of the avocado-lemon mayonnaise. A Sauvignon Blanc from a slightly warmer region with less gravelly soils gener-ally produces a wine with more melon and citrus flavors. This medium-bodied wine will match the weight and texture of the scallops and sauce with enough acid to refresh the palate.

Although we usually make our mayonnaise by hand, using a mortar and pes-tle and a whisk, I use a food processor for this recipe. Because of the amount of oil in the avocado, less oil is used in the preparation. A processor purées the avocado and incorporates the oil well, preventing the mayonnaise from sepa-rating. You can use a blender, but it's harder because of the size of the jar. The small work bowl of a mini-chopper is perfect. You can also make it by hand, but it won't be as smooth.

AVOCADO-LEMON MAYONNAISE

1 avocado, peeled and pitted

1 egg yolk

2 teaspoons lemon juice, more if desired

1/2 cup olive oil

Kosher salt and freshly ground white pepper

CHAMPAGNE VINAIGRETTE

1 teaspoon champagne vinegar

1 teaspoon finely minced shallot

1/2 teaspoon Dijon-style mustard

1 tablespoon extra-virgin olive oil

2 tablespoons olive oil

1 pound sea scallops

1/2 pound organic baby lettuces

To prepare the mayonnaise: In a small food processor or blender, com-bine the avocado, egg yolk, and lemon juice. Process until smooth. With the motor running, slowly add the olive oil. Season to taste with salt and white pepper. Set aside in the refrigerator until ready to use.

To prepare the vinaigrette: In a bowl, combine the champagne vine-gar, shallot, and mustard. Whisk in the extra-virgin olive oil.

To prepare the scallops: Over high heat, heat a nonstick sauté pan. Add the olive oil. When very hot, add the scallops. Cook, turning once, until nice-ly browned on both sides, 3 to 5 minutes per side (depending on the size of the scallops). Drain onto paper towels.

To serve, toss the lettuces in the vinaigrette and divide among 4 plates. Top with the scallops. Spoon the avocado mayonnaise over the scallops and serve immediately.

CHAMPAGNE OR SPARKLING WINE?

What is Champagne? What is *méthode champenoise*? What is sparkling wine?

By definition, Champagne is an effervescent wine made in the Champagne region of northeastern France. Everything else made around the world from various grape varieties with various methods is referred to as a sparkling wine. Most people consider the two terms interchangeable, but "champagne" is the more commonly used. My family released its first *méthode champenoise* sparkling wine in 1983 in celebration of our winery's hundredth anniversary.

The grape varieties used to produce the true French Champagne are chardonnay, pinot noir, and pinot meunier. In California, the finest sparkling wines use these same varieties and may also include a bit of pinot blanc in the blend. Traditional Champagne is made by putting a *cuvée* (or blend) of still wine in a bottle along with sugar and yeast to start a secondary fermentation. During the second fermentation, the yeast converts the sugar to alcohol and carbon dioxide in the sealed bottle. The trapped carbon dioxide creates the natural effervescence characteristic of this wine. The wine is then aged on the yeast for a period of time (two to three years). As the yeast breaks down, it imparts additional flavor and complexity to the sparkling wine, usually giving it a yeasty or toasty flavor. The yeast is then worked down into the neck of the bottle by a process called riddling, where it is disgorged. This is done by freezing the neck of the bottle, removing the cap, and allowing the frozen plug of yeast and wine to be pushed out by the pressure inside the bottle. A dosage consisting of some amount of sugar, usually combined with wine, is added back to balance the sparkling wine, and then the bottle is corked. This entire process of fermenting the wine in a bottle is called *méthode champenoise*, the French term for this classic technique.

Sparkling wine is generally considered a special-occasion or celebration wine, but those of us involved in the production of this wonderful elixir believe it has far more versatility than just a toast during the reception hour. It is possible to serve it throughout a meal—not just at the familiar beginning or end. When selecting a sparkling wine to go with savory foods, the best choice is a brut. This category of sparkling wine is generally one of the driest. Because of its acidity, it can be a wonderful accompaniment to fried foods, mildly spicy recipes, or saltier dishes. Try a sparkling wine with more delicate foods, where the effervescence will refresh the palate and enhance the subtlety of the dish.

It's possible to serve various styles of sparkling wine throughout an entire meal. Starting with a salad dressed with champagne vinegar, you can serve a brut or natural (the driest sparkling wines). Continue with a soup having a bouillon broth base, which will pair nicely with a dry sparkling wine. The textures of the two are complementary. Follow with an entrée of roasted squab, switching the sparkling wine to a brut rosé, more full in body and richer in style. This sparkling wine is usually made with a predominance of pinot noir grapes that have been allowed to take on a slight blush during the first pressing. Finish the meal with a crème brûlée with raspberry purée paired with a crémant, a sparkling wine with a greater dosage added to it at bottling, resulting in more residual sugar, which matches the sweetness found in the dessert.

At your next meal when you are thinking about what wine to serve, why not try a Champagne or sparkling wine?—CW

PIZZA AND PASTA

MAKES FOUR 12- TO 14-INCH PIZZAS

Pizza with Oven-Dried Tomatoes, Goat Cheese, and Duck Sausage

This pizza is wonderful with the duck sausage, but it can also be made with about 8 ounces of just about any other sausage. Rather than using an aged cheese, I like to use a fresh style of goat cheese, which is softer and creamier, so the rest of the ingredients are not overwhelmed.

DUCK SAUSAGE

2 duck leg-thighs, about 1 pound total

1/2 teaspoon minced fresh oregano leaves

1/2 teaspoon minced fresh thyme leaves

1/2 teaspoon minced fresh flat-leaf parsley leaves

1/2 teaspoon minced garlic

1/2 teaspoon fennel seed

Kosher salt and freshly ground pepper

1 leek, white part only, sliced in half lengthwise

1 cup chicken stock (page 206)

1 (16-ounce) can whole peeled tomatoes in juice

1/4 cup grated Parmesan cheese

1 cup goat cheese (fresh style)

Pizza dough (page 203)

To prepare the sausage: Remove the skin from the duck and carve the meat from the bones. Remove as much of the tendons from the legs as you can. Trim the fat from the meat and add enough of the fat to the duck meat to equal about 10 percent of the total. Cut the meat into small pieces.

In a bowl, combine the duck meat with the oregano, thyme, parsley, garlic, and fennel seed and season with salt and pepper. Place in the freezer for 1 hour. Pass through a meat grinder or finely chop the mixture by hand.

To prepare the leek: In a saucepan over medium heat, combine the leek and chicken stock and bring to a simmer. Season with salt and pepper to taste and simmer until tender, about 25 minutes. Remove the leek from the stock, cool, and coarsely chop. Reserve the stock for future use.

To dry the tomatoes: Preheat the oven to 300°. Drain the tomatoes, cut them in half lengthwise, and remove the seeds. Lay the tomatoes on a parchment-lined baking sheet, cut side down. Slowly roast in the oven until dried but not colored, about 1 hour. Reserve.

To make the pizza: Prepare the oven for pizza as described on page 204 and preheat to 550°. Shape the pizza dough into 4 rounds, each 12 to 14 inches in diameter. Divide the sausage, leek, tomatoes, and cheeses among the rounds and place in the oven. Bake until golden brown, 6 to 8 minutes. Serve immediately.

Calzone with Artichokes, Westphalian Ham, Ricotta, and Parmesan

SERVES 4

We usually make this recipe with ricotta salata—a drier, sharper-tasting ricotta. It's more difficult to find, but the flavor is quite different from regular ricotta. True Westphalian ham comes from Germany and is prized for its smoky, velvety texture. The pigs that the ham is made from are raised on a special diet of acorns. The hams are then cured with salt and slowly smoked. If you cannot find Westphalian ham, use another dry, cured, smoked ham. Any leftover filling will make great ravioli.

1/2 recipe pizza dough (page 203)

2 cups coarsely chopped artichoke hearts
  (the hearts of 2 large artichokes, page 209)

2 ounces Westphalian ham, cut into very thin julienne

1 3/4 cups ricotta (to make your own, see page 200)

1/4 cup grated Parmesan cheese

1/2 cup grated mozzarella cheese

2 teaspoons lemon juice

1/4 teaspoon finely chopped fresh rosemary leaves

1/8 teaspoon whole celery seed

Kosher salt and freshly ground pepper

Olive oil, for brushing calzone

Prepare and preheat the oven to 550° as described on page 204. Shape the pizza dough into 4 rounds.

Combine the artichoke hearts, ham, cheeses, lemon juice, rosemary, and celery seed. Taste for seasoning and add salt and pepper if necessary.

Place a quarter of the filling on half of each of the 4 rounds of dough. Moisten the edges with water, fold the dough over the filling, and seal the edges. Bake in the oven until golden brown, about 10 minutes. Remove from the oven, brush lightly with olive oil, and serve immediately.

WINE NOTES

During college, I had the opportunity to study in Florence, Italy. A favorite student meal was calzone, made with a variety of fillings and served with the local red wine. A predominant varietal in Tuscany is Sangiovese, which has a number of California producers. This is a well-constructed wine with a reasonably soft, tannic structure and good flavor, which complements the saltiness of the ham and cheeses and is not confounded by the artichoke. A medium-bodied Zinfandel would also pair nicely with this calzone.

Fettuccine with Prawns, Leek Purée, Blood Oranges, and Spinach

SERVES 4

🌺 WINE NOTES

Try a medium- to full-bodied Chardonnay. This dish requires a wine compatible with the weight of the leek purée and the richness of the prawns, but one that won't conflict with the astringent quality of the spinach. A slightly chilled, light-bodied, nontannic Gamay or Pinot Noir would also work well with this combination of flavors. It is not taboo to chill a lighter-style red wine. This often makes it even more refreshing as an accompaniment to food.

Most of the prawns that you find in your fish market have been frozen. One of the reasons is that prawns break down very rapidly after they have been caught. We use fresh prawns in the restaurant, but they are expensive and difficult to find. If they are not available, fresh frozen prawns are a good alternative. In place of the leeks, you can use other members of the onion family, such as shallots, spring onions, or red onions to make the sauce. Although the cream sauce is rich, the acidity of the blood orange balances it nicely.

> 2 tablespoons olive oil
>
> 4 large leeks, white part only, sliced in half lengthwise
>
> 1/2 cup sliced onion
>
> 2 cups heavy whipping cream
>
> 1 pound prawns (16 to 20 per pound)
>
> Kosher salt and freshly ground pepper
>
> 1/2 pound fresh spinach (about 5 cups)
>
> 1 1/2 pounds fettuccine, fresh or dried
>
> 6 tablespoons lemon juice, more if needed
>
> 5 teaspoons finely chopped lemon zest
>
> 4 blood oranges, peeled and divided into segments (page 209)

In a nonreactive pan over low heat, heat the olive oil. Add the leeks and onion, cover, and cook until softened, 15 to 20 minutes. Do not brown. Add the cream and continue cooking, uncovered, over very low heat for 1 hour. Purée and strain through a medium sieve.

Put a pot of salted water on the stove to boil. Prepare a bowl of ice water.

Clean the prawns, remove the shells, and butterfly them down the back side. Remove anything dark (this is the digestive tract). Season with salt and pepper to taste. Reserve in the refrigerator.

Blanch the spinach in the boiling water for 30 seconds, or until just wilted, then plunge into the ice water. Drain and place in a clean kitchen towel. Wring out the water. Chop.

Cook the pasta in boiling water until done, about 7 minutes for dried or 3 to 4 minutes for fresh.

In a pot, heat the cream sauce to a simmer. Add the prawns and simmer until cooked, 8 to 10 minutes. Add the spinach and warm through. Add the pasta, lemon juice, and finely chopped lemon zest and warm through. Taste for seasoning, adding more lemon juice if necessary.

To serve, divide the pasta and prawns among 4 plates. Top with the blood orange segments.

Angel–Hair Pasta with Toasted Sesame Seeds, Aged Asiago, and Cilantro

Be sure to use aged Asiago in this recipe. It is a harder, drier cheese than the softer, more mellow regular Asiago, which can get stringy and gummy. If you can't find aged Asiago, substitute a fine Parmigiano-Reggiano. If I don't have any homemade chicken stock on hand, I use Glace de Poulet Gold, a staple in my pantry. When made using 1 part concentrated formula to 6 parts water, it creates a very rich broth. Serve this pasta as a first course on individual plates or as the main course of a light supper. Accompany with a butter lettuce salad with mustard–Meyer lemon dressing and bruschetta with chopped sundried tomatoes or eggplant tapenade. —CW

1/4 cup olive oil

2 tablespoons chopped garlic

1/4 cup finely minced shallot

1 1/2 cups chicken stock

3/4 cup Chardonnay

1 pound dried angel-hair pasta

1/4 cup sesame seeds, toasted (page 210)

Grated aged Asiago cheese

1/2 cup fresh cilantro leaves

In a large pot, bring 3 quarts of salted water to a boil.

In a large skillet over medium heat, heat the olive oil. Add the garlic and sauté for 4 minutes. Add the shallot and continue sautéing until the garlic is crisp, toasty, and browned, 4 to 5 minutes. Add the chicken stock and wine and lower the heat to a low simmer.

Meanwhile, add the pasta to the boiling water and cook until just tender (al dente). Drain and add to the mixture in the skillet. Add the sesame seeds and toss thoroughly.

To serve, divide the pasta among 4 plates, sprinkle with Asiago to taste, and garnish with whole cilantro leaves.

SERVES 4

WINE NOTES

The simple, pure flavors of this dish make it a wonderful complement to an aged white wine such as a Chardonnay or a Sauvignon Blanc–Sémillon blend. This type of dish is excellent to showcase the wine as the feature of the meal.

Ravioli with Salmon, Fennel, and Tangerine Butter

If you can get it in your area, wild steelhead salmon from the Pacific Northwest is wonderful in this dish. It has a rich flavor without being oily. Other meaty fish can be used in this recipe in place of the salmon. Crab is a great alternative.

TANGERINE BUTTER

2 tablespoons unsalted butter, at room temperature

1 teaspoon tangerine zest

Kosher salt and freshly ground pepper

RAVIOLI

1 fennel bulb (reserve tops for garnish)

1 leek, white part only, cut in half lengthwise

1/2 teaspoon fennel seed

1 tablespoon tangerine juice

2 cups vegetable stock (page 205)

Kosher salt and freshly ground pepper

2 tablespoons olive oil

1 pound salmon fillets with skin

1/4 cup crème fraîche (page 199)

Lemon juice to taste

Double recipe pasta dough (page 202)

1 tablespoon toasted, skinned finely chopped hazelnuts (page 210)

To prepare the butter: In a small bowl, blend the butter and tangerine zest together and season with salt and pepper to taste.

To prepare the ravioli filling: Preheat the oven to 350°.

Cut the fennel bulb in half, top to bottom, and remove the core. In a baking dish, combine the fennel bulb, leek, fennel seed, tangerine juice, and vegetable stock. Add salt and pepper to taste. Cover and braise in the oven for 1/2 hour, or until very tender.

Remove the leek and fennel from the stock, cool, and chop coarsely. Strain the stock. In a nonreactive saucepan over medium heat, reduce the stock by half. Set aside.

In a nonstick sauté pan over medium heat, heat the olive oil. Season the salmon with salt and pepper. Add the salmon, skin side down, cover, and reduce heat to medium-low. Cook for 5 to 7 minutes. Turn, cover, and cook for another 5 to 7 minutes. It should be still pink inside and flaky. If you are using a tail section, it will cook in about half the time. When cool, remove the skin.

SERVES 4

WINE NOTES

Pastas can be delicate or robust—it is the filling and sauce that most affect the wine choice. The salmon filling is the dominant flavor in this dish, with the sauce being a bit more delicate. Select a medium-bodied Sauvignon Blanc with a slight citrus to herbal flavor profile to complement the fennel and leeks.

In a bowl, flake the salmon into bite-sized pieces. Add the fennel-leek mixture, and crème fraîche and mix. Taste for seasoning. Add lemon juice, a little at a time, until the flavors are balanced.

To assemble the pasta: Bring a large pot of salted water to a boil to cook the pasta. Separate the pasta dough into 4 pieces, keeping them covered. Roll out a piece in a pasta machine set to the thinnest setting, as described on page 202. Cut in half to form 2 rectangular pieces the width of the pasta machine. Lay a piece down on a flat surface and place 1/4 cup of filling in the center of the dough, about 2 1/2 inches from a short edge. Continue placing 1/4 cup of filling every 5 inches along the length of the dough. Moisten the edges of the pasta dough, including the spaces between the filling, lightly with water. Place the other rectangular piece over the piece with the filling, slowly and gingerly stretching it so that it covers the filling and dough. Press down on the edges to seal, and cut between the stuffing, forming 5-inch square ravioli. Trim any loose edges. Repeat with the remaining 3 pieces of dough.

KIMBALL'S PANTRY

People always wonder how I cook at home. What do I keep in my pantry for daily meal preparation as well as special occasions? I feel that I can't be as spontaneous or creative without a solid selection of ingredients at home. Some ingredients can be purchased only through mail order or specialty food stores, and I definitely want to have them in my pantry. I supplement these basic ingredients with daily shopping for produce, meats, or fish.

Dried goods—porcini, chiles, currants, cherries, figs, cranberries

Dried beans—lentils, flageolets, pintos, cranberry beans, Great Northern beans

Flours, grains, and baking supplies—cake flour, bread flour, all-purpose flour, cornmeal, polenta, dry yeast, baking soda, and powder

Rice—carnaroli, jasmine

Nuts—pine nuts, pistachios, whole and sliced almonds, hazelnuts, pecans, walnuts

Sugars—light and dark brown, powdered, granulated

Chocolate product—cocoa; semi-sweet, unsweetened, and white chocolates; chocolate chips (for my kids)

Vinegars—6- and 12-year-old balsamic, red wine, champagne, apple cider, sherry

Oils—Wente extra-virgin olive oil, regular olive oil, peanut oil

Olives—green, black, salt cured

Dairy—buttermilk, milk, heavy cream, Plugrá butter, cage-free eggs

Miscellaneous—good canned tomatoes, Rustichella d'Abruzzo pastas, Parmigiano-Reggiano cheese, French Dijon mustard, honey (different flavors like lavender, clover, and so on), maple syrup (the real stuff!), kosher salt, black and white peppercorns in their own grinders, pink peppercorns, lemons, apples

In a pot, reheat the reduced stock. Cook the ravioli in the boiling water until al dente, approximately 3 minutes. Drain from the water and finish cooking in the stock for a few minutes.

To serve, divide the ravioli and stock among 4 bowls. Top with the tangerine butter. Garnish with a few fennel sprigs. Sprinkle with the hazelnuts.

CAROLYN'S PANTRY

My husband always kids me about my "inventory control." Because we live about half an hour from the nearest grocery, I keep at least two of everything in my pantry and a running list of items that we are getting low on or have used up. What I keep on hand is a reflection of my own personal approach to cooking, which is a combination of family traditions and recipes, tidbits picked up from my experiences in the world of food and wine, and the personal tastes and preferences of myself and my family.

Because my mother's family comes from Georgia, rice is very important in my menus. It's always been an easy side dish for a wide variety of meats, fish, and poultry. I like to perk up white rice with the addition of simple things like citrus (lemon, lime, orange) peels or zests when serving with fish or poultry. Wild rice is a favorite of mine, and I sometimes add raisins, toasted pine nuts, or pecans for a bit more crunch and flavor. I serve risotto frequently, made with what is fresh in the market. Glace de Poulet Gold makes a wonderful

stock for soups, sauces, and risottos if you don't have time to make your own. Polenta is also popular in our house, both creamy and grilled. And, of course, I always keep various flours on hand for making breads, rolls, quick breads, and such. I enjoy making pasta and do it when I have the time. However, as a time-saver, I always have on hand dried pasta, and usually a variety of fresh raviolis or tortellini in the refrigerator. A mélange of dried fruits and nuts is a good additive for all sorts of recipes, including steamed vegetables, rices, and salads. I depend on fresh herbs, which grow year-round for me in pots or in my vegetable garden. I keep a selection of some of the more exotic dried herbs on hand as well.

Dried goods—porcini and oyster mushrooms, raisins, dried cranberries, apricots, prunes, candied fruit (for breads and some desserts)

Dried beans—red kidney, cranberry, black-eyed peas, lentils

Flours, grains, and baking supplies—white and whole wheat flour, cornmeal, couscous, tapioca (for desserts), Glace de

Poulet Gold, dry packaged yeast

Rice—arborio, white, wild

Nuts—pine nuts, walnuts, peanuts, pecans, cashews, hazelnuts

Vinegars—balsamic, white balsamic, white and red wine, rice, apple, raspberry, blackberry, and sherry

Oils—olive oil, extra-virgin olive oil, and walnut, grapeseed, canola, sesame, and peanut oils

Pastas—trenne, angel-hair, orzo, penne, gemelli, fettuccine, ravioli, tortellini

From the garden—cilantro, Italian parsley, sage, lemon thyme, thyme, tarragon, rosemary, mint (assorted varieties), lavender, oregano

Dried herbs—saffron, curry, and cumin

Dairy—cream, butter, eggs, yogurt, sour cream

Miscellaneous kitchen necessities—A variety of mustards, and a variety of cheeses such as Parmigiano-Reggiano, Asiago, and fresh mozzarella

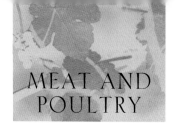

SERVES 8

A robust Cabernet Sauvignon, Syrah, or Pinot Noir are all excellent selections for this flavorful meat. Here is a classic recipe that reinforces the guideline of "red wine with red meat."

Chuck Williams's Sunday Supper Chuck Roast with Mashed Potatoes and Creamed Spinach

To celebrate his eightieth birthday, I was asked to prepare a traditional Sunday supper, updated for the '90s, for Chuck Williams, the founder of Williams-Sonoma. We served 250 people family-style. Some of the great table additions we did were homemade dill pickles, pickled jalapeños, and an updated relish tray with baby carrots, celery root slaw, herb-garlic marinated olives, Toy Box cherry tomatoes, and Flambo radishes.

CHUCK ROAST

4 pounds beef chuck roast

Kosher salt and freshly ground pepper

1/2 bunch fresh thyme

1/2 bunch fresh rosemary

2 tablespoons olive oil

1 (8-ounce) can whole, peeled tomatoes with juice

2 small carrots, diced

1 small onion, diced

1 rib celery, diced

6 cloves garlic, peeled

1 cup Cabernet Sauvignon

MASHED POTATOES

5 pounds new potatoes, thoroughly cleaned

12 tablespoons unsalted butter

2 tablespoons kosher salt

1 teaspoon freshly ground pepper

1/2 cup heavy whipping cream

1/2 cup crème fraîche (page 199)

1/4 cup coarsely chopped parsley leaves

1/4 cup chopped scallions, green part only

CREAMED SPINACH

2 pounds fresh spinach

1 tablespoon olive oil

1 tablespoon butter

1 onion, sliced

1 cup heavy whipping cream

Kosher salt and freshly ground pepper

To prepare the roast: Season the beef with a liberal amount of salt and pepper. Coarsely chop half of the thyme and rosemary and press into the meat. Marinate overnight.

Preheat the oven to 325°.

In a roasting pan over medium-high heat, heat the olive oil. Brown the beef on all sides until golden. Combine with the tomatoes and their juice, carrots, onion, and celery. Cook until the vegetables are soft, about 15 minutes. Add the garlic, wine, remaining herbs tied in a bouquet garni (page 211), and enough water to cover the roast. Bring to a simmer, cover, and place in the oven. Cook for 3 to 4 hours, or until very tender.

When done, remove the meat from the liquid and set aside. Remove the bouquet garni. Purée the vegetables in the liquid. Over medium heat, reduce until the liquid is the consistency of applesauce, and season with salt and pepper to taste. Slice the beef and return it to the sauce to keep warm. This can be cooked a day ahead and reheated before serving.

To prepare the mashed potatoes: Place the potatoes in a pot and cover with cold water. Bring to a boil and lower the heat to a simmer. Cook the potatoes until they are easily pierced with a knife and their jackets start to crack.

Drain the potatoes, including the skin, and place in a mixing bowl. Add the butter, salt, pepper, cream, and crème fraîche. Mash together with a hand masher. Do not overmix. Check for seasoning. Keep warm in a hot water bath. Garnish with the parsley and scallions just before serving.

To prepare the spinach: Put a pot of salted water on the stove to boil. Prepare a bowl of ice water. Blanch the spinach in the boiling water for 30 seconds, or until just wilted, then plunge into the ice water. Drain and chop. In a saucepan over medium-low heat, warm the oil and butter. Add the onion, cooking slowly until lightly browned. Pour off any excess oil. Add the cream, bring to a low simmer, and reduce until it coats the back of a spoon, approximately 1/2 hour. Toss in the spinach and just warm though. Season with salt and pepper. Serve immediately.

Braised Lamb Shanks with Tangerine Gremolata and Fried Winter Vegetables

SERVES 4

❮WINE NOTES

This is a braised or stewed red meat and so requires a red wine. The cooking method, ingredients, and thick sauce point toward a fuller-bodied, robust wine with good intensity of flavor. Try a Petite Sirah or Zinfandel from a warmer climate.

I can barely wait each year for the first chill of winter. That's when I start cooking slow-braised meat dishes like lamb shanks. Because the shank is one of the muscles used most by the lamb, it is full of flavor but can be fairly tough if not cooked slowly over a long period. Cooking in liquid also helps to break down the tightly wound muscle fiber. You can prepare the lamb shanks up to two days in advance, keeping them in the refrigerator until ready to serve. They are wonderful accompanied with creamy polenta (page 204).

4 lamb shanks

Kosher salt and freshly ground pepper

2 tablespoons olive oil

1/2 cup diced carrot

1/2 cup diced onion

12 cloves garlic, peeled

1 stick cinnamon

2 bay leaves

2 cups canned, peeled Roma tomatoes in juice
   (about one 16-ounce can)

2 cups red wine

2 cups chicken stock (page 206)

8 sprigs fresh flat-leaf parsley

1 tablespoon tangerine zest

FRIED WINTER VEGETABLES

1 whole carrot, peeled

1 whole parsnip, peeled

1 cup peanut oil for frying

To prepare the lamb: Season the lamb with salt and pepper, cover, and let sit 8 hours or overnight in the refrigerator.

Preheat the oven to 325°.

In a heavy-bottomed, nonreactive pan over medium-high heat, heat the olive oil. Add the lamb, carrot, and onion. Cook, turning often, until light golden brown. Drain off any fat remaining in the bottom of the pan. Add 10 cloves of the garlic, the cinnamon, bay leaves, tomatoes with juice, red wine, and stock. Scrape the caramelized bits from the bottom of the pan. Remove the leaves from the parsley and set aside. Tie the stems together with kitchen twine and add to the pot. Bring to a boil, cover, and place in the preheated oven. Cook for 1 1/2 to 2 hours, or until the lamb is tender and almost falling off the bone. Cooking time will depend on the size of the shanks.

Remove the lamb from the braising liquid and set aside. Discard the cinnamon, bay leaves, and parsley stems. Purée the remaining liquid and strain through a medium sieve. Over medium heat, reheat to a simmer and reduce by half. Taste and adjust the seasoning, if needed. Return the shanks to the liquid.

To prepare the gremolata: Mince the remaining 2 cloves of garlic with the reserved parsley leaves and tangerine zest.

To prepare the vegetables: Using a peeler, peel ribbons of carrot and parsnip until you get to the center. In a small sauté pan over medium-high heat, heat the peanut oil. Fry the ribbons in batches until light golden brown. Do not overcook or they will become bitter. Drain on paper towels.

To serve, reheat the lamb in the sauce by bringing it to a simmer on the stove top. If you have had the shanks in the refrigerator, bring the sauce and shanks to a simmer on the stove top and then pop them into a 325° oven until warmed through, about 30 minutes.

Place a shank on each of 4 plates. Spoon sauce over the top, add the fried vegetables, and sprinkle with gremolata.

Veal Scallops with Meyer Lemon and Tarragon Sauce and Lemon–Flavored Rice

SERVES 4

ᐁ WINE NOTES

In this dish, the sauce has more influence on the wine choice than the light, white veal. A fuller-bodied Chardonnay will complement the Meyer lemon, shallot, butter, and garlic flavors, and will also match the weight and texture of the veal. Pinot Noir, a lighter-style red wine, will work well with the weight and texture of the dish, as well as with the tarragon, parsley, and pepper flavors.

This recipe comes from my repertoire of quick meals that pair well with wine. The ease of cooking veal scallops in less than 30 minutes is crucial when unexpected dinner guests need to be entertained while I prepare an elegant repast. The only ingredient that is not in my pantry or garden is the veal itself, and my local butcher always saves the day. If it is not Meyer lemon season, I substitute regular Eureka lemons. This makes the recipe slightly more tangy, but still good with a rich Chardonnay or even a Pinot Noir. —CW

8 medium-sized veal scallops (about 2 by 4 inches and $1/2$ inch thick)

$1/4$ cup unsalted butter

2 tablespoons olive oil

$1^1/2$ teaspoons minced garlic

2 tablespoons minced shallot

$3/4$ cup dry white wine

$1/4$ cup Meyer lemon juice

1 tablespoon coarsely chopped fresh tarragon leaves

1 tablespoon arrowroot blended with 1 tablespoon hot water

Kosher salt and freshly ground pepper

LEMON-FLAVORED RICE

2 cups chicken or veal stock (page 206)

1 cup long-grain white rice

2 tablespoons butter

1 tablespoon finely chopped Meyer lemon zest

Thinly sliced Meyer lemon rounds

2 tablespoons chopped flat-leaf parsley leaves, for garnish

To prepare the veal: Place each scallop between 2 sheets of waxed paper or plastic wrap. With a mallet or cleaver, flatten each scallop to about 1/4 inch thick. Pat each scallop with a paper towel to dry. This will help them brown nicely without the need to dredge them in flour.

In a large skillet over medium-high heat, heat 2 tablespoons of the butter and the olive oil. When the butter begins to brown, place several scallops in the pan. Don't crowd them. Sauté on one side for about 2 minutes, then turn and cook for another 2 minutes. Monitor the heat so that the butter does not get too hot and burn, but still sautés the veal. The veal should be just browned and the pink juices beginning to turn pale yellow. When done, place on a plate and continue to cook the remaining scallops in the same manner. Do not overcook or the veal will lose its tenderness.

To prepare the sauce: Place the same skillet, with the veal juices, oil, and butter remaining in the pan, over medium heat, add the remaining 2 tablespoons of butter, and the garlic and shallot. Sauté for about 2 minutes, or until transparent. Add the white wine, lemon juice, and tarragon and reduce until there is about 3/4 cup liquid. Add the arrowroot-water mixture and stir until the sauce has thickened. Add salt and pepper to taste.

To prepare the rice: In a saucepan over high heat, bring the stock to a boil. Add the rice and butter. Cover, turn to low, and simmer for 20 minutes or until the rice is cooked and the stock has been absorbed.

When done, mix in the finely chopped lemon zest while fluffing the rice.

To serve, place the scallops back in the skillet and warm over medium heat, turning once to cover with the sauce and to heat through, about 4 minutes. Remove from the heat, place the scallops on a platter, and spoon the sauce over the top. Garnish with the parsley. Place the rice in a serving bowl with overlapping lemon slices arranged around the rim. The lemon slices add a nice flavor to the rice and veal and are easily eaten when sliced so thinly.

Goat Cheese–Stuffed, Roasted Chicken Breast with Olive Oil and Lemon Mashed Potatoes

SERVES 4

🎋 WINE NOTES

This is a subtle dish without any dominant flavors. The citrus notes brought out by the tangerine juice, and the lightness of the mashed potatoes flavored with olive oil suggest a Sauvignon Blanc or a light, stainless steel–fermented Chardonnay.

When you sauté or roast meat, fish, or poultry, you leave a lot of flavor in the pan. The simple sauce, or *jus*, in this dish, created by deglazing the pan with citrus juice, leaves none of that flavor behind. Experiment by deglazing with other liquids such as fruit juices, wine, liqueurs, and even vegetable juices. If the liquid is too acidic or sharp, you can finish the *jus* with a little whole butter swirled in at the last moment to balance the flavors.

The olive oil, which replaces the usual butter and sour cream in this mashed potato recipe, makes it a much lighter preparation. These potatoes are equally good with chicken or shellfish such as scallops and prawns.

This recipe calls for a fresh goat cheese. This means that the cheese has not been aged, cured, or colored and usually has not had any flavoring agents added. It is very creamy and soft. Fresh, steamed asparagus would add a nice touch.

OLIVE OIL AND LEMON MASHED POTATOES

2 pounds Yukon Gold potatoes, peeled

1/4 cup extra-virgin olive oil

1/4 cup heavy whipping cream

6 tablespoons lemon juice

1 tablespoon plus 1 teaspoon finely chopped lemon zest

Kosher salt

4 large chicken breasts with wing attached
    (we call them airline chicken breasts)

1 cup fresh goat cheese

2 tablespoons olive oil

Kosher salt and freshly ground pepper

1 cup honey tangerine juice (or regular tangerine juice)

To prepare the potatoes: Place the potatoes in a large pot and cover with cold water. Bring to a boil and reduce to a simmer. Cook for about 30 minutes, or until the potatoes are tender and easily pierced with a sharp knife. Drain and return to the pot. Add the olive oil, cream, lemon juice, and finely chopped lemon zest and mash with a hand masher or heavy whisk. Season with salt. Keep warm in a double boiler.

To prepare the chicken: Preheat the oven to 350°. On the thick side of each chicken breast, near the wing bone, cut a pocket in the flesh. Fill each pocket with 1/4 cup goat cheese.

182

In a large, ovenproof sauté pan over high heat, heat the olive oil. Season the chicken with salt and pepper. Add the chicken to the sauté pan, skin side down. Lower the heat to medium-high. Cook until the skin is nicely browned, about 5 minutes. Turn the chicken breasts over and place in the oven. Cook for 20 minutes. The internal temperature of the chicken should be at least 140°. Remove the chicken from the pan and let rest on a plate.

To make the glaze: Pour out any fat remaining in the pan, add the honey tangerine juice, and stir over medium heat, scraping up the browned bits from the bottom of the pan. Pour any juice that has accumulated on the plate with the chicken back into the saucepan. Bring to a boil and strain.

To serve, place a chicken breast on each plate. Spoon the tangerine jus over the chicken. Serve the mashed potatoes on the side.

Winery cellarmen surround C.H. Wente (standing in center with mustache), his wife Barbara (standing next to large puncheon), and their children seated in front—Ernest (with pitchfork), May, Herman, Carolyn, Frieda (standing on puncheon), and Carl.

Pan–Seared Ahi Tuna with Tapenade and Lentils

SERVES 4

❧ WINE NOTES

Although this is a fish dish, the method of preparation calls for a red wine. The earthy lentils, the salty tapenade, and the meaty fish are a good balance for a Pinot Noir or Syrah. These wines tend to have a good balance of earthiness, fruit, and especially acid, making them a fun and tasty match.

Good olives are very important in this recipe. Niçoise olives are the best, but any good-quality brined olives will work. I don't recommend salt-cured olives for this preparation because the texture is not firm enough. The canned California black olives that are available everywhere lack flavor and are neither ripe nor black. They are picked green (all olives start out green and gradually turn black as they ripen on the tree) and are then manipulated with chemicals, lye, and brine to erase any flavor they once had. Any small-sized lentils can be used in this recipe if you can't find the green variety. Green lentils tend to hold their texture better and not become mushy.

TAPENADE

1/4 cup pitted, minced niçoise olives

1/2 teaspoon minced garlic

1/2 teaspoon finely minced fresh thyme leaves

1/2 teaspoon Cognac

1/2 teaspoon chopped capers

1/2 teaspoon finely minced anchovy

1 teaspoon lemon juice

1/4 teaspoon tangelo zest

LENTILS

1 tablespoon olive oil

1/2 cup finely diced carrot

1/2 cup finely diced onion

1/2 cup finely diced fennel bulb

1/4 cup diced celery

1 tablespoon minced garlic

2 cups small green lentils, cleaned and sorted

4 cups chicken stock, more as needed (page 206)

1 small dried red chile

1 bay leaf

2 tablespoons olive oil

4 portions ahi tuna (5 to 6 ounces each)

2 tablespoons tangelo juice

To prepare the tapenade: In a small bowl, combine the minced olives with the garlic, thyme, Cognac, capers, anchovy, lemon juice, and tangelo zest. Check for seasoning. It probably will not need additional salt, as the capers and anchovies are very salty.

To prepare the lentils: In a large saucepan over medium heat, heat the olive oil. Add the carrot, onion, fennel, and celery. Cook for 10 minutes, stirring often. Add the garlic and cook, stirring, for 1 minute. Add the lentils, chicken stock, chile, and bay leaf and bring to a simmer. Reduce the heat to a low simmer and cook until the lentils are tender, about 40 minutes, adding more stock if necessary. The lentils should be cooked but not mushy. Remove the chile and the bay leaf.

In a large sauté pan over high heat, heat the olive oil. Sauté the tuna on one side for about 3 minutes and turn. Baste with tangelo juice. Continue cooking for another 3 minutes. The tuna should be medium-rare to medium inside.

To serve, divide the lentils among 4 plates. Top each with a piece of tuna and then the tapenade. Serve immediately.

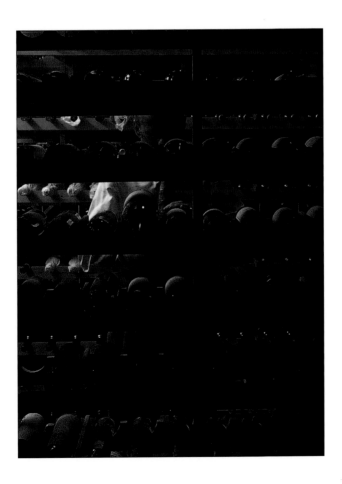

Grilled Swordfish with
Spicy Remoulade Sauce

Remember to consider the texture of the fish as well as the flavor in pairing fish with wine. Swordfish is more meat-like and delivers more flavor when grilled. Also consider the sauce—in this recipe, it is somewhat spicy from the peppercorns, capers, and cayenne. A red wine rather than a white is the most likely match. Look for medium body and soft tannins to pair with the fish's texture, and a youngish character to deliver good fruit and spice to play off the sauce. Examples would be a Cabernet Sauvignon or a Zinfandel.

A cooking technique such as broiling or even pan-searing imparts less flavor to meats or fish, giving them a simpler, purer flavor. In contrast, the flavors from grilling permeate a food and make the final dish more complex, adding caramelized, smoky, almost acrid flavors. Because of this overriding character, smoked and grilled preparations are always harder to pair with wine.

SPICY REMOULADE SAUCE

1 cup basic aioli or mayonnaise (page 207)

1 tablespoon minced dill pickle

1 teaspoon chopped capers

1 1/2 teaspoons chopped fresh tarragon leaves

1 teaspoon crushed pink peppercorns

1/4 teaspoon cayenne

Kosher salt and freshly ground pepper

Lemon juice (optional)

4 swordfish steaks, each about 1 inch thick

1 tablespoon olive oil

To prepare the sauce: Combine the aioli with the pickle, capers, tarragon, pink peppercorns, and cayenne. Season with salt and pepper. Add a little lemon juice if the acidic flavors of the pickle and capers need a boost.

To prepare the swordfish: Prepare a medium-sized fire in your barbecue. Season the swordfish steaks with salt and pepper and rub with the olive oil.

When the fire is ready, place the swordfish on the grill and cook for 4 to 5 minutes. Turn and cook another 4 to 5 minutes. The swordfish should be cooked through but still moist inside. Serve each steak with a dollop of the remoulade.

Pan-Roasted Sea Bass with Porcini Crust and Mushroom-Leek Ragout

Local sea bass is one of my favorite fish; it is meaty yet flaky, with a strong taste of the sea. When you sauté fish, place the skin side down first. The fat that was stored under the skin, which still remains even if the fish has been skinned, helps to season the pan. The skin side is usually the darker side.

MUSHROOM LEEK RAGOUT

2 tablespoons olive oil

1 pound portobello mushrooms, stems and gills removed, sliced

2 leeks, white part only, sliced

1 tablespoon finely diced carrot

1 tablespoon finely diced celery

2 sprigs fresh thyme (reserve several leaves for garnish)

1 sprig fresh tarragon (reserve several leaves for garnish)

2 cups vegetable stock (page 205)

Kosher salt and freshly ground pepper

1/2 ounce dried porcini mushrooms

4 (5-ounce) portions sea bass, skinless

Kosher salt and freshly ground pepper to taste

2 tablespoons olive oil

To prepare the ragout: In a sauté pan over medium-high heat, heat the olive oil. Add the portobellos and sauté until golden brown, stirring often. Add the leeks, carrot, and celery. Reduce the heat to low and cook until the vegetables have softened, 8 to 10 minutes. Tie the thyme and tarragon together in a cheesecloth bag. Add the stock, thyme, and tarragon and bring to a simmer. Simmer until the liquid has reduced by half. Season to taste with salt and pepper.

To prepare the sea bass: Preheat the oven to 500°. Place the porcini in a spice grinder or a coffee grinder. Grind to a very fine powder.

Season the sea bass with salt and pepper and coat both sides in the ground porcini.

In an ovenproof pan over medium-high heat, heat the olive oil. Add the sea bass, skin side down. Cook until brown, 3 to 4 minutes. Turn over and place in the oven. Roast until the internal temperature is 140° when checked with an instant-read thermometer, about 10 minutes.

To serve, slowly reheat the ragout, if necessary. Remove the herbs. Divide among 4 plates. Serve the sea bass on top of the ragout, garnished with a few leaves of thyme and tarragon.

SERVES 4

≈WINE NOTES

Depending on the type of fish, the preparation, and the other ingredients, many fish dishes go against the often-repeated "white wine with fish" rule. Meatier fishes such as sturgeon, salmon, and sea bass, the slow-cooked flavors found in stocks or braises, and deep, earthy flavors pair very well with red wines—particularly Pinot Noir or a fruity Sangiovese. These less tannic wines complement this recipe's slow cooking and earthy, mushroom flavors.

THE WINES AT OUR VINEYARD TABLE

When the restaurant opened in 1986, we operated under our winegrower's permit, which allowed us to serve any beverage made from grapes. In addition to wine, we offered brandy, port, sparkling wines, and grappa. As we developed the wine list, it seemed natural to feature wines produced here in the Livermore Valley by the glass, supported by a broader wine list focused on wines from the various appellations in California. Within those appellations, I sought out producers of particular varietals who were recognized in their regions because of their soils and climates or winemaking expertise. We put together a wonderful selection of approximately 400 wines, even featuring older vintages from some of California's most venerable and long-lived wineries such as Krug, Martini, Mirassou, Simi, Heitz, Ridge, and Stony Hill. We are particularly proud of the depth (the vintages and number of bottles in storage) and breadth (the number of varietals from different appellations) of our wine list.

Although it is always a work in progress, the wines we showcase are chosen to reflect the daily and seasonal changes in the menu, providing an opportunity for our frequent guests to try new varietals and vintages from the local wineries and for out-of-town visitors to experience the wines of our region. We emphasize Livermore Valley wines because we believe the best way to enjoy the food from a particular wine region is with its wine.

Several wineries in the Livermore Valley best demonstrate the various microclimates and soils found in the valley and the talent of the winemakers at each property. Each of these wineries focuses on grape varieties from France, Italy, and Spain.

Concannon Vineyard was established in 1883, the same year my great-grandfather started the Wente family winery. Today, the winery is still considered one of the jewels in the California wine industry and is a top producer of Sauvignon Blanc and Petite Sirah. Concannon has broadened its offerings to Rhône varietals from the south of France by planting viognier, rousanne, marsanne, and syrah grapes. Each vineyard site was chosen because its soils and microclimate closely reflect the conditions of its native appellation.

Murrieta's Well produces wine from traditional French grape varieties originating in the Bordeaux region, including sauvignon blanc, sémillon, cabernet sauvignon, merlot, malbec, and cabernet franc. The grapes are grown in a certified organic vineyard and are blended to create elegantly rich, complex, and full-bodied wines. The winemaker, Sergio Traverso, adds a twist to his blends that he calls Vendimia. Modeling them on a true Bordeaux blend, or what we in California refer to as Meritage blends, Sergio adds a bit of Zinfandel to his red wine and a percentage of Muscat de Frontignan to his white blend, producing some very distinctive wines. (Meritage is a name created by California producers to recognize the best wines from their wineries that are not pure varietals but are made solely from the grape varieties grown in the Bordeaux appellation in France. There are both red and white blends, usually bearing a proprietary name from the winery.) Again, both of these red and white blends reflect the specific 90-acre vineyard block in which they are grown in the Livermore Valley. Sergio is also experimenting with growing grape varieties from Spain. The wines have not yet been released, but they echo the emerging varieties coming from California.

Iván Tamás is the one winery in the Livermore Valley focusing on producing Italian varietals such as Trebbiano, Pinot Grigio, and Sangiovese. These wines are gaining in popularity among consumers, as they are moderately priced and very versatile wines to pair with food. When featured at the restaurant, the Pinot Grigio and Trebbiano are great starters for many of the appetizers on our menu. They are light and well balanced, with good fruit and a crisp finish. The Sangiovese is reminiscent of berries and spice, a medium-bodied red wine that is easy to drink and enjoy—another "by the glass" winner. —CW

Dungeness Crab with Frisée, Fennel, and Citrus Salad

Of course, the best crab for this dish is one that you bought live, cooked, and cleaned yourself. I know it's a lot of work, but the results are far superior. The trouble I have with most precooked Dungeness crab is the high levels of salt that are added to the cooking liquid. The salt seems to leach out most of the flavor and also makes the crab watery. You can substitute other types of crab such as blue, stone, king, or snow in this recipe with great results.

1 tablespoon orange juice

$1/2$ teaspoon minced orange zest

1 tablespoon sherry vinegar

1 tablespoon Dijon mustard

1 teaspoon granulated sugar

$1/4$ cup extra-virgin olive oil

1 head frisée, washed, cored, and torn into bite-sized pieces

Kosher salt and freshly ground pepper

2 fennel bulbs, cored and very thinly sliced
   (reserve the tops for garnish)

$1/4$ cup very thinly sliced red onion, cut into julienne

Segments of 2 oranges (page 209)

1 pound Dungeness crabmeat (more if you like)

In a bowl, whisk together the orange juice, zest, vinegar, mustard, sugar, and olive oil. Check for seasoning by dipping a piece of frisée in the dressing. Adjust with salt and pepper to taste. The amount of vinegar used will depend on the sweetness of the orange. Add the frisée, fennel, onion, and orange segments. Toss.

Pick through the crabmeat thoroughly, removing any shells.

To serve, divide the salad among 4 plates and top with the Dungeness crabmeat. Garnish with fennel tops.

SERVES 4

WINE NOTES

Because of the combination of greens and citrus, I immediately gravitate toward dry, white wines such as a Sauvignon Blanc, Trebbiano, or Chenin Blanc. The variety of flavors that evolve in the different soils and climates where these varieties are planted develop characteristics ranging from very herbal and grassy to citrus. The acid backbone or structure of these varietals will provide a balance to the fruit flavors in this dish.

DESSERTS

Aunt Frieda's Carrot Pudding with Brandied Sauces

SERVES 12, WITH APPROXI-
MATELY 2 CUPS OF EACH
SAUCE

❧WINE NOTES

A late-harvest Riesling is wonderful with this dessert, or try a
glass of vintage port.

My family's Christmas dinner was never complete without the flaming steamed pudding placed before my grandfather for serving, complete with custard sauce (we called it soft sauce) and hard sauce. The lights would dim and my Aunt Frieda would emerge from the kitchen with the pudding ablaze, to applause from all of us. As the tradition is now mine to carry on, it is an honor and a treat to make this pudding. The dessert does take some preparation time, but it is well worth it. Traditionally, all steamed puddings were made with suet or animal fat. My aunt's original recipe called for suet, but I use either butter or vegetable shortening. I have also reduced the steaming time a bit. My mold, which was handed down from my great-grandmother, is made of fluted metal with a clamp-on lid. You can still buy pudding molds, but you can also use a ceramic dish. Cover the top with greased parchment, secured with a rubber band, and then cover again with aluminum foil. You can also divide the batter among a couple of molds. This recipe makes a bit more than Aunt Frieda's mold would hold, so she would also make a small pudding in a Planter's Peanut tin, steam it by itself in another pot, freeze it, and serve at a later occasion. —CW

3 to 4 cups mixed dried fruit (raisins, currants, figs, prunes, apricots, and so on), covered with apple juice and soaked overnight (enough to yield 2 cups ground fruit)

About 3 large carrots, peeled

About 3 small white potatoes, peeled

1/2 cup walnuts or pecans

1 cup vegetable shortening, at room temperature

1 cup dry bread crumbs

1 cup all-purpose flour

1 cup light brown sugar

1 teaspoon kosher salt

1 teaspoon baking soda

1/2 teaspoon ground cinnamon

1/2 teaspoon ground cloves

1/2 teaspoon ground nutmeg

3 tablespoons molasses

6 tablespoons apple or orange juice

3 eggs, beaten

BRANDIED HARD SAUCE

10 tablespoons unsalted butter, at room temperature

2 cups sifted confectioners' sugar

$1/4$ teaspoon kosher salt

2 tablespoons brandy

1 teaspoon vanilla extract

1 egg, beaten

BRANDIED CUSTARD SAUCE

$1/3$ cup unsalted butter, at room temperature

1 cup sifted confectioners' sugar

3 tablespoons brandy

2 egg yolks

$1/3$ cup heavy whipping cream

$1/4$ to $1/3$ cup brandy

To prepare the pudding: Drain the whole dried fruit after it has soaked overnight. Put the fruit through a food grinder, measuring out 2 cups of ground fruit.

Grease and flour the molds, using vegetable shortening or butter. This recipe yields about 11 cups of batter, so you may have to use 2 molds. A small metal aspic mold would work well for any leftover batter.

With a grater, grate the carrots and potatoes. Then with the food grinder, grind the carrots, potatoes, and nuts and combine in a large bowl. (You should have $1^1/2$ cups each of the ground carrots and potatoes.) Drain off any liquid that accumulates. Blend the shortening into the ground vegetables. In another bowl, combine the bread crumbs, flour, brown sugar, salt, baking soda, cinnamon, cloves, and nutmeg. Mix the dry ingredients into the vegetable-nut mixture. Add the drained ground fruits, molasses, juice, and eggs, and mix well.

Fill greased and floured molds $2/3$ to $3/4$ full. Cover the top of the mold with buttered parchment paper or waxed paper and secure with the lid.

To steam the pudding, use a deep pot with a tight-fitting lid and a small wire rack that fits on the bottom of the pot. My Aunt Frieda used a folded dish towel in the bottom of the pot to protect the pudding from direct heat. If you use this method, be very careful not to boil the pot dry! I have also used an inverted lid from another pot as a rack.

Carefully place the filled mold in the large pot and add boiling water about halfway up the sides of the mold. Cover the pot and let the water simmer for approximately 3 hours, or until a cake tester comes out clean. As the water evaporates, replenish it with boiling water, keeping the water level halfway up the mold's sides.

Remove the mold from the pot and let it sit for about 15 minutes before turning it out of the mold onto a heat-resistant serving platter.

To prepare the hard sauce: In a bowl with an electric mixer, cream the butter until soft and smooth. Gradually add the sugar and beat until fluffy, 2 to 3 minutes. Add the salt, brandy, and vanilla. Blend in the egg thoroughly. Pour into a serving dish and chill for a couple of hours. You can make this the day before.

To prepare the custard sauce: In the top of a double boiler over boiling water, beat the butter until smooth with an electric hand mixer. Gradually add the sugar, beating until creamy, 2 to 3 minutes. Slowly blend in the brandy. Remove from the heat and beat in one egg yolk at a time. Return to the heat and blend in the cream. Cook until slightly thickened. Serve hot over steamed pudding.

To serve, warm the brandy in a small pot. Now it's showtime! Pour the heated brandy over the top of the pudding and light with a match. Allow the alcohol in the brandy to burn off before cutting slices. Serve with a dollop of hard sauce and pass a tureen of custard sauce.

Banana Cream Tarts with Lime Syrup

In this variation of a banana cream pie, you could substitute sweet pastry dough for puff pastry with equally glorious results. Virtually any fruit in season can be used, such as peaches, strawberries, blueberries, oranges, pineapple, or mango. There are some good commercial puff pastries on the market, or you can make your own from the recipe on page 202.

LIME SYRUP

Juice of 2 limes

1/4 cup granulated sugar

4 pieces puff pastry (page 202), rolled 1/4 inch thick and cut into 51/2-inch rounds

Pastry cream (page 199)

4 bananas, thinly sliced on an angle

To prepare the syrup: Add enough water to the lime juice to yield 1/4 cup liquid, then combine with the sugar in a small saucepan. Cook over medium heat until slightly thickened.

To prepare the tarts: Preheat the oven to 400°.

With a fork, thoroughly pierce the rounds of puff pastry. Place on a parchment-lined baking sheet and bake until golden brown, about 15 to 20 minutes.

To serve, divide the pastry cream among the puff pastry rounds and smooth into a mound.

Arrange the bananas on top of the pastry cream in a circle around each tart, overlapping the slices. Drizzle the lime syrup on top.

SERVES 4

❧ WINE NOTES

The very perfumey aromas and sweet finish of a late-harvest Muscat will pair well with this dessert. Muscat grapes originated in France and northern Italy and when being used for a late-harvest wine must be watched very carefully during harvest—if they are picked too late, the acidity is gone and the wine tastes flat. A sauterne dessert wine, made from a blend of Sauvignon Blanc and Sémillon, will be too full bodied for this tart; you want a simple wine with this simple dessert.

Apple Fritters with Armagnac Cream

MAKES 25 FRITTERS

WINE NOTES

The richness and apple tones of a late-harvest Riesling will pair with this dessert, even if you substituted peaches and pears for the fruit. You could also try a demi-sec sparkling wine or a Malvasia Bianca sparkling wine. The malvasia bianca grape is a Greek variety and is usually made into a dessert wine or sparkling wine. It is very fruity, with berry characteristics.

I first developed this recipe to serve at Sunday brunch, but it is equally good as a dinner dessert. Other fruit such as pears or peaches can be substituted. The Armagnac cream is also wonderful spooned over fresh summer berries. You can use other styles of brandy if Armagnac is not available.

ARMAGNAC CREAM

1 cup sour cream

2 tablespoons brown sugar

2 teaspoons Armagnac

APPLE FRITTERS

3 eggs, separated

2 tablespoons plus 2 teaspoons granulated sugar

1 1/2 teaspoons melted butter

1/2 cup flour

1/8 teaspoon kosher salt

1/4 teaspoon baking powder

2 tablespoons apple juice

1/4 teaspoon ground cinnamon

3/4 cup peeled, cored, and diced Granny Smith apple (about 1 apple)

2 cups peanut oil for frying

Confectioners' sugar, for sprinkling over fritters

To prepare the cream: In a small bowl, combine the sour cream, brown sugar, and Armagnac. Mix well. Refrigerate.

To prepare the fritters: In a large mixing bowl, combine the egg yolks and sugar. Add the melted butter, flour, salt, baking powder, apple juice, and cinnamon and mix until all ingredients are well blended. Fold in the apples.

Whip the egg whites until they form soft peaks. They should hold their shape but not be too stiff. Combine 1/3 of the whites with the apple mixture. This loosens up the mixture, making it easier to fold in the remaining whites without breaking them down. Fold the apple mixture into the remaining egg whites.

In a pot over medium-high heat, heat the oil to 375°. Using a tablespoon, drop a spoonful of the fritter batter at a time into the hot oil. You should be able to cook 4 to 6 fritters in one batch. When the first side of each fritter is golden brown, gently turn it over to brown the other side. Make sure to turn the fritters away from you so that you aren't splattered with oil. Drain on paper towels. Repeat with the remainder of the batter.

To serve, pool a couple of tablespoons of the Armagnac cream on each plate. Place 2 to 3 fritters on top of the sauce, and sprinkle with confectioners' sugar.

Chocolate, Almond, and Citrus Cake

Living in Northern California, I get a little citrus happy in the winter. This is one of my favorite cakes—it's rich, yet the citrus really keeps it light. It is a variation of a recipe that I learned from Bo Friberg, my pastry instructor at the California Culinary Academy. You can substitute different nuts or play with other types of citrus and still have great results. The ground almonds replace flour in this recipe.

2 tablespoons fine dry bread crumbs

1¹/2 cups whole almonds

³/4 cup granulated sugar

¹/2 pound semisweet chocolate, grated

2 teaspoons finely chopped lemon zest

2 teaspoons orange zest

2 teaspoons grapefruit zest

8 eggs, separated

1 teaspoon vanilla extract

¹/2 teaspoon almond extract

1 orange, separated into segments (page 209)

1 grapefruit, separated into segments

Sweetened whipped cream, for garnish

Butter a 10-inch round cake pan and line the bottom with parchment paper. Butter the bottom again and sprinkle the bottom and sides with a thin coating of the fine bread crumbs. Shake out any excess.

Preheat the oven to 350°.

In a food processor or blender, grind the almonds very fine. In a bowl, combine the nuts, sugar, chocolate, citrus zests, egg yolks, vanilla, and almond extract.

Beat the egg whites until they hold stiff peaks. Fold one-fifth of the whites into the chocolate-nut mixture. Add this mixture back into the egg whites and quickly fold it in. This technique helps to combine the heavy and light ingredients quickly without breaking down the egg whites. Bake for about 30 minutes, or until set. The cake is done when it starts to pull away from the sides of the pan and there is no wiggle in the center.

Remove from the oven and cool a bit. While still warm, turn the cake out of the baking pan onto a plate and then back onto a cooling rack. Let it cool completely before serving. It's best to let the cake cool all day or overnight so that the chocolate gets nice and hard.

Serve each slice with a couple of segments each of orange and grapefruit and a dollop of lightly sweetened whipped cream.

MAKES ONE 10-INCH CAKE

WINE NOTES

Select a tawny port to reflect the almond flavors in this awesome dessert. The citrus characteristics of the cake will be a nice contrast to the aged wine. A tawny port is aged in wood and is pale, dry, and relatively smooth. Tawnies tend not to be as full and rich in flavor as vintage ports and usually have nutty characteristics.

APPENDICES

Basic Recipes

Crème Anglaise and Ice Cream

MAKES 3 CUPS

Crème anglaise (or English cream) is a custard sauce used as the basis of virtually all ice creams. Served hot or cold, it can also be used as a sauce with cakes, fruits, desserts, and so on. It is easily flavored.

1 cup heavy whipping cream

4 egg yolks

7 tablespoons granulated sugar

1 cup milk, or as needed

In a saucepan, bring the cream to a boil. In a bowl, mix the egg yolks and sugar together until smooth. Slowly add the cream to the eggs, a little at a time. Completely blend in each addition before adding more, bringing the temperature of the eggs up to the temperature of the cream without scrambling them. This is called tempering the cream into the eggs. Pour the mixture back into the saucepan and cook over medium heat, stirring constantly with a wooden spoon, until thickened. Do not boil. The cream should be thick enough to coat the back of a spoon. When you run a finger through the cream on the back of the spoon, the line your finger makes should remain and not run together. Strain into a bowl. Cool immediately over ice set in a larger bowl. Stir occasionally. When the mixture is cool, add the milk, a little at a time, until the cream is the desired consistency.

If the cream does scramble, immediately place it in a blender and purée. Thin with cold milk, strain, and cool.

To add different flavors: Add a flavoring, such as almond, rum, vanilla, chocolate, and so on, to the cream after it has cooked. To use a solid flavoring, such as a vanilla bean, heat the cream and let it steep in the cream for an hour, and then strain out the solids and use the flavored cream to make the crème anglaise.

To make ice cream, freeze the crème anglaise in an ice cream machine.

Crème Fraîche

Although not limited to France, crème fraîche is the French version of our American sour cream. I have had excellent versions in such disparate places as Moscow and Mexico. The French distinguish the soured cream we talk about in this recipe by the name of *épais* (heavy sour) as opposed to whipping cream, which they call *crème fraîche liquide*. It is very easy to make at home and has a much better flavor than commercial sour cream. Additionally, it doesn't separate when you cook with it. All you have to do is plan ahead so that it is ready in time. Once thickened, it will keep at least a week in the refrigerator. Use an active cultured buttermilk as the lactic acid bacteria it contains is needed to sour the cream.

7 parts heavy whipping cream

1 part cultured buttermilk

Warm the cream to body temperature. Whisk in the buttermilk and transfer to a bowl or jar. Cover tightly and place in a warm place until it thickens, 8 to 24 hours. Refrigerate.

Pastry Cream

MAKES ABOUT 3 CUPS

Pastry cream is the glue that holds many desserts together. It provides a rich, custardy texture while having enough body to hold together desserts such as napoleons, cream puffs, and shortcakes. You can use it as the filling for éclairs or cream pies. Flavor pastry cream either by adding ingredients or by steeping ingredients in the milk, as described at the end of the recipe.

(Pastry Cream, continued)

2 cups milk

$^1/_2$ cup granulated sugar

2 tablespoons plus 2 teaspoons cornstarch

2 large eggs

$^1/_4$ cup unsalted butter, melted

In a heavy-bottomed saucepan, combine $1\,^1/_2$ cups of the milk and the sugar and bring to a boil. In a separate bowl, whip together the cornstarch and the remaining $^1/_2$ cup milk, making sure there are no lumps. You may need to check with your fingers to make sure the cornstarch is dissolved. Whisk the eggs into the cornstarch-milk mixture. Add this egg mixture to the boiling milk and sugar and whisk continuously until it returns to a boil. The addition of cornstarch prevents the eggs from curdling, but you still need to stir the mixtures rapidly as you blend them. Remove from the heat and stir in the melted butter. Transfer to a mixing bowl. To prevent the formation of a film on the surface of the cream, cover with plastic wrap, placing it directly on the surface of the cream. Refrigerate until cool.

You can flavor the pastry cream by adding any of the following:

$1\,^1/_2$ teaspoons minced citrus zest, such as lime, orange, or lemon

$^1/_2$ teaspoon vanilla or almond extract

Another way to flavor the cream is to steep ingredients, such as nuts, coffee beans, a vanilla bean, or herbs such as lemon verbena or lavender, in the milk-sugar mixture. To do so, bring the milk and sugar to a boil with the flavoring agent, let it sit until the flavor comes through, usually 1 to 2 hours, strain the liquid, and proceed with the remainder of the recipe.

Homemade Ricotta

MAKES ABOUT $1\,^1/_2$ CUPS

Making your own ricotta is simple, but you will need to start a day ahead if you are going to use it in a recipe. This little bit of preplanning produces results that are far superior to the store-bought varieties. When you suspend the ricotta to drain it, the length of time it hangs determines how wet or dry the final product will be. In the restaurant, we usually hang the cheesecloth bag from a refrigerator rack with a bowl underneath. If your refrigerator has flat shelves with nothing you can attach a string to, tie the bag to a spoon laid over the top of a tall plastic container.

4 cups whole milk

1 cup buttermilk

1 tablespoon champagne vinegar

In a noncorrosive pan over medium-high heat, combine the milk and buttermilk. Bring to a simmer and cook until the mixture curdles, which happens pretty quickly. Add the vinegar and cook for 1 minute. Strain through cheesecloth draped over a colander. Pull the corners of the cloth together and tie, enclosing the curds inside. Drain in the refrigerator overnight, either in the colander or suspended over a bowl. If you prefer, let the ricotta drain longer than 8 hours, which will make it drier. Remove from the cheesecloth and serve.

Simple Syrup

MAKES 2 CUPS

This syrup is great for iced tea because the sugar is already dissolved. Use it any time you want a dissolved, untextured sweetener, such as to sweeten fruit in desserts. It can be used as a sauce by itself or flavored using mint, cinnamon, citrus peel, vanilla, lemongrass, ginger, and liqueurs. To flavor it, steep the ingredients in the syrup. Fresh mint makes a cooling dessert sauce. Use it for glazing, in jams and jellies, and to add moisture to cakes. I like to brush it between the layers of cakes to keep them moist.

Originally, this syrup was made because raw, unrefined sugar had lots of impurities. Bringing the sugar-water mixture to a boil made it possible to skim the impurities off of the surface. Using simple syrup when making caramel also gives you more control.

1 cup granulated sugar

1 cup water

Combine the sugar and water and bring to a boil. You can increase or decrease the amounts in equal proportions as needed.

Sweet Pie Dough

MAKES TWO 9 BY 2-INCH PIE SHELLS OR
ONE 11 BY 1-INCH TART SHELL (WITH A LITTLE
LEFT OVER)

The sugar in this recipe makes the dough much more forgiving when rolled out. Although not as flaky as unsweetened pie dough, it is very tender and holds together well in small and large tarts. The dough can also be pressed into tart pans or shells, making it much easier to fill smaller baking pans. It will keep 4 to 5 days in the refrigerator or 1 month in the freezer.

5 cups all-purpose flour

3/4 cup granulated sugar

1 tablespoon kosher salt

1 1/2 cups cold butter, cut into small pieces

1/3 cup egg yolks (about 5 large egg yolks)

1/4 cup cold water, more as needed

To prepare by machine: In the bowl of a mixer, using the paddle attachment on low speed, combine the flour, sugar, and salt. Add the butter in small pieces and mix for about 2 1/2 minutes. Remove the bowl from the mixer. Using your hands, check to see that there are not too many big lumps of butter. A few actually help to make the pastry more flaky. Return the bowl to the mixer and add the egg yolks and water. Mix until the dough just begins to hold together. You may need to add more cold water if it is too dry. Remove the dough from the mixer, wrap in plastic wrap, and flatten slightly with your hands. Refrigerate for 30 minutes.

To prepare by hand: In a mixing bowl, combine the flour, sugar, and salt. Cut the butter into the dry ingredients with a pastry cutter, a fork, or your hands. Continue blending the mixture until it resembles coarse cornmeal. Add the egg yolks and water and mix until the dough just holds together. You may need to add more cold water if it is too dry. Remove the dough from the bowl, wrap in plastic wrap, and flatten slightly with your hands. Refrigerate for 30 minutes.

To roll out: Lightly dust your rolling surface and the top of the dough with flour. Working from the center with a rolling pin, roll the dough into a circle about 1/4 inch thick. Roll the dough onto the rolling pin, and then roll it off into the tart or pie pan, centering the dough in the pan. Press the dough into the bottom and sides of the pan. With a sharp knife, trim the excess dough from the top. Use the trimmings to patch any holes that may occur. Place the shell in the refrigerator for 30 minutes.

To bake an unfilled pie or tart shell: Preheat the oven to 350°. Press a piece of aluminum foil into the shell and place an empty pie tin on top of the aluminum. This will help to decrease the amount of shrinkage in the shell as you cook it. Another method is to line the shell with parchment paper and fill it with beans or pie weights. For a partially baked shell, bake until the middle of the shell has lost its rawness, 10 to 15 minutes. A partially cooked shell will appear to be an even blond color throughout. For a fully cooked shell, remove the extra tin and aluminum foil (or beans) after partial cooking, return to the oven, and cook until golden brown throughout, about 15 minutes more.

Puff Pastry

MAKES ENOUGH FOR APPROXIMATELY
4 DESSERTS

It may take you a few tries to perfect the technique of making this very versatile dough. Once you master it, however, you will never go back to the store-bought variety. I usually divide the dough in half and freeze what I don't use. Don't throw away the scraps after rolling and cutting the dough. These can be rolled in sugar and used to make palmier cookies. (Roll out the sugared dough into a rectangle. Then roll opposite edges of the rectangle inward (as you would a scroll), until they meet in the middle. Slice into cross-sections 1/4 inch thick and lay each piece flat on a parchment-lined baking sheet. Bake at 375° until golden brown.)

> 2 pounds unsalted butter, at room temperature
>
> 6 cups all-purpose flour
>
> 1/2 pound cold unsalted butter
>
> 2 teaspoons kosher salt
>
> 1 1/2 cups ice water

In the bowl of a mixer, with the paddle attachment, combine the soft butter with 1 cup of the flour. Mix until just incorporated. If you don't have a mixer, combine the soft butter and flour in a bowl with a wooden spoon. Place 2 pieces of plastic wrap, each 1 1/2 feet long, side by side on a flat surface with the long edges overlapping. Put the butter-flour mixture in the middle and fold over the edges, wrapping the mixture inside. Smooth the butter out and push it to the edges until you have formed a block approximately 1 inch thick by 8 inches wide by 10 inches long. Place on a baking sheet and put in the refrigerator.

Cut the cold butter into very small, pea-sized pieces. In a mixer with the paddle attachment or in a very large food processor, combine the butter with the remaining 5 cups flour and the salt. Blend until it is the texture of cornmeal. Add the ice water and mix until smooth, 4 to 5 minutes.

Turn the butter block over in the refrigerator to chill it evenly. Remove the dough from the mixer bowl and wrap the ball in plastic wrap. Set aside in the refrigerator.

When the butter in the refrigerator matches the consistency of the dough, roll the dough into a rectangular shape a little bit larger than twice the size of the butter block (18 inches by 12 inches). Use as little flour as you can when rolling out the dough. Unwrap the butter block and place it on one half of the dough. Fold the other half of the dough over the butter and pinch the edges of the dough to it seal in the butter. Press the butter down evenly so that it gets into the edges of the dough. Roll it out to about double its size (14 inches by 28 inches). Using a pastry brush, remove the excess flour from the surface. Fold the edges into the center, and then fold the whole thing in half again, making 4 layers of dough. (This is called a double turn.) Place on a baking sheet, cover, and refrigerate for 1 hour. Halfway through the hour, turn the dough over. Repeat the rolling out, folding, and refrigerating 3 more times, each time rolling the dough out into a rectangle 4 times its original size. This in effect turns the dough 90 degrees each turn. When all 4 double turns are done, refrigerate the dough for 1 more hour. Roll out to desired thickness, then cut and bake as called for in the recipe.

Pasta Dough

MAKES ABOUT 1/2 POUND FRESH PASTA, ENOUGH FOR 4 LARGE RAVIOLI

When making fresh pasta, the trick is to work in only as much flour as the egg will hold when you first put the dough together. It is a delicate balance. If you add too much flour, it is very difficult to roll out. Not enough flour and the finished pasta is tough and rubbery. I like to press it together until it starts to come together. I then wrap it in plastic wrap and let it rest. This allows the liquid to absorb more of the flour, making it easier to roll out. It also lets the flour rest a little so it stretches better when you shape it.

I use my trusty hand-crank pasta machine for the task of rolling out the pasta, but I have even rolled it out with a wine bottle when a machine was not available. A rolling pin works, too. Just make sure the surface is well-dusted with flour so the dough doesn't stick.

> 1 cup flour
>
> 1 tablespoon olive oil
>
> 1 large egg
>
> 1 tablespoon water
>
> Pinch kosher salt

Place the flour on a clean work surface and make a well in the center. Add the olive oil, egg, water, and salt to the well. Using a fork, whisk the liquid together and then slowly work the flour into the liquid mixture. Create a soft but not sticky ball.

Knead with your hands until the dough just comes together. If the dough is too soft or sticky, roll it in some flour. Use only as much flour as the liquid can handle. Don't force the flour into the dough. Alternately, you can make the dough in a mixer with the paddle attachment. Flatten and wrap in plastic wrap. Let rest for 30 minutes.

Roll the dough through the widest setting of a pasta-rolling machine a few times, each time folding the dough onto itself in thirds and changing the direction that it goes through by a quarter turn. If the dough is too wet, add a little flour each time you roll it through the machine. Then narrow the rollers by a notch and roll the dough through again. Repeat, each time narrowing the setting, until it has been rolled out at the thinnest setting. Use the sheets for ravioli or lasagna, machine-cut them into various shapes, or hand-cut them into pappardelle.

Pizza Dough

MAKES EIGHT 8- TO 10-INCH PIZZETTAS OR
FOUR OR FIVE 12- TO 14-INCH PIZZAS

This pizza dough is designed to rise fairly quickly, with a good, stretchy structure. The sugar and warm water added at the beginning help activate the yeast. If the water is too hot, the yeast cells will be killed. Salt inhibits the growth of yeast, so it is added with the rest of the ingredients, after the yeast has been activated. You can make this dough using less yeast, but it will take longer to rise.

Kneading the dough activates the gluten, toughening the dough, and giving it structure. I use bread flour in this recipe because it has a higher gluten content, making a stronger dough for stretching and shaping into pizza or calzone. Letting the dough rest and rise gently lightens it, allowing it to be stretched out. You may need to use more or less flour than called for in the recipe. The capacity of the flour to retain water changes from month to month, depending on the weather, and from harvest to harvest. In the restaurant, our chefs don't measure, preferring to determine the right amount by eye and feel.

2 cups warm water

1 tablespoon plus 1 teaspoon dry yeast

1 tablespoon granulated sugar

1 tablespoon kosher salt

6 tablespoons olive oil

4 1/4 cups bread flour, more as needed

To prepare the dough using a mixer: In the bowl of a mixer, mix together the water, yeast, and sugar. Make sure that the yeast and sugar are dissolved. Let rest for approximately 10 minutes. The yeast should start to bloom or form a film on the top of the water. With the dough hook attached and the mixer on low speed, add the salt and olive oil. Slowly add the flour until the dough starts to pull away from the sides of the bowl. The dough should be fairly wet and sticky to the touch. Knead with the dough hook at high speed for a few minutes, then lower to medium for 5. Remove from the mixer bowl and knead by hand for a few minutes, until smooth.

To prepare the dough by hand: In a large mixing bowl, dissolve the yeast and sugar in the water. Let sit for 10 minutes, until the yeast starts to bloom. Add the olive oil and salt. Slowly stir in the flour until a dough is formed. Add just enough flour to be able to work the dough; it should still be a little sticky. Transfer to a floured surface and knead for 15 minutes.

To knead: Fold the dough over on itself, pushing hard to work up the gluten. Turn the dough 90 degrees, changing the direction each time you fold it. Continue kneading for 15 minutes. Thorough kneading strengthens the gluten in the flour, allowing the dough to stretch nicely without breaking.

To let the dough rise: Oil the sides of a mixing bowl that is a least twice the size of the dough, place the dough in the bowl, and cover with a towel. Let rise in a warm place until double in size.

Remove the dough from the bowl and punch it down to release any air bubbles. Divide into 8 equal portions for pizzettas or 4 or 5 portions for pizza. On a lightly floured surface, roll each portion into a tight ball. Place on a lightly floured baking sheet and cover with plastic wrap. Let rest in the refrigerator for 1/2 hour before using. It is possible

(Pizza Dough, continued)

to leave it in the refrigerator for 3 to 4 hours, or you can freeze it. If you freeze the dough, let it defrost in the refrigerator for at least 3 to 4 hours before using. I pull it out of the refrigerator in the morning for use that evening.

To prepare the oven and shape and bake the pizza: Place a pizza stone or bricks in the bottom of your oven. Turn the temperature to the highest baking setting possible, usually 550°. Your oven will take a bit longer to reach the required temperature with the addition of the stone or bricks. Place some flour on a pizza paddle or on the back side of a baking sheet. Dust your hands with flour and begin slowly stretching the dough, always working from the outside edge. If you don't feel comfortable with this method, use a rolling pin to roll the dough out on a lightly floured surface. The dough should be 8 to 10 inches in diameter for a pizzetta and 12 to 14 inches for a pizza. Place the dough on the pizza paddle or on the back of a baking sheet. Arrange the toppings on the dough and slide the pizza off the paddle onto the stone in the oven. Cook for 6 to 8 minutes, or until golden brown. If you do not have a stone or bricks for your oven, simply place the dough on a baking sheet after shaping, arrange the toppings, and place the pizza on the lowest rack of your oven. It may take a few minutes longer to cook.

For a sheet of focaccia, spread all of the dough out on a lightly oiled baking sheet (11 by 17 inches). Let rise, covered, in a warm area of the kitchen until double in size. Dimple the top with your fingers, drizzle with extra-virgin olive oil, and sprinkle with kosher salt. Bake in a preheated 400° oven for approximately 20 minutes, or until golden brown on top.

Creamy Polenta

MAKES ABOUT 3 CUPS

Like tomatoes, cornmeal came to Italy from the New World and has become an integral part of the cuisine. Legend has the first cornmeal polenta being made in the great port city of Venice. Polenta had been made before using various other grains such as barley and chestnut meal, but corn supplanted them all.

Good polenta requires slow cooking since it is a coarser milled corn meal. You need enough cooking liquid so that the grains of cornmeal cook evenly. It is also important to add the polenta slowly to the boiling liquid, stirring constantly as you add. This helps to prevent lumps. I like to use a whisk for this part of the cooking and then switch to a wooden spoon. If the mixture becomes too dried out, the polenta clumps up. I always keep a pot of boiling water on the stove to add, as needed, to the cooking polenta. As with all dried grains and beans, the amount of water absorbed while cooking depends on various things, including humidity. Just be sure to cook it until the graininess has disappeared. If you are going to grill or fry the polenta, cook it a little longer, stirring often, until any extra water evaporates.

> 1 cup water
>
> 1 cup milk
>
> $^1/_2$ cup polenta
>
> $^1/_2$ cup heavy whipping cream
>
> 3 tablespoons freshly grated Parmesan cheese
>
> Kosher salt and freshly ground pepper

In a saucepan, bring the water and milk to a boil. Slowly whisk in the polenta. Turn the heat down to very low and continue cooking, stirring every few minutes. As the polenta begins to dry out, add the cream, a little at a time. When the polenta has lost its graininess (after about an hour of cooking), add the Parmesan. Season to taste. Serve immediately, or keep warm in a hot water bath.

For crispy polenta, spread the polenta onto a $4^1/_2$ by 8-inch loaf pan after the initial cooking, cool, cut into pieces, and fry in olive oil.

Stocks

A good stock is the backbone of great soups, braises, and sauces. Although stocks need to cook for a long time, the actual preparation work involved is minimal. I like to make a large quantity at once and freeze what I don't immediately need in resealable bags or ice cube trays. When you make your own stock, you control what goes into it. I don't add any salt to my stocks when I make them; this allows them to be reduced or cooked for long periods without becoming overly salty. Salt and MSG are added to most commercial stocks to boost the flavor. This can be accomplished in your own home with good ingredients and slow cooking.

When skimming meat stocks, skim around the outside edge. This is where the fat accumulates. Always start a stock with cold water. It allows the meat used to release its impurities (soluble proteins) slowly into the stock, where they rise to the top and are easily skimmed. This makes for a clearer stock.

VEGETABLE STOCK

MAKES ABOUT 8 QUARTS

2 tablespoons olive oil

1 cup thinly sliced leek (about 1 whole leek, green and white parts)

1 cup peeled, sliced yellow onion (about 2 onions)

1/2 cup chopped celery

1 1/2 cups chopped carrot

1 fennel bulb, chopped

2 whole heads garlic, cut in half

4 cups peeled, whole canned tomatoes with their juice

1 2/3 cups white wine

8 quarts water

1/2 cup lentils

Stems from 1/2 bunch fresh parsley (leaves removed)

1/2 bunch fresh thyme

1 tablespoon black peppercorns

4 bay leaves

In a noncorrosive 5-gallon stockpot over medium heat, heat the olive oil. Add the leek, onion, celery, carrot, and fennel, and sauté for 10 minutes, stirring often. Add the garlic, tomatoes, wine, water, lentils, parsley stems, thyme, peppercorns, and bay leaves, and bring to a simmer. Simmer lightly for 5 to 6 hours. Strain.

You can add other ingredients to the stock depending on the season and how the finished stock will be used. Mushrooms, summer or winter squash, celery root, potatoes, peppers, chiles, other herbs, and corn are all possibilities.

COURT BOUILLON

MAKES ABOUT 8 QUARTS

2 tablespoons olive oil

1 cup thinly sliced leek (about 1 whole, green and white parts)

1 cup peeled, sliced yellow onion (about 2 onions)

1/2 cup chopped celery

1 bulb fennel, chopped

2 whole heads garlic, cut in half

1 2/3 cups white wine

8 quarts water

Stems from 1/2 bunch parsley (leaves removed)

1/2 bunch fresh thyme

1 tablespoon black peppercorns

4 bay leaves

In a noncorrosive, 5-gallon stockpot over medium heat, heat the olive oil. Add the leek, onion, celery, fennel, and garlic and sauté, stirring often, for 10 minutes. Add the wine, water, parsley stems, thyme, peppercorns, and bay leaves, and bring to a simmer. Simmer lightly for 1 hour. Strain.

CHICKEN STOCK

MAKES ABOUT 8 QUARTS

10 pounds chicken bones,
    preferably backs and necks

8 quarts water

1 cup thinly sliced leek (about 1 whole leek,
    green and white parts)

1 cup peeled, sliced yellow onion
    (about 2 onions)

$1/2$ cup chopped celery

$1 1/2$ cups chopped carrot

2 whole heads garlic, cut in half

$1 2/3$ cups white wine

Stems from $1/2$ bunch parsley
    (leaves removed)

$1/2$ bunch fresh thyme

1 tablespoon black peppercorns

4 bay leaves

Place the chicken bones and water in a non-corrosive 5-gallon stockpot and bring to a boil. Lower the heat to a simmer and stir the bones with a spoon. This will bring most of the impurities to the surface as well as the fat. Skim the stock very well at this point. Add enough water to bring the stock back to the original level, add the leek, onion, celery, carrot, garlic, wine, parsley stems, thyme, peppercorns, and bay leaves, and bring to a boil. Lower the heat to a simmer and cook for 6 to 8 hours, skimming once an hour. Strain. If you cook the stock at too high a temperature, it will be cloudy.

VEAL DEMIGLACE

MAKES ABOUT 4 QUARTS

8 pounds veal bones, preferably shanks
    and marrow bones

1 cup thinly sliced leek, white part only
    (about 2 to 3 leeks)

1 cup peeled, sliced yellow onion
    (about 2 onions)

$1/2$ cup chopped celery

$1 1/2$ cups chopped carrot

$1/4$ cup olive oil

$1 2/3$ cups red wine

8 quarts water

2 whole heads garlic, cut in half

2 cups canned peeled tomatoes with juice

Stems from $1/2$ bunch parsley
    (leaves removed)

$1/2$ bunch fresh thyme

1 tablespoon black peppercorns

4 bay leaves

Preheat the oven to 350°. In a heavy roasting pan, combine the veal bones, leek, onion, celery, and carrot. Toss with the olive oil and place in the oven. Roast for 40 to 50 minutes, or until golden brown, turning every 15 minutes. Transfer the roasted bones and vegetables to a 5-gallon stockpot. Drain off any excess oil or fat left in the roasting pan. Add the red wine to the pan and stir over medium heat to scrape up the browned bits from the bottom of the pan. Add to the stockpot along with the water, garlic, tomatoes, parsley stems, thyme, peppercorns, and bay leaves. Bring to a boil, then lower to a simmer. Skim the stock very well at this point. Add enough water to bring the stock back to the original level. Lower the heat to a simmer and cook for 12 to 24 hours, skimming occasionally as fat rises to the top and adding water as needed to keep the stock at the same level. The longer you let the stock simmer, the better the flavors will be. If you cook the stock at too high a temperature, it will become cloudy. Strain, place in a pot half the size of the original, and very slowly reduce by half.

Mayonnaise and Aioli

Some form of mayonnaise is made throughout southern France, Spain, and Italy. The basic ingredients, egg yolk and olive oil, remain the same, but potatoes are added in some recipes to bind the sauce together. It is traditionally made in a mortar and pestle. This seems to be the most gentle way to incorporate the oil without making it bitter, as olive oil is a very delicate creature and doesn't like to be overworked. I usually begin the process in a mortar and pestle and then move to a bowl and whisk once the initial emulsification is completed. If the mayonnaise breaks, or becomes very liquidy at any point, start over, using another egg yolk and adding the broken sauce to it a little bit at a time, as you would add olive oil. A little bit of prepared mustard also helps emulsify the sauce and flavor it.

Commercial mayonnaise enriched with a bit of extra-virgin olive oil and fresh garlic is a quick aioli and can approximate the flavors of a good aioli. Plus you can make it in small quantities. (Thank you, Faith Willinger, for this tip.)

Aioli is simply a mayonnaise with added garlic. To make it, start with the chopped garlic in the mortar and pestle and continue as you would with mayonnaise. Omit the garlic in the basic aioli recipe given here if you want to make mayonnaise. You can flavor aioli and mayonnaise in many ways. I've included a couple of variations to give you some ideas.

BASIC AIOLI

MAKES 1 CUP

- 1 teaspoon chopped garlic
- 1 egg yolk
- 2 tablespoons lemon juice
- 1 teaspoon Dijon-style mustard
- 1 cup olive oil
- Kosher salt and freshly ground pepper

In a mortar and pestle, crush the garlic until it forms a smooth paste. Add the egg yolk and lemon juice and combine until smooth. Transfer to a noncorrosive, heatproof bowl, place over simmering water, and whisk constantly until the mixture starts to thicken. Remove from the heat and whisk in the mustard. Whisk the olive oil into the mixture, a few drops at a time at first, and then in a slow, steady stream, until all is added. Season with salt and pepper to taste. Refrigerate until needed.

BASIC MAYONNAISE

MAKES 1 CUP

- 1 egg yolk
- 1 teaspoon lemon juice
- 1 teaspoon Dijon mustard
- 1 cup olive oil
- Kosher salt and freshly ground pepper

In a noncorrosive, heatproof bowl, combine the egg yolks and lemon juice. Whisk in the mustard and olive oil as described in the basic aioli recipe. Check for seasoning. Refrigerate until needed.

FRIED CAPER AND LEMON AIOLI

MAKES 1 CUP

- 1 cup olive oil
- 2 tablespoons small capers
- 1 teaspoon chopped garlic
- 1 egg yolk
- 6 teaspoons lemon juice
- 1 teaspoon Dijon mustard
- 2 teaspoons finely chopped lemon zest
- Kosher salt and freshly ground pepper

In a small saucepan over medium-high heat, heat the olive oil. When hot but not smoking, add the capers and cook for about 1 minute, or until they are a bit crispy. Drain the capers, reserving the oil, and set both aside. Cool the oil completely.

Continue as described in the Basic Aioli recipe, using the cooled olive oil. Fold in the fried capers and finely chopped lemon zest. Season with salt and pepper to taste. Be careful with the amount of salt you add, as the capers are already very salty. Refrigerate until needed.

Techniques

CLEANING WILD MUSHROOMS

I like to use a clean towel or pastry brush to clean the dirt and twigs off of wild mushrooms. If they are really dirty, wash them quickly in cold water and immediately pat dry with a towel. Mushrooms absorb water like a sponge, which greatly dilutes their flavor when cooked.

FLAMING

There is an old cook's story involving alcohol that was not cooked off—or flamed—before being used in a recipe. It seems that someone, to remain nameless, was cooking a ham (it could have been a turkey or prime rib) with copious amounts of whiskey. The whiskey was poured over the roast and placed in the oven. About an hour later, a loud boom was heard coming from the kitchen. The alcohol had finally ignited and blew the door off the oven.

To avoid having this happen to you, be careful to keep the bottle away from the flame. If ignited, it could shoot across the room like a rocket or explode in your hands. Also make sure none of your appendages or clothing are close to the flame.

On a gas stove, heat the pan you will be using to cook with over high heat. Remove the pan from the stove and add the liquor. Return the pan to the fire and tilt it away from you. Watch the fire flame up. Level the pan out and cook, gently shaking, until the flame goes out. If you are using an electric stove, light a long-stemmed match, tilt the pan away from you and place the match on top of the liquid. It should flame up. Remove the match and proceed as for a gas stove.

In general, wine and beer are low enough in alcohol content that they do not need to be flamed. You can still try it if it makes you feel safer or you like pyrotechnics. Definitely flame anything that is over 15 percent alcohol. Doing so makes the liqueur or liquor more stable, but does not eliminate all of the alcohol content.

PEELING AND SECTIONING CITRUS

Cut off the stem end and blossom ends of the citrus fruit, slicing all the way to the flesh. Place the fruit with one of the cut ends down on a cutting board and trim off the remaining skin, again cutting all of the way to the flesh. To remove the sections, place the citrus in your hand and cut out the segments, using the membranes in between each segment as your guide. Set aside in a bowl and squeeze any juice that is left in the membrane over the segments.

PEELING AND SEEDING TOMATOES

With a sharp knife, cut out the stem end of the tomatoes and lightly score the other end. Slip the tomatoes into boiling water for a few minutes, or just until the skin starts to split. Remove from the boiling water and immediately plunge them into ice water. The skins should easily peel off. If they don't, return the tomatoes to the hot water and repeat the process. To remove the seeds, cut the tomato in half widthwise and gently press the seeds out.

PREPARING ARTICHOKE HEARTS

Trim off the stem of the artichoke and remove the lower leaves. With a sharp paring knife, cut under the first layer of lower leaves all around the base of the artichoke. Remove the leaves in this manner until you get to the more tender and lighter-colored inner leaves. Cut the inner leaves off the top of the artichoke heart. With a spoon, remove the fuzzy inner choke. Cut a lemon in half and rub the cut half all over the artichoke heart. Cook in boiling salted water until tender when pierced with a sharp knife.

PREPARING PARMESAN SHARDS

Using a vegetable peeler, shave off long strips from a chunk of Parmesan cheese.

PREPARING TOASTS

Preheat the broiler. Slice a baguette thinly on an angle so that you end up with pieces about 2 inches long. Brush one side of each piece with olive oil. Toast the oiled sides under the broiler until golden brown.

ROASTING, PEELING, AND SEEDING PEPPERS AND CHILES

Roast the peppers and chiles over an open flame, such as a gas burner, or under a broiler, lightly blackening the entire outside. (Turn them as each side blackens.) Place in a bowl and cover tightly. Let them steam for 10 to 15 minutes. Remove from the bowl and peel off the blackened skins. Do not run the peppers under water as this removes flavors. Keep a bowl of water close by and dip your hands in it as needed to remove pieces of the skin. Cut out the stem and remove the seeds. Slice into thin strips. Be very careful with chiles, as the residue on your fingers can be transferred to your eyes and mouth, causing irritation. In the restaurant, we use surgical gloves, which are widely available, to protect our hands, as the chile oil can sting tiny cuts.

SEASONING WITH SALT AND PEPPER

Why do we season with salt and pepper? Salt enhances the flavors in a dish. I prefer to use kosher salt because it doesn't have any additives that can taste metallic and bitter. Besides adding flavor, pepper opens up our sinuses, which helps us perceive aromas and flavors. Be sure to use freshly ground pepper.

SHUCKING OYSTERS

My tools of choice when opening oysters are a plastic-handled oyster knife and a rubber glove. I like to use a knife with a long, dull blade with a slightly rounded tip. The glove protects the hand holding the oyster from the sharp edges of the oyster and from the knife, which slips quite often when prying the oyster open.

If you are not going to eat the oysters the day you purchase them, place them in a colander with a drain pan underneath, pack the colander with ice, and refrigerate.

Wash the outsides of the oysters thoroughly. Place a dry dish towel on a flat surface. The oyster has two sides—a flat side, which is the top, and a more rounded, bowl-shaped side, which is the bottom. Place the oyster on the towel with the flat side up. This will keep the juice in the oyster shell when you open it, rather than having it run all over your countertop. There is a hinge between the top and the bottom, which you should place closest to you. Wedge your knife into this hinge and pry the top open. Once you have the hinge open, gently scrape the inside of the top shell to release the oyster. Use your knife to cut the muscle holding the oyster to the shell on the bottom. Serve immediately.

TOASTING SEEDS

Preheat the oven to 300°. Sprinkle the seeds on a baking sheet and place in the oven. Shake the sheet or stir very frequently until the seeds are lightly toasted and crisp—just beginning to turn golden brown. An alternate method is to place the seeds in an ungreased skillet over medium heat until lightly toasted and crisp, stirring very frequently to prevent burning.

To toast fennel seeds, sprinkle on a hot skillet and cook for 1 to 2 minutes, stirring constantly.

TOASTING AND SKINNING NUTS

Be sure to store nuts in airtight containers, as the oil in them can turn rancid. To toast them, which enhances the flavor of many nuts, preheat the oven to 350°. Spread the nuts on an ungreased baking sheet. Bake until lightly toasted and crisp but not browned. Stir or shake the pan very frequently to avoid burning, about every 3 minutes. The total time will vary depending on the kind of nuts you are toasting. Smaller nuts, such as pine nuts or sliced almonds will toast quicker than large nuts. All burn quickly, so watch very carefully. To remove the skins from toasted nuts, such as hazelnuts, rub them between your palms after they have cooled.

Glossary

COOKING GLOSSARY

BOUQUET GARNI—A collection of herbs and/or flavorings that are tied together with string or tied up in cheesecloth (sachet bag). Herbs in a traditional bouquet garni are thyme, parsley, and bay leaf. Bouquets garnis are mostly used in long-cooked preparations such as stocks and braises. To make a bouquet garni using cheesecloth, cut a piece of cloth large enough to enclose the flavorings. Place contents in the center of the cloth, gather the corners together to form a bag, and tie them with kitchen twine. This method allows for easy removal.

BRAISE—A wet method of cooking used for tougher cuts of meat and poultry. The meat is first seared and then placed in a pot or roasting pan with liquid, vegetables, and aromatics and tightly sealed with a lid. Braises generally cook for a long time at a low temperature.

BRINE—A method of preserving vegetables, fruits, meat, fish, and poultry. A brine is a combination of water and salt that may contain vinegar (or other acid such as citrus juice), sugar, spices, herbs, or vegetables. It is used for pickling and curing.

CHIFFONADE—Vegetables or herbs such as lettuce, sorrel, sage, and mint that are cut into very thin strips before being used in a recipe.

DEGLAZE—A method of retaining all of the wonderful flavors of the little bits of meat, poultry, or vegetables that are left in the bottom of the pan after sautéing or roasting. The meat is first removed from the pan, the fat is poured off, and liquid such as wine, beer, stock, or fruit juice is added to the pan. All of the bits of flavor are scraped up from the bottom of the pan, enriching the liquid.

FLAMING (FLAMBÉ)—This method can be used to dramatic effect at the table to impress guests, or in the kitchen to lower the alcohol content of the wine or spirit you are using before adding it to a dish. See page 209.

INCORPORATE—To thoroughly blend one ingredient into another so that there are no streaks or lumps.

JULIENNE—Strips of food that are cut into matchstick-sized pieces.

MACERATE—To marinate fruit.

MARINADE—There are two types of marinades, wet and dry. Wet marinades usually contain liquids such as wine, vinegar, or fruit juices and vegetables, fruits, spices, and herbs. Dry marinades are composed of vegetables, fruits, spices, and herbs and sometimes olive oil. Marinades are used to impart flavor and, in the case of marinades with an acid component, tenderize meats. The trade-off with tenderization is that although the acid breaks down the tough fibers, it also pulls moisture from the meat.

RENDER—To slowly cook animal fats or skins. The fat can be used for sautéing, and the leftover skins or rinds (such as duck or pork) are called crackling. Crackling can be used as a garnish or eaten out of hand.

SACHET BAG—A piece of cheesecloth, with herbs or other flavorings placed inside, that is then tied with string. It is essential to use when you want to flavor a dish without having the flavoring agent (usually herbs) floating around in the final preparation.

STEEP—To infuse a liquid with dry flavorings such as coffee, tea, fresh or dried herbs, spices, and aromatics. The flavoring is usually strained out after the desired taste has been incorporated into the liquid.

SWEAT—To cook vegetables, covered, over low heat without browning until they literally sweat out their moisture and become translucent.

SWIRL—To add one ingredient into another without using a spoon or whisk to blend it. It usually refers to the addition of butter to a sauce. The cold butter is slowly added, a little at a time, to the warm sauce, off the fire. The pan is gently shaken in a clockwise motion until all the butter is incorporated.

TEMPER—To add a little bit of a hot liquid to an egg mixture to raise the temperature of the egg mixture before adding all of the egg mixture to the remaining hot liquid. This keeps the eggs from curdling.

WINE GLOSSARY

ACID BALANCE—A balance achieved by the proper degree of acidity, giving the wine a balance on the palate. If the acid is too high, a puckering, sharp tartness is evident. If the wine is too low in acid, it will taste flat and soapy. It is the wine-maker's job to bring the organic acids in grapes into balance.

BALANCE—A harmonic proportion of fruit, alcohol, acidity, pH, and tannins in a wine.

BODY—The weight or feel of the wine in your mouth. The alcohol content of the wine will contribute to the body; light-bodied wines have less than 12 percent alcohol by volume, while fuller-bodied wines have 13 to 14 percent, sometimes even more.

DRY—A dry wine is one without perceptible sweetness. It has been fermented completely so that there is no residual grape sugar left; it has all been converted to alcohol.

FLAVOR—The recognized variation of a wine's taste, influenced by the bouquet and aroma.

FORWARD FRUIT—A tasting term referring to the intensity of fruit character that comes from the grape. Fruitiness is not necessarily an indication of sweetness in a wine.

INTENSITY—The depth or strength of flavors and aromas in a wine.

MALOLACTIC FERMENTATION—A secondary fermentation that involves the natural conversion of malic acid to lactic acid. Malic acid can be likened to the sharp, tart acid found in green (pippin) apples, while lactic acid is a softer acid found in milk, cream, and butter. When a white wine goes through malolactic fermentation, it becomes softer, reducing the tartness and adding the flavor complexities of butter to butterscotch.

OFF-DRY—An off-dry wine has some amount of residual grape sugar. The threshold for tasting "sweetness" is measured as approximately 0.5 percent residual sugar. Wines at this level or greater will begin to taste sweet.

pH—A scientific term for measuring acidity in wine in the form of hydrogen ions. A high pH range will cause instability in wines, while one that is too low will be recognizably acidic and perhaps undrinkable.

SUR LIE—A French term referring to the practice of aging a wine on the yeast sediment (the lees) after the fermentation process has been completed. The lees enhance the flavor, texture, and complexity of the wine, adding yeasty, toasty, baked bread, and nutty characteristics.

TEXTURE—The actual feel of the wine on the palate, a combination of the weight and body, the alcohol, the tannin, and the acid feel. Thin, viscous, and chewy are some of the adjectives used to describe the texture of a wine.

WEIGHT—The feel of the body of the wine on the palate, usually described as being light or heavy.

Mail Order Resources

Aroma Wheels
Colored, laminated plastic wine aroma
   wheels are available from:
Ann C. Noble, Professor of Enology
Dept. of Viticulture and Enology
University of California
Davis, CA 95616
(530) 752-0387
fax (530) 752-0382
acnoble@ucdavis.edu

All profits support wine sensory research.

Corti Brothers
5810 Folsom Boulevard
Sacramento, California 95819
(800) 509-3663 or (916) 736-3800
fax (916) 736-3807

Olive oils, vinegars, spices, etc.

D'Artagnan
280 Wilson Avenue
Newark, New Jersey 07105
(800) DARTAGN
fax (973) 465-1870
www.dartagnan.com
celine@dartagnan.com

Game birds, foie gras, demiglace, etc.

Dean & DeLuca
Call or fax for locations and catalog.
(800) 221-7714
fax: (800) 781-4050
www.dean-deluca.com
WebHost@dean-deluca-catalog.com

Spice, preserves, meats, cheese, etc.

Katz and Company
101 South Coombs, Suite Y3
Napa, California 94559
(800) 676-7176
fax (707) 254-7846
www.katzandco.com
katzandco@aol.com

Extra-virgin olive oils, vinegars, preserves, etc.

Manicaretti
5332 College Avenue, Suite 200
Oakland, California 94618
(800) 799-9830
fax (510) 655-2034
www.manicaretti.com
mail@manicaretti.com

Italian risotto rices, artisanal pastas, etc.

Marché aux Delices
P.O. Box 1164
New York, New York 10028
(888) 547-5471
fax (718) 858-5288
www.auxdelices.com
staff@auxdelices.com

Truffles, wild mushrooms, etc.

Maytag Dairy Farms
P.O. Box 806
Newton, Iowa 50208
(800) 247-2458
fax (515) 792-1567

Maytag blue cheese

Melissa's
P.O. Box 21127
Los Angeles, California 90021
(800) 588-0151
fax (323) 588-9774
www.melissas.com
hotline@melissas.com

Specialty produce

More Than Gourmet
115 West Bartges Street
Akron, Ohio 44311
(800) 860-9392
fax (330) 762-4832

Demiglace, foie gras, pâté, etc.

Mozzarella Company
2944 Elm Street
Dallas, Texas 75226
(800) 798-2954 or (214) 741-4072
fax (214) 741-4076
www.mozzco.com
mozzco@aol.com

Fresh mozzarella

Petrossian
419 West 13th Street
New York, New York 10014
(800) 828-9241
fax (212) 337-0007

Caviar, foie gras, smoked fish, etc.

Sur La Table
(800) 243-0852
www.surlatable.com

*Over 12,500 products for the professional and
   home chef*

Urbani
(800) 281-2330
www.urbani.com
urbaniusa@aol.com

Truffles, truffle oil, wild mushrooms, etc.

Urbani USA
29-24 40th Avenue
Long Island, New York 11101
(718) 392-5050
fax (718) 392-1704

Urbani West
5851 West Washington Boulevard
Culver City, California 90232
(323) 933-8202
fax (323) 933-4235

Zabar's Gourmet Foods
2245 Broadway
New York, New York 10024
(800) 697-6301
fax (212) 580-4477
info@zabars.com

Smoked fishes, caviar, etc.

Zürsun, Ltd.
754 Canyon Park Avenue
Twin Falls, Idaho 83301
(800) 424-8881
phone/fax (208) 735-1044
www.soberspace.com/zursun.htm
glynn@computer-depot.com

Heirloom and unusual legumes

Bibliography

The American Baker by Jim Dodge with Elaine Ratner (New York: Simon and Schuster, 1987)

James Beard's American Cookery by James Beard (Boston: Little, Brown, 1980)

American Vineyards by Barbara Ensrud (New York: Stewart, Tabori & Chang, 1988)

Back to Square One by Joyce Goldstein (New York: William Morrow, 1992)

The Chez Panisse Menu Cookbook by Alice Waters (New York: Random House, 1982)

The Fannie Farmer Cookbook by Marion Cunningham (New York: Knopf, 1996)

The French Menu Cookbook by Richard Olney (New York: Simon and Schuster, 1970)

The Greens Cookbook by Deborah Madison with Edward Espe Brown (New York: Bantam, 1987)

Italian Food by Elizabeth David (New York: Penguin, 1999)

Joy of Cooking by Irma S. Rombauer and Marion Rombauer Becker (Indianapolis: Bobbs-Merrill, 1931)

Larousse Gastronomique by Prosper Montagné (New York: Crown, 1988)

The Los Angeles Times Book of California Wines by Robert Lawrence Balzer (New York: Harry N. Abrams, 1984)

Mastering the Art of French Cooking by Julia Child, Louisette Bertholle, and Simone Beck (New York: Random House, 1961)

Mastering the Art of French Cooking, Volume 2 by Julia Child and Simone Beck (New York: Random House, 1970)

The New Food Lover's Companion, second edition, by Sharon Tyler Herbst (New York: Barron's, 1995)

The New Frank Schoonmaker Encyclopedia of Wine, completely revised by Alexis Bespaloff (New York: William Morrow, 1988)

The New Larousse Gastronomique: The Revised American Edition of the Encyclopedia of Food, Wine and Cookery by Prosper Montagné (New York: Crown, 1988)

On Food and Cooking by Harold McGee (New York: Charles Scribner's, 1984)

Red Wine with Fish by David Rosengarten and Joshua Wesson (New York: Simon and Schuster, 1989)

Taste Tour Collection: Fine Wines of the World by Ronn Wiegand and Brenda Boblitt (Napa: Taste Tour Collection Publications and Seminar, 1996)

Ten Vineyard Lunches by Richard Olney (New York: Olympic Marketing Corporation, 1988)

The University of California Sotheby Book of California Wine by Doris Muscatine, Maynard Amerine, and Bob Thompson (Berkeley: University of California Press, 1984)

The Way to Cook by Julia Child (New York: Knopf, 1989)

The Wente Family and the California Wine Industry by Ruth Tieser (Berkeley: University of California, Bancroft Library, Regional Oral History Office, 1992)

Wine Lover's Companion by Ron Herbst and Sharon Tyler Herbst (New York: Barron's, 1995)

The World Atlas of Wine: A Complete Guide to the Wines and Spirits of the World by Hugh Johnson (New York: Simon and Schuster, 1994)

Index